LESBIANISM IN SWEDISH LITERATURE

LESBIANISM IN SWEDISH LITERATURE

AN AMBIGUOUS AFFAIR

Jenny Björklund

CONTENTS

ACKNOWLEDGMENTS

Writing this book has been a long process, and many people have been involved along the way. Some of them have read parts or all of the manuscript at various stages and provided helpful and insightful comments. Without them, this book would not be what it is today. Others have invited me as a visiting scholar, which has given me invaluable time to write, or to give lectures that have developed into chapters. Some have helped with practical issues, such as sending me books from Sweden when I lived in California or providing emotional and practical support at home. I am extremely grateful to everyone listed as follows, and I would like to thank them deeply for their time and investment in my project: Rebecca Ahlfeldt, Marika Andræ, AnnaCarin Billing, Elisabeth Björklund, Kenneth Björklund, Annelie Bränström Öhman, Jacob Bull, Matthew Davidson, Sigrid Ekblad, Lars Elleström, Stina Ericsson, Peter Forsgren, Charlotte Furth, Jack Halberstam, Robert Höglund, Christina Kullberg, Lisa Folkmarson Käll, Ursula Lindqvist, Ann-Sofie Lönngren, Benjamin Martin, Piia Posti, Magnus Rodell, Linda Sjögren, Cecilia Steen-Johnsson, Tim Tangherlini, and Anna Williams. I am also grateful to the anonymous reviewers, whose readings improved the manuscript significantly. A special thank you goes to everyone who has been involved in the project at Palgrave Macmillan, including my editor Brigitte Shull and her editorial assistants Ryan Jenkins and Naomi Tarlow.

While writing this book I have been part of a few different academic environments: The Centre for Gender Research at Uppsala University has been my base camp, but I have also spent time at the Center for Feminist Research at the University of Southern California; in the Scandinavian Section at University of California, Los Angeles; and at the School of Language and Literature at Linnæus University. I would like to thank all my colleagues, past and present, in these departments for providing intellectually engaging and friendly spaces to work in.

I have been very fortunate to receive generous financial support from many different sources: The Swedish Academy (Stina och Eriks Lundbergs stiftelse); Gästrike-Hälsinge nation (Göransson-Sandviken stipendium); Birgit och Gad Rausings stiftelse för Humanistisk Forskning; Stiftelsen Lars Hiertas Minne; Knut and Alice Wallenberg Foundation; Magnus Bergvalls Stiftelse; Stiftelsen Torsten Amundsons fond; Helge Ax:son Johnsons stiftelse; The Royal Swedish Academy of Letters, History and Antiquities (Stiftelsen Wallenbergsstiftelsens fond); The Wenner-Gren Foundations; Sven och Dagmar Saléns Stiftelse; and Stiftelsen Karl Staaffs Fond för frisinnade ändamål. I am very grateful to these benefactors who decided to support my project—without them, this book would have been much more difficult to write.

Different versions of some of the text in Chapter 1 have already appeared in print as "Frihet, jämlikhet, systerskap: Samkönat begär och gränsöverskridande kärlek i Agnes von Krusenstjernas *Fröknarna von Pahlen*" in *Tidskrift för litteraturvetenskap* 35 (3–4): 65–83 (2006); "Kärlekens gränsland: Kvinnlig homosexualitet i Agnes von Krusenstjernas *Fröknarna von Pahlen*" in *Gränser i nordisk litteratur/Borders in Nordic Literature, IASS XXVI 2006*, vol. 2, edited by Clas Zilliacus, Heidi Grönstrand, and Ulrika Gustafsson (Åbo: Åbo Akademis förlag, 2008); and "Angela + Stanny = sant: Samkönad kärlek som politik i Agnes von Krusenstjernas *Fröknarna von Pahlen*" in *Tänd eld! Essäer om Agnes von Krusenstjernas författarskap*, edited by Jenny Björklund and Anna Williams (Stockholm: Norstedts Akademiska Förlag, 2008). A summary of the main arguments in this book has been published as "En ambivalent historia: Kärlek mellan kvinnor i svensk litteratur" in *Fält i förvandling: Genusvetenskaplig litteraturforskning*, edited by Eva Heggestad, Anna Williams, and Ann Öhrberg (Hedemora: Gidlunds, 2013). I would like to thank these publishers, who have made it possible for me to further develop the ideas in these texts and include them here.

Introduction

In a world of ever-changing understandings about human sexuality, Sweden is often seen as one of the most gay-friendly countries. Same-sex sexual activity has been legal since 1944, the first national organization for gays and lesbians was founded in 1950, and Swedish law today is among the most progressive on lesbian, bisexual, gay, transgender, and queer (LGBTQ) issues in the world. However, Swedish literature tells a different, more nuanced story. This book examines representations of lesbianism in Swedish literature across the twentieth century, revealing a discourse that challenges the straightforward understanding of a progressive and tolerant Sweden. Moreover, it calls into question Sweden's role as a representative and even a pioneer in the broadly accepted Western discourse on homosexuality.

The way same-sex love is viewed in society has undergone several changes during the twentieth century, but the development has followed a similar path in most North American and European countries. The parallel courses of the history of same-sex love in these countries suggest that there is a common Western understanding of homosexuality—an understanding that has developed from what began with the repression and persecution of homosexuality in the beginning of the twentieth century but transformed into more open and tolerant attitudes toward the end (Norrhem, Rydström, and Winkvist 2008; Rizzo 2006; Tamagne 2006). As one of these European countries, Sweden can be seen as representative of this Western way of understanding homosexuality, and being viewed as one of the most liberal and progressive countries, Sweden thus has a kind of pioneer status (Hekma 2006).

This book uncovers a Swedish literary discourse on lesbianism between 1930 and 2005 by studying novels with lesbian themes. Throughout, the investigation explores the ways literary discourse confirms and/or challenges the broader, generally established sociopolitical discourse on homosexuality briefly described in the previous paragraph. Central to this book is the idea that this broader discourse on a progressive understanding of homosexuality in Sweden should be reexamined to include a literary discourse, which does not always coincide with the sociopolitical. On one hand, Swedish literature shows that there were other, more progressive ways of understanding lesbianism in the 1930s than what is suggested by the sociopolitical discourse, which focuses on medicalization. On the other hand, the subtle medicalization of lesbianism in contemporary, turn-of-the-millennium Swedish literature challenges the image of Sweden as one of the most gay-friendly societies in the world. The study of the literary discourse on lesbianism can thus contribute to a better and more nuanced understanding of the general Swedish discourse on lesbianism.

In the late nineteenth century, a common Western understanding of homosexuality as a concept and identity began to emerge with the new science of sexuality, *sexology*, and it spread quickly across Europe (Foucault [1976] 1990). Sexologists—and later psychologists—became interested in mapping sexuality, particularly what they saw as deviant. Same-sex sexuality was understood in several different ways—as inherent deviance or acquired disease, for example—but what all these understandings had in common was a medicalization of homosexuality: it became associated with pathology. While many Western countries used this medicalization to argue against the criminalization of homosexuality in the twentieth century, it still remained criminalized in many of these countries until the latter half of the century. As a result homosexuals suffered from repression and persecution, a legacy that remains today. The "invention" of homosexuality also led to the emergence of a homosexual identity, facilitating the growth of related subcultures, especially in cities, during the early twentieth century. Another turning point in the history of Western discourse on homosexuality was the new era of activism and liberation that began in the 1960s. For instance, in 1969, gays and lesbians filled the streets of Greenwich Village in New York City for what became known as the Stonewall riots, protesting the police raids of the gay and lesbian bar Stonewall Inn. This era of activism and liberation raised visibility for gays and lesbians and led to increased recognition for homosexuals as human beings and citizens. Although the general tendency is to view the history of homosexuality in the Western world as progressive—as a development from repression, persecution, and medicalization to liberation, visibility, and civil rights—it is important to remember that the course of development is not a simple success story. For example, increased visibility has led to antihomosexual campaigns and hate crimes, and heterocultural dominance is still strong in the Western world.[1]

In many ways, the progression of attitudes and views on homosexuality in Sweden follows the same pattern. A discourse on homosexuality with medicalization at its center quickly gained influence in the early twentieth century and eventually led to decriminalization in 1944. However, this change did not promote increased tolerance, and the 1950s were as homophobic in Sweden as elsewhere in the Western world. In the 1970s, gay and lesbian liberation movements thrived, and homosexuality was removed from the National Board of Health and Welfare's manual of psychological disorders in 1979. Political parties (mainly on the left) have worked for legal recognition for homosexuals since the 1970s, and parliament has taken several measures to extend rights to gay and lesbian individuals and couples. In the spring of 2009 the Swedish parliament passed legislation that replaced the 1996 law validating domestic partnership, now making marriage gender-neutral and allowing same-sex couples to marry on the same terms as heterosexual couples. Currently, Swedish gay and lesbian couples have the right to be considered as adoptive parents, and female same-sex couples are eligible for assisted reproduction in Swedish hospitals.[2]

The idea of Sweden's progression from repression to tolerance of homosexuality has not gone unchallenged. For instance, Sara Edenheim (2005)—who has studied Swedish governmental reports on homosexuality, transsexualism, and intersexualism from the twentieth century—emphasizes that rather than reflecting a progression in understandings about the nature of homosexuality, these reports showed a continuity; the beliefs the authors expressed had not fundamentally changed. Despite more tolerant attitudes reflected in later reports, the authors still imply that heterosexuality is the norm and homosexuality is an "other" that has to be normalized and adjusted to heterosexual norms.

If the Western history of homosexuality is already fairly well established, why study literature in order to learn more about lesbianism? Edenheim's critique suggests that the persistence of the belief in homosexuality as an "other" indicates that there is reason to question this history, and the study of literature can be part of such a project. Sherrie A. Inness (1997) argues that popular culture affects a society's general understanding of homosexuality; she views popular culture as "one of the most influential forces shaping lesbian identities and heterosexual perceptions of lesbianism" (3). Since lesbians are a group marginalized both in society and in mainstream culture, these representations might constitute the reality of lesbianism for many people, especially for those who have no acquaintance (to their knowledge) with "real" lesbians. Inness acknowledges this to be true for many marginalized groups, but, uniquely, gays and lesbians' identities are not always visible as such, and their sexualities might go unnoticed by people around them. Therefore, "[t]his real or imagined absence of the lesbian allows representations to take on unusual importance" (3). Along the same lines, Niall Richardson argues that cultural representations of homosexuality help shape a sense of identity for many of those gays and lesbians who grow up in isolation, outside of metropolitan areas, since they may never have met another openly gay person (Richardson 2010, 2). Since these representations provide many people with the only image of gays and lesbians, a study of these works is an essential part of an analysis of the discourse on lesbianism. While both Inness and Richardson are primarily concerned with contemporary popular culture, I would like to emphasize what should be acknowledged as one of the points of departure for this study: not only contemporary popular culture but also critically acclaimed or "high" cultural representations from different historical periods can be influential in creating a discourse on lesbianism in society.

The relationship between cultural representations and social reality has long been debated. The idea of literature and art as separate from and a reflection of the "real" world has been examined by various critics, including cultural studies scholars such as Stuart Hall, who argues that the material world has no meaning in itself. Instead, meaning is created through language when we describe or represent the world. Thus the relationship between cultural representations and social reality is dynamic rather than mimetic; when we represent something through literature or art, the representation itself produces the meaning of the social reality it depicts (Hall 1997). As Richardson states, "representations are *never* innocent—they do not just suddenly happen by accident—but are always a construct in accordance with a specific set of politics and ideas" (2010, 3). With this approach to cultural representations and social reality, literature can be seen as part of a discourse in Michel Foucault's sense: it is a group of statements that provide a language for that which can be said about and thought of a certain topic in a given context—that is, a kind of knowledge production. Thus literary representations of different phenomena contribute to setting boundaries for how these phenomena can be described in that culture (Foucault [1969] 2002; Foucault [1976] 1990). For instance, our understanding of lesbians comes from different areas of society such as laws, mass media, and political debate as well as from literature. Close readings of literary texts can thus contribute to our understanding of the discourses in a given culture, revealing a complexity that might not be visible in law texts and policy documents.

This book is, of course, not the first to address literary representations of lesbianism. The field of research is large, especially in the Anglo-American world, large enough to write an Anglo-American lesbian literary history. Early scholarship such as Lillian Faderman's *Surpassing the Love of Men*, originally published in 1981, and Bonnie Zimmerman's *The Safe Sea of Women* from 1990 have strongly influenced the shaping of this literary history. Most later scholars agree with and confirm, or at least relate to, the representations of lesbian literary history as it is created out of Faderman's and Zimmerman's studies. Even those who do not agree with the Faderman/Zimmerman model still use it as a point of departure and a foil for their own studies.

Before turning to Swedish lesbian literature, it is important to understand what the Anglo-American version of lesbian literary history looks like, both because of its broadness in scope and because of the aforementioned interconnectedness of Western ideas. Prior to the turn of the twentieth century, Anglo-American literature offered positive depictions of love between women, or "romantic friendships" as Faderman ([1981] 2001) refers to them. According to Faderman and Zimmerman (1990) this changed with the emergence of sexology at the turn of the twentieth century, when literature was invaded by lesbian vampires and monsters as well as representations of female homosexuals as lonely and misunderstood. Faderman finds two basic types depicted in writing during the early and mid-1900s: "the lesbian as sickie" and "the lesbian as martyr." Zimmerman views 1969—the year of the Stonewall rallies—as a watershed year. After Stonewall, lesbianism was redeemed, and novels that celebrated lesbians and a "lesbian lifestyle" were published. Zimmerman (but also Faderman, who briefly covers post-Stonewall lesbian literature in the end of her book) connects the themes of lesbian literature after 1969 to second-wave feminism. Both scholars write that this literature portrays lesbianism not only as a sexual identity but also as a political statement, a way of leading a life outside of patriarchy.[3]

Anglo-American lesbian literary history is strikingly similar to the Western history of homosexuality. On a social level, lesbianism was medicalized by the science of sexuality, and at the same time, early twentieth-century literature was invaded by images with medically judgmental connotations: "the lesbian as sickie" or "the lesbian as martyr," the latter implying that lesbians were to be seen as victims of a medical condition rather than as criminals. After Stonewall, lesbianism was redeemed by the gay liberation movement and by a more open society, and novels that celebrate women, lesbians, the lesbian lifestyle, and feminism were published. Anglo-American literary history thus appears to confirm the progressive view of the history of homosexuality. Sociopolitical developments and literary representations seem to coincide.

In contrast, lesbianism in Swedish literature is not a large field of research. Only two detailed studies have been published on this topic: Eva Borgström's (2008) book on desire between women in nineteenth-century literature and Liv Saga Bergdahl's (2010) dissertation on identity and (in)visibility in Swedish twentieth-century lesbian novels—and only Bergdahl's study covers the period this book explores.[4] While these texts are important contributions to the Swedish literary history of lesbianism, they are not primarily concerned with the ways literature relates and contributes to sociopolitical discourse.

Swedish twentieth-century novels contain a surprising number of lesbian characters,[5] and because this book conducts close readings of each text, it cannot cover all these novels. Instead this study covers representative material from three different periods: the 1930s, when homosexuality (including same-sex eroticism between women) was still criminalized in Sweden; the 1960s, when homosexuality was defined as a psychological disorder by the Swedish government; and the turn of the millennium, with its more liberal laws and attitudes toward homosexuality. By studying Swedish literary representations of lesbianism between 1930 and 2005, this book aims to contribute to a better and more nuanced understanding of the Swedish discourse on lesbianism. As mentioned, Sweden is representative of the Western way of understanding homosexuality but is generally seen as being even more open and tolerant. The previously described Western history of homosexuality—not based particularly on literature but on other sources such as medicine, legislation, policy making, and historical documents—indicates that society has come to view lesbians less as deviants and more as humans and citizens during the twentieth century; the course of history seems to follow a progression of ideas. However, this book examines the way literary representations challenge this idea, even in the context of a nation that is thought to have an unusually liberal attitude toward homosexuality. Swedish literary representations of lesbianism show remarkable continuity during the twentieth century, suggesting that the clear divisions between early twentieth-century thought, the 1960s sexual revolution, and present-day norms may deserve a second look.

This study is grounded in literary and cultural studies, and the point of departure will be textual analysis. It will also rely on historical and sociological research on lesbianism (and homosexuality) in Sweden, using different materials as resources in an ambition to contribute to the understanding of the Swedish discourse on lesbianism. This methodology builds on a set of approaches that Judith Halberstam (1998) calls a "queer methodology," grounded in her understanding of the drawbacks that different approaches to sexuality research pose. For example, ethnographical methods have their shortcomings since there is no way for the scholar to observe people in the bedroom. Surveys are unreliable since people do not tend to be reliable when reporting on their sexual behavior: men tend to exaggerate and women tend to downplay. On the other hand, text-oriented, cultural studies scholars are criticized by proponents of social science for not paying enough attention to the everyday realities of queer life. Halberstam is critical of "this belief in the real and the material as separate from the represented and the textual," since it recreates "some essential divide between the truth of sexual behavior and the fiction of textual analysis" (12). Her resulting "queer methodology" is an interdisciplinary approach. Following Halberstam's lead, this book uses a variety of sources in order to avoid the downsides of a purely textual focus, and as a result, it will not particularly focus on the formal and aesthetic aspects of the literary texts. However, since the aim is to study literary representations of lesbianism, the book will, of course, look at *how* the literary texts create lesbianism and, hence, how they work as literature.

Chapter 1 focuses on the 1930s, a period when Agnes von Krusenstjerna (1894–1940) was the only author who wrote extensively on the subject of lesbianism. She was extremely productive, making it impossible to cover all her work. This study explores *Fröknarna von Pahlen* (1930–35; *The Misses von Pahlen*), Krusenstjerna's series of novels that is perhaps her most famous work and also the texts that feature love between women most prominently. These seven books contain several different, sometimes contradictory, representations of lesbianism. The portrayals of love between women create a kind of political arena, where different views of lesbianism at that time are tried out by the characters. In this arena, ideas of deviance and disorder coexist with depictions of love between women as empowering and as a way to escape a male-dominated society. The end of the chapter connects ideas in these novels to similar representations of lesbianism in two other novels published in the 1930s: Margareta Suber's *Charlie* and Karin Boye's *Kris* (*Crisis*).

Chapter 2 examines the work of Annakarin Svedberg (1934–), the author who wrote the most extensively on the subject of lesbianism during the 1960s. The representations of lesbianism in her novels show remarkable continuity with those in Krusenstjerna's novels from the 1930s. The connection between homosexuality and the medical discourse established at the turn of the century is even more strongly articulated in Svedberg's work than in Krusenstjerna's, but this discourse is also challenged more explicitly. Moreover, her work is concerned with discrimination based on sexual identity and describes the injustices lesbians face in this society. Writing plays a key role in Svedberg's novels, and it becomes a political means of influencing society for the better both for lesbians and for women in general. The end of the chapter connects Svedberg's work to a few other novels with lesbian themes from the 1960s, exploring how lesbianism is represented through the same ambiguous discourse.

Chapter 3 is devoted to three key lesbian-themed novels from the turn of the millennium: Louise Boije af Gennäs's (1961–) *Stjärnor utan svindel* (1996; *Stars without Vertigo*) and Mian Lodalen's (1962–) *Smulklubbens skamlösa systrar* (2003; *The Shameless Sisters of the Scraps Club*) and *Trekant* (2005; *Three-some*). These three novels reached a wide audience and were published internationally, thus becoming important in shaping the turn-of-the-millennium discourse on lesbianism. *Stjärnor utan svindel* was the first Swedish novel with a prominent lesbian theme to reach a wide audience during this period. Mian Lodalen's first two novels take place in a similar environment and are concerned with the same theme—lesbian life in contemporary Stockholm. In these texts lesbianism is connected to gay and lesbian rights and women's empowerment, but the connections to the medical discourse have not disappeared entirely. Writing also plays a prominent role in these novels, and as in Svedberg's novels, writing can be seen as a political strategy. Again, the end of the chapter connects the three novels to similar representations of lesbianism in other novels from this time period, all with lesbian themes as well.

The conclusion explores these three periods together and in relation to sociopolitical discourses on lesbianism. In contrast to the Anglo-American literary history, the Swedish literary discourse does not mirror the Western progressive view on the history of homosexuality. Literary representations and sociopolitical development do not always coincide. Instead, negative images of lesbianism as a medical condition or disorder are prevalent during the entire period, which indicates the lasting power of this discourse in the ideas and understandings of lesbianism across the twentieth century. On the other hand, lesbianism is also connected to positive images throughout the twentieth century, and even as far back as the 1930s, Agnes von Krusenstjerna depicted love between women as ideal love, connecting it to women's empowerment almost half a century before radical feminism and lesbian feminism movements took form.

Through careful readings of literary texts, this book attempts to build a better understanding of the idea that discrimination and marginalization are measured not only by political successes or setbacks. Throughout the twentieth century and into the twenty-first, literature tells a nuanced story about lesbianism in Sweden, a story not always in line with the sociopolitical discourses of the time. On one hand, we can find seeds for more recent societal changes in literature from the 1930s, at a time when the sociopolitical discourse on lesbianism tended to be dominated by the medical discourse. On the other hand, if traces of discrimination persist in contemporary literature despite long-standing initiatives for equity in the law, we as a society need to look further for additional models and approaches to create a truly open and progressive society.

CHAPTER 1

THE POLITICAL SCENE OF LOVE
AGNES VON KRUSENSTJERNA AND THE 1930S

The 1930s was a time of discursive change in Sweden, especially in terms of sexuality. The Social Democrats came to power in 1932 and started building the foundation of the welfare state—or "the people's home" (*folkhemmet*) as Social Democrat leader Per Albin Hansson called it. Further, during the 1930s Sweden underwent a process of industrialization and urbanization as well as economic and population crises. The population crisis and the building of the welfare state brought issues of family planning and sexuality to the political agenda, and RFSU, the Swedish association for sexual education, was founded in 1933. Several reforms were passed by parliament that allowed greater sexual freedom, and a new discourse gained influence, emphasizing sexuality as intrinsically good and something that could increase happiness in the population. These new ideas gradually replaced the former discourse, represented by the church, which focused on the reproductive aspects of sexuality (Lennerhed 2002).

However, this change in attitude toward sexuality was strongly tied to the heterosexual couple. Voices both within and outside RFSU argued for the decriminalization of homosexuality, but this issue was not a priority for the organization. Moreover, many different ways of understanding homosexuality and its causes and effects were fighting for discursive space in Swedish society in the 1930s. The medical discourse dominated; homosexuality was generally seen as a disease or psychological deviance, but there was no consensus on its causes, whether it could be treated, and how society should deal with people "suffering" from this "condition" (Lennerhed 2002; Rydström 2003). Adding to the complexity, several scholars have observed how different attitudes toward same-sex sexuality could exist, side by side, within the same organization or even within the same text (Lennerhed 2002, 159–71; Lindeqvist 2006, 8; Lundahl 2005, 268). While the medical discourse gained influence during the 1930s, homosexuality was not decriminalized until 1944, and several cases of same-sex offenses went to court or were handled by the police during the 1930s and 1940s (Lennerhed 2002; Rydström 2003).

In the 1930s, love between women gained increased attention in literature. Radclyffe Hall's *The Well of Loneliness* (1928) was translated into Swedish in 1932, and several Swedish novels with lesbian themes came out: Margareta Suber's *Charlie* (1932), Karin Boye's *Kris* (1934; *Crisis*), and Agnes von Krusenstjerna's seven-volume suite *Fröknarna von Pahlen* (1930–35; *The Misses von Pahlen*). The main focus of this chapter is Agnes von Krusenstjerna (1894–1940), one of the most radical writers in Swedish literary history. At first glance her novels might not seem that radical, as they depict upper-class women and the protected environments where they led their lives. However, under the neat and quiet surface, the novels present themes such as women's sexuality, same-sex desire, and even incest— taboo ideas in Swedish society at the time, particularly for an aristocratic woman such as Krusenstjerna. In fact, the book series *Fröknarna von Pahlen* caused one of the most heated newspaper debates in Swedish literary history. The novels were criticized for being too explicit and graphic on the subject of sexuality and were accused of being immoral. The first three novels were released by the prestigious publishing house Albert Bonniers Förlag, but editor Karl Otto Bonnier refused to take on the remaining four novels because he thought publishing them would discredit his press. Instead the last four novels were released by a small independent publisher, Spektrum (Svanberg 1989, 45–46; Williams 2013, 335–93).

Krusenstjerna was an extremely productive writer. She made her debut at the age of 23 with the novel *Ninas dagbok* (1917; *Nina's Diary*) and continued to publish novels as well as short stories and some poetry until her death. Her marriage to writer and critic David Sprengel was unconventional at the time; he more or less set his own career aside in order to support his wife, whom he believed to be a more talented writer than himself. He read her manuscripts and helped her with editing. Early scholarship argued that Sprengel played an important part in Krusenstjerna's work, suggesting that she was not herself responsible for the radicalism of her work (Ahlgren 1940; Lagercrantz [1951] 1980). This has been disputed by feminist scholars such as Birgitta Svanberg (1989), who studied the original manuscripts of *Fröknarna von Pahlen* in detail and argued that Sprengel's additions suggest that his literary style was not as strong as his wife's. She concludes with saying that it is impossible to know exactly to what extent Sprengel was involved in his wife's authorship, but that her high level of productivity at least indicates that he was a supportive husband (19–23, 37–41).

At the time of her death in 1940, Krusenstjerna was one of the most famous female writers in Sweden but also one of the most controversial. In some libraries her novels were kept in restricted areas, only available to readers who requested them at the information desk (Svanberg 1989, 7). Her authorship has inspired many scholars; seven book-length studies as well as many articles and book chapters have been written on her work.[1] Previous scholars have discussed lesbian themes in her work, but not many have focused exclusively on them.

This study will explore two examples of love between women in *Fröknarna von Pahlen* in the light of historical research on sexuality and gender to see how these fictional representations relate to the contemporary sociopolitical discourse. Krusenstjerna's book series depicts two very different ideas about lesbianism in the character Bell von Wenden, who is explicitly and exclusively drawn to other women, and in the relationship between Angela von Pahlen and Agda Wising. The character Bell represents the deviant, diseased, and threatening, while the relationship between Angela and Agda is one of the most beautifully portrayed love affairs in the entire book series. By depicting Angela and Agda's love in a positive light, Krusenstjerna's work challenges some of the judgmental attitudes associated with the 1930s and presents a new image of lesbianism that is empowering for women—today's readers may even view Krusenstjerna's portrait of this relationship as radical feminist. However, at the same time, the imagery used to portray Angela and Agda's love has connections to the medical discourse on female same-sex love. Several different and even conflicting views representing different attitudes about lesbianism from the 1930s intersect in their relationship. These views seem to allude to a larger discourse on same-sex love, making the book into a kind of political arena where different attitudes are tried against each other.

BELL VON WENDEN AND THE MEDICAL DISCOURSE

Readers of *Fröknarna von Pahlen* are introduced to several characters and settings throughout the seven novels, but the main plot line follows two misses von Pahlen, Petra and her niece Angela, for nearly a decade. The books begin in 1906 when Petra, 27 years old and unmarried, takes in 11-year-old Angela after the death of Angela's parents. The novels mostly take place in the Stockholm area and in Eka, the mansion that Petra owns in Småland, a province in southern Sweden. In the last novel, Petra and Angela start a women's commune in Eka, "a big and loving land for children and women"[2] (*Av samma blod*, 478). Both Petra and Angela remain unmarried, but they have relationships—both friendships and love affairs—with men and women throughout the novels. In the end of the final novel, Angela gives birth to a child that Petra and Angela plan to raise together in the women's commune without any help from the father, Thomas Meller, who is already out of the picture.

The book series includes one female character, Bell von Wenden, who is exclusively and openly attracted to women. When Bell is first introduced in the second volume, she works as a teacher at the school of home economics for girls that Angela von Pahlen attends as a teenager. In many ways Bell is represented as a stereotypical lesbian according to 1930s medical theories: "She looked at women as the way a man looks at them: with heated desire. For her it was natural to desire a young woman, whose body blossomed and smelled good"[3] (*Kvinnogatan*, 160). This quote seems to embody the sexological theory of the female homosexual—or the inverted woman, as she was often called—as a body stuck between genders. Sexologists such as Richard von Krafft-Ebing and Havelock Ellis viewed homosexuality primarily as a congenital inversion of the sexual drive, connected to androgyny. In his famous study of deviant sexual behavior, *Psychopathia Sexualis*, Krafft-Ebing describes the lesbian as follows: "The masculine soul, heaving in the female bosom, finds pleasure in the pursuit of manly sports, and in manifestations of courage and bravado. There is a strong desire to imitate the male fashion in dressing the hair and in general attire, under favourable circumstances even to don male attire and impose in it. Arrests of women in men's clothing are by no means of rare occurrence" (Krafft-Ebing [1886] 1998, 264). In his book Krafft-Ebing defines various degrees of homosexuality, but they all have in common an emphasis on the homosexual's androgynous traits; the gay man was thought of as being feminine and the lesbian woman as masculine. This is particularly obvious in Krafft-Ebing's case studies (Krafft-Ebing [1886] 1998, 35–36, 186–88). Ellis, too, understands homosexuality as a congenital deviance, but he argues that this deviance can become stronger due to social and psychological circumstances. According to Ellis, the development that makes us into either men or women has not proceeded "normally" in the homosexual, and he or she is therefore in an androgynous state. Thus lesbians have masculine traits, but Ellis also emphasizes that all androgynous individuals are not necessarily sexually inverted (Ellis [1901] 1920, 196, 310–11, 322).

Sexologists like Krafft-Ebing and Ellis viewed homosexuality as primarily innate, but other understandings of homosexuality existed at the turn of the century. Sigmund Freud and his psychoanalytic followers viewed homosexuality mainly as a result of an abnormal psychosexual development—that is, primarily socially and psychologically acquired. Freud himself did not establish any direct connections between homosexuality and pathology, although his theories have been used to support the medicalization of homosexuality that took place in the twentieth century. Moreover, some of his theories on homosexuality are similar to the sexologists'. For instance, Freud, too, emphasizes a connection between homosexuality and androgyny, at least in female inverts who, according to Freud, often have masculine traits (Freud [1905] 1953, 136–48; Freud [1920] 1955, 147–72).

As previously mentioned, the science of sexuality gained influence in the Western world during the twentieth century and contributed to the medicalization of homosexuality. Prior to sexology, sexuality was viewed as practices that did not determine an individual's identity in any way, but with the rise of sexology, sexuality came to be seen as part of what shaped our identities. Hence homosexuality as an identity or a sexual orientation did not exist before the science of sexuality. As a part of this change in beliefs, nonheterosexual practices were medicalized, and same-sex sexuality became part of the medical discourse on so-called deviant sexual behavior (Foucault [1976] 1990).

This process occurred in Sweden as well, and several scholars have discussed how the medicalization of homosexuality was particularly intense in the 1930s (Lennerhed 2002; Rydström 2003). Further, Pia Lundahl (2001) argues that a shift of paradigms—similar to the late-nineteenth-century discursive change described by Foucault—took place in Sweden around 1930. Lundahl focuses on the descriptions of intimacy between female prisoners in charts, reports, and other written accounts. She finds that eroticism between women before 1930 was not labeled as "homosexual" or "lesbian," or viewed as part of the identity of these women; same-sex erotic practices of these women were thought to coexist with other erotic practices, including heterosexual. Erotic relationships between female prisoners were seen as a substitute; lacking men in the prisons, the women looked for erotic fulfillment in each other. Hence intimacy between women was not connected to a homosexual or lesbian identity but was viewed rather as an expression of immorality or oversexuality in general. However, around 1930 a change took place. Erotic practices between women were now generally understood in the light of medical science and sexology, which had its breakthrough around the turn of the century but started to gain influence in Sweden around 1930. Now intimacy between women came to be viewed as an expression of a homosexual identity.[4]

Since the science of sexuality gained influence in Sweden in the 1930s when Krusenstjerna wrote *Fröknarna von Pahlen*, it is not surprising that the character Bell's same-sex desire is explained with references to sexological and psychoanalytical theories. As we have seen, Krafft-Ebing, Ellis, and Freud all emphasize masculinity as a prominent trait in the female homosexual, and in Krusenstjerna's novel, Bell's behavior is, accordingly, compared to that of a man. However, looking beyond her actions—which include a range of behaviors attributed to masculinity and femininity as well as female homosexuality—Bell von Wenden is not presented as androgynous; she is described as feminine with curly blond hair and red lips. However, by desiring women and looking at them "as a man," Bell claims masculinity. She competes with men for women, and since her desire for women is said to be natural, it comes across as congenital—like Krafft-Ebing's "invert," she seems to have a male soul (which desires women) in a female bosom.

Krusenstjerna describes Bell's background in one chapter, alluding to another explanation of female homosexuality as connected to motherhood, a theory that is discussed by Freud. In "The Psychogenesis of a Case of Female Homosexuality" (1920), Freud describes a young female patient who has fallen in love with an older woman. He primarily views her love object as a mother substitute. At an early stage in life, the young woman had an ambivalent relationship with her mother, and when the girl reached puberty, her mother gave birth to a sibling. The young woman was at a stage of puberty associated with regression to an infantile Oedipus complex: She wishes to have a child with her father, but, instead, her competitor, her mother, has a child with him. In disappointment she turns away from her father and from men in general and searches for a new object for her libido. The real mother is not a possible object for love, so the girl finds a mother substitute. Giving up men was also a benefit of this "illness"; her mother still liked male attention, so by giving up men and leaving them to her mother, the young woman eliminated the competition that used to make her mother hostile (Freud [1920] 1955, 156–59). Thus according to Freud and his followers, some cases of female homosexuality could be understood as a way of finding a substitute for a mother who, for various reasons, could not meet the needs of her child. Allusions to this explanation of lesbianism can be found in the chapter on Bell von Wenden's background: Bell grew up in an orphanage, but she was taken care of by a widow when she was 12 and received a good education. Thus Bell's mother was literally absent, which, according to psychoanalytic theory at the time, might cause her to love women. While an older woman might function better as a mother substitute according to this explanation, Bell usually falls in love with young women. However, Frank S. Caprio ([1954] 1958), who builds on Freudian theories, argues that older lesbians who had dysfunctional relationships with their mothers might fall in love with young women and love them as daughters to compensate for the love they never received from their mothers (123).

Previous scholars have acknowledged that most representations and theories of female homosexuality as a disease or deviance can be summarized in three Ms: *masculinity*—lesbianism as a man's soul captured in a woman's body; *mothering*—lesbianism as caused by a troubled relationship between daughter and mother, which makes the daughter search for a mother substitute in her love relationships; and *mirrors*—lesbianism seen as an expression of narcissism (Allen 1996, 89; Fjelkestam 2002, 112–19; O'Connor and Ryan 1993). The first introduction of Bell quoted previously alludes to two of the Ms: *masculinity* and *mothering*. However, this portrayal is not representative of her character in the book series as a whole; Bell is usually described as feminine, and her background as an orphan is hardly ever referred to.

Instead, the third *M*, *mirrors*, dominates passages about Bell. This explanation can be traced to Freud, who discusses the connection between love and narcissism in "On Narcissism" (1914). As previously mentioned, Freud himself did not pathologize homosexuality, but his theories have been used as support in the medicalization of same-sex desire that took place in the twentieth century. Freud argues that, from birth, human beings originally have two love objects: themselves and their caregivers, the mother/woman. Men usually choose their love object with their mothers as a model, while most women have themselves as a model. The narcissistic object choice can but does not have to indicate homosexuality, and Freud emphasizes that people with a disordered libido development (e.g., "perverts and homosexuals") often model their love object based on themselves and not their mother (Freud [1914] 1957, 87–90).

Allusions to narcissistic object choice recur in the passages describing Bell and, more directly, when Bell herself speaks. One afternoon at the housekeeping school, Angela visits Bell in her room, and Bell gives her own explanation of lesbian love:

Girlfriends can love each other also. I know that. That kind of love is easier to understand. That's what I think. Men are so different from us. They never understand us. They live in their own little worlds made only for themselves. I have never met a man who was not an egotist. A man gets his nourishment from his own strength. A woman always needs someone else to love, to sacrifice for, to cry and laugh together with. Then she is her strongest. Shouldn't love be the happiest when the person you love is similar to yourself—also in terms of your body? You admire your own graces in someone else, even to a greater extent. You cannot fondle yourself or caress yourself. That's called narcissism. But to embrace an image similar to you, yet more beautiful and more developed, that is to try to mold yourself after perfection. Then you mature and become a whole woman. I think that we have to reach outside of ourselves, but we lose ourselves and become entirely lost if we search for a soul-mate as different from us as a man. Do you understand?[5] (*Kvinnogatan*, 190)

Bell validates lesbian love based on the idea that men and women are different; women will therefore be happier if they love other women, who can understand them fully. But importantly, the quote also presents a connection between homosexuality and narcissism, although Bell seems not to see the connection herself; according to her, lesbian love is a substitute for and connected to a woman's love for herself.

In line with twentieth-century discourse, narcissism as an explanation for female homosexuality is medicalized by Krusenstjerna as Bell totters into insanity. One day Bell takes the students on a trip in the forest. Bell is in love with Angela and jealous of the close friendship between Angela and another girl, Stanny Landborg. When they are ready to eat, Angela and Stanny are missing, and Bell goes to look for them. While she is looking, she comes to think of all the girls she has loved over the years, and she sees them ahead of her as visions. While following the false images she suddenly discovers her own shadow on the ground, "a young woman's body"[6] (*Kvinnogatan*, 224) with "a little strange head with hair like crawling snakes"[7] (*Kvinnogatan*, 224). Bell bends over the shadow and realizes eventually that it is her own shadow and not a beloved woman: "she had loved herself, enjoyed herself, eaten up her own heart, so that blood now dripped from her lips"[8] (*Kvinnogatan*, 224). She loses consciousness, and the same night, after the girls have found her and carried her back to the school, she is taken to a mental institution.

The Medusa allusion—Bell's hair looks like crawling snakes—makes Bell monster-like. This image, presented in conjunction with images alluding to her sexual orientation, suggests that lesbianism in general is threatening and dangerous. In addition, the third *M, mirrors*, is again strongly emphasized in this passage. Bell is said to have loved herself, and the dangerous and almost deadly results of that kind of love are laid out through the bloody imagery. The heart is connected to both life and love, so her love, too, is tied to destruction and death in this passage. The bloody metaphors and the allusions to threatening characters such as Medusa portray the lesbian as a monster or vampire. As Lillian Faderman ([1981] 2001) argues, this image can be found in other literary works from the beginning of the twentieth century. Bell von Wenden is depicted as a "lesbian evil" character, as Faderman describes them in her book, and her sexual orientation is portrayed as deviant and pathological. The fact that Bell's breakdown leads up to her confinement in a mental institution could be read as a final verdict on lesbian love as connected to mental illness, as least in the case of Bell von Wenden.

Bell is associated with deviance and disease at an early stage; the chapter that describes her upbringing indicates that she had masochistic tendencies as a child. She found pleasure in being physically punished by the director of the orphanage, and this drive is so strong that she breaks rules in order to be punished:

> Gradually, out of the first terrible fear of being punished grew a strange desire to be punished. A raging, itching desire that made her throat dry and burning and that chased her all the way into her dreams at night. When the director fumbled with the buttons of her pants, she clung to her, sobbing, with wide-open eyes, jerking in spasms. The shame, feelings of shyness, everything melted away for this longing for the burning pain those hands caused her. She lurched and twisted over the director's knees only to feel the pleasure of the whips stronger, the heat in her body, the throbbing beat of her pulse. She committed infractions that were seen as mischief and evil just to be led again, trembling, to the director and receive the punishment.[9]
> (*Kvinnogatan*, 161–62)

The erotic overtones are clear in this passage, where images such as "heat in her body," "the throbbing beat," and "jerking in spasms" can be connected to sexual desire and even orgasm. Both Richard von Krafft-Ebing and Sigmund Freud discuss masochism as deviance in their writings, and Krafft-Ebing argues that masochism and homosexuality are sometimes connected, both in men and in women. Freud points out that the childhood physical punishment of whipping the child's behind can lead to masochistic tendencies in adulthood (Krafft-Ebing [1886] 1998, 86–143; Freud [1905] 1953, 157–60, 193). Thus Bell is doubly pathologized; she is not only lesbian but also a masochist.

Furthermore, Bell is referred to as "the perverse child"[10] (*Kvinnogatan*, 162), and she is described as a flower in the swamp: "She looked like one of those light red flowers, which thrive in the swamps and twist their slimy roots deeper and deeper into the mud. They blossom in the sunshine with their heads over the glossy water surface, while they get all their nutrition and all their life from the dark, subterranean decay that they're firmly rooted to. Like these flowers Bell led a double life, forced into it by dark drives and the environment she grew up in"[11] (*Kvinnogatan*, s. 162). This quote is based on contrasts: the beautiful, tranquil, and light oppose the dark and rotten. The beautiful is visible from the outside, above the surface, while the dark is invisible and subterranean. However, these two parts are interconnected; the beautiful flower gets its nutrition from the dark and subterranean. Kristina Fjelkestam, when discussing another passage in *Kvinnogatan*, mentions that Bell's homosexuality is said to be a curse in her blood but also caused by her upbringing, and she argues that Bell thus embodies the two most common views of the time— homosexuality as caused by inheritance and by environment (Fjelkestam 2002, 94). This quote can be read as an expression of both views of that time, where Bell's double life is said to be caused by inheritance, "dark drives," as well as "the environment she grew up in."

As we have seen, Bell represents many contemporary explanations of female homosexuality, and her desire for women is continually medicalized. Her character could thus be read in line with the Swedish debate on homosexuality in the 1930s. As previously mentioned, several different and sometimes contradicting understandings of homosexuality existed side by side in the debate, and different attitudes were expressed within the same organization or even in the same text. This confusion applies to Bell von Wenden, too. Her sexuality is seen as both congenital and acquired, and she embodies explanations of homosexuality connected to *masculinity, mothering,* and *mirrors.* She is even described as masochistic. However, all these conflicting explanations have one thing in common: medicalization. The portrayal of Bell can thus be said to reflect the debate in the Swedish 1930s and read as a claim for seeing lesbianism as a disease rather than a crime.

BELL VON WENDEN VERSUS ANGELA AND AGDA: THE MADWOMAN IN THE ATTIC

In the final novel of *Fröknarna von Pahlen,* Angela von Pahlen falls in love and starts a relationship with another woman, Agda Wising. At this point Angela and Agda live together with a few other women at Petra's mansion, Eka. Three of the women—Angela, Agda, and Frideborg—are pregnant, but the fathers are out of the picture, and the women plan to raise the children together at Eka. The relationship between Angela and Agda provides a foil for the negative portrayal of lesbian love that Bell von Wenden embodies. The distance between these portrayals is established through imagery; in contrast to Bell's lesbian lust as detailed in the previous section, Angela and Agda's love is depicted as light, pure, fertile, and natural—and as the ideal kind of love. The novel's description of Angela and Agda's relationship as natural and good contradicts the 1930s sociopolitical context, which presented lesbianism as deviant and diseased. However, the imagery describing their relationship also is connected to the medical discourse found in the representations of Bell. These two kinds of images exist side by side in the text and create a conflict between the contemporary negative and medicalized image of homosexuality and the more positive view, less common in the sociopolitical context of the 1930s.

Bell's traits contrast sharply with the qualities emphasized in Angela and Agda. Angela's name alludes to angels, and Agda is sometimes depicted as a Christ character, offering salvation to people in need of it. For instance, she marries Count Gusten Sauss af Värnamo in order to save him from his sinful life and make him pure. Moreover, the imagery describing Angela and Agda's relationship often suggests purity and health. One beautiful winter day they go out on a trip on the grounds of the mansion. The description of the winter landscape is dominated by the color white, the open fields, and the refreshing cold, images connected to purity, freedom, and health, respectively. These ideas are also presented more generally in the passage: Angela and Agda's outdoors adventure is contrasted with Frideborg's choice to stay inside in front of the fireplace, even though she knows that fresh air is good for her condition— Frideborg is also pregnant. During the trip Agda reflects on how her love for Angela has made her feel free: "Never before had she had this sense of freedom of both body and soul"[12] (*Av samma blod*, 257). These positive ideas contrast with images of death, destruction, disease, and decay used to describe Bell in the previous section.

Some scholars argue that Bell is being condemned in *Fröknarna von Pahlen* because she represents the wrong kind of love: a love based on inequality and exploitation of the female body (Lagercrantz [1951] 1980, 212; Mazzarella 1992, 118–19; Paqvalén 2007, 315–16). However, Bell is not entirely condemned and dismissed as diseased. Both Angela and Agda are drawn to Bell, and her philosophy on love in the second part of the book series (*Kvinnogatan*, 190), discussed in the previous section, is, in fact, similar to the ideas about love advocated in the book series as a whole. Agda even refers to Bell's rationalization of lesbian love when she talks to Angela about their own love (*Av samma blod*, 259). In addition, Bell's description of men as egotistical beings who live for themselves and do not understand women matches what the women in *Fröknarna von Pahlen* experience when interacting with men. These negative experiences with men finally lead the women to distance themselves from men in the end of the series. Instead they start a women's commune at Eka, where they plan to live in love and happiness with each other and with the new children who are to be born—this is indeed the very same lifestyle that Bell advocates for in the second book.

On the other hand, Bell is represented as the kind of lesbian debated in contemporary Swedish society: a pathologized and sad figure who could not help her desire for women. She stands for everything that the good love between women is distanced from. Even though Agda uses Bell's words to define

Angela and her love, she still draws a boundary between her love for Angela and what Bell represents by arguing that Bell is probably not a real woman and that she has a twisted emotional life (*Av samma blod*, 259). Interestingly, despite the fact that Agda has just validated Bell's perspective, she then follows by dismissing Bell with a description that falls in line with contemporary medicalized images of lesbians.

How then is Bell von Wenden to be understood? She could be read as a lesbian version of the madwoman in the attic. In their classic study *The Madwoman in the Attic* from 1979, Sandra M. Gilbert and Susan Gubar argue that women writers of the nineteenth century had to rebel against the images of women that hitherto had dominated (male) literary history: the woman as angel and the woman as monster. Gilbert and Gubar view Charlotte Brontë's *Jane Eyre* as a paradigmatic novel; the perfect heroine Jane Eyre contrasts with her evil double Bertha Mason, the madwoman hidden in the attic but also the wife of the man, Edward Rochester, who Jane wants to marry. Women writers from this time often created perfect heroines who adjust to the norms of patriarchy (angels) but also wrote independent and crazy women (monsters) into the stories—women who try to break down the patriarchal structures that both the heroine and the writer seem to accept. Thus the writer projects all her rebellious impulses on a mad character instead of on her heroine. Gilbert and Gubar argue that this is a way for the writer to phrase her own ambivalence in relation to the patriarchal rules: she wants to adjust to the rules (like the angel-heroine) but also rebel against them (like the monster). From this perspective, the madwoman in the text can be seen as the writer's double and an image of her own rage (Gilbert and Gubar [1979] 2000, 17, 77–78, 86, 336–71).

Bell fits into this model to a certain extent, and some previous scholars have used Gilbert and Gubar's framework in their readings of Krusenstjerna's novels, though not so much in regards to Bell. Birgitta Svanberg has a more conciliatory view of Bell von Wenden than many other scholars, and she argues that Bell can be seen as a foil for Angela and Agda's idyllic love. She also mentions briefly, but in a different context, that it is possible to see Bell as a monster character in Gilbert and Gubar's sense (Svanberg 1989, 186, 376–79, 385–86). However, she never connects these two arguments. Piecing these two ideas together, Bell von Wenden can be read as a madwoman in regards to the book series' lesbian theme. Merete Mazzarella views Krusenstjerna's supporting characters as aspects of the main characters and argues that these, in turn, are aspects of herself. She suggests that the lesbian or bisexual character Maud Borck in *Tony växer upp* (1922) could be read as a projection of Krusenstjerna herself and her inability to control her own erotic impulses (Mazzarella 1992, 44–45, 47). Mazzarella does not refer to Gilbert and Gubar in this context, but their argument has been applied to *Fröknarna von Pahlen* by other scholars; both Birgitta Svanberg and Eva Adolfsson have read another character, Adèle Holmström, as a madwoman in the attic, and this is a reasonable interpretation from a heterosexual perspective (Svanberg 1989, 131–35; Adolfsson 1983, 207–15; Adolfsson 1991, 41–46).

However, moving beyond the heterosexual frame of interpretation, Bell von Wenden can also be viewed as a monster character in the Gilbert and Gubar sense—especially if she is read as a foil for Angela and Agda, who have many similarities to the angelic heroines in these two scholars' study. Putting aside Gilbert and Gubar's connections between the author's position as a woman writer in a male-dominated society, the angel/monster dichotomy also plays an important role within the context of the book. There are several similarities between Gilbert and Gubar's monster character and Bell. First, the locations of Bell's homes suggest that she is a kind of attic character: In the beginning at the school of home economics, Bell lives in a room on the upper floor of the house, and when she later returns to the book series she lives in Stockholm in an apartment with "many stairs" to climb. Second, Bell is directly connected to Medusa, as explored in the previous section. Gilbert and Gubar also refer to Medusa in relation to the monster woman: the character has a Medusa face that kills female creativity—therefore the woman writer has to get rid of the monster, kill it (Gilbert and Gubar [1979] 2000, 17).

While Bell's sexual desire is continually emphasized in the book series as she tries to seduce the women she encounters, Angela and Agda's relationship comes across as fairly innocent. On one occasion their love is expressed erotically, but aside from that it is depicted as platonic. But more important, it never seriously threatens the moral system of the 1930s society. Both Angela and Agda have love relationships with men, and their love for each other is portrayed as a possible alternative that can coexist with heterosexual love. Implied in their relationship is an understanding that heterosexuality is still the norm and, in a country suffering through a population crisis, reproduction is still promoted, so lesbian love does not substitute for love between man and woman entirely. Bell, on the other hand, is exclusively drawn to women and rebels against male hegemony because she competes with men for women. For instance, she becomes Thomas Meller's rival for Angela and is depicted as threatening from Thomas's perspective. Women like Bell nauseated him, but they also scared him: "in particular he feared them, when they tried to infiltrate young women whom he himself wanted to protect or love"[13] (*Porten vid Johannes*, 256). In the same chapter, Bell and Thomas run into each other by coincidence and have a heated discussion about which one of them has the most right to Angela.

Bell thus embodies all the dangerous and pathologized aspects of lesbianism in the book series: she is a lesbian madwoman in the attic, to whom the angelic heroines are both repelled and attracted. Putting these ideas back in the context of the 1930s, the Swedish government's sexual reforms strongly promoted heterosexuality and the family in the 1930s; good sexuality was tied to the male/female couple, and homosexuality became more and more pathologized. By projecting all the dangerous and threatening parts of lesbianism onto Bell, she becomes a foil and a scapegoat, allowing Angela and Agda to keep their innocence. In this process their love comes across as a good, ideal kind of love—even if it is lesbian love.

ANGELA AND AGDA: CONFIRMING
AND CHALLENGING 1930S
SOCIOPOLITICAL DISCOURSES

Several passages in the first volumes of *Fröknarna von Pahlen* indicate that Agda—who is a nanny for Angela's cousins in the first novel—and Angela have a special relationship, but they do not begin their love affair until the last novel. When Angela and Agda first realize that they love each other, they are sitting together in a room at the mansion Eka, sewing. A new year has just begun, and emerging from the dark Swedish winter, the days are getting lighter and longer. Angela is thinking about the child she will soon give birth to and is happy about the fact that a new generation will grow up at the mansion. Aside from the longer days, a few more signs of spring are mentioned in this passage, and coming of spring is intertwined with the children who will be born: "A pale, light yellow ray of sunlight fell through the window. Angela thought it looked like a daffodil as it flickered on the wallpaper: an early message that spring was just around the corner. Then, in April, she would give birth to her child. It would awaken with the sun and grow with the spring flowers"[14] (*Av samma blod*, 244). The quote brings forward light, life, growth, and warmth. The Swedish name for daffodil is *påsklilja* (Easter Lily), and in a Christian context Easter is a celebration of reconciliation, rebirth, and renewal. The daffodil reappears later in the same passage; while Angela is being touched by Agda she is looking at the same flower-shaped ray of sunlight while smiling happily.

However, the daffodil reference holds other connotations. This flower belongs to the narcissus family, and according to Greek mythology, the beautiful young man Narcissus became lost in his own reflection in the water and eventually turned into a narcissus flower. This more negative association with the daffodil can be connected to *mirrors*, a connection that is suggested in another the depiction of Angela and Agda's love: right before they fall into each other's arms, they are standing in front of a large mirror, looking at each other side by side, realizing how similar they look.

The flower and the mirror tie Angela and Agda's love to the third M: the medicalized explanation of same-sex love as *mirrors* or narcissism. The mirror image suggests that the two women can merge because of their likeness, or sameness. In the description of the erotic encounter that follows, the pronouns *they* and *them* dominate instead of singling out each woman as an individual, and the two women are described as almost enclosed in each other. This contrasts the descriptions of erotic encounters between men and women in the book series, where the pronouns *he* and *she* dominate and where the lovers are portrayed more as separate individuals.

Merging can also exclude other beings, and this idea is expressed in the image of a sparrow, which sits at the windowsill right before Angela and Agda embrace, looking at them. The bird later flies up to the closed window as if it wants to come in. The sparrow can also suggest love; Birgitta Svanberg mentions the bird as a positive love symbol in the book series (Svanberg 1989, 114–15). However, in this particular scene, the glass of the window separates the two lovers from the sparrow and the rest of the world, and the glass of the mirror encloses them in each other.

In the previous quote, blooming and growth were connected to the children who will be born, but these same images later become metaphors for the love between Angela and Agda as well: "The room was a greenhouse where the flower of their sudden love blossomed. It overpowered them with its scent. They were drawn close to each other, trembling with desire. [. . .] It was like when life began, when nobody had eaten from the tree of knowledge yet. It was light and purity and a blessed calmness"[15] (*Av samma blod*, 246). This quote portrays their love as something overwhelming and growing. The greenhouse and flower metaphors emphasize the strength of their love and its connections to life. Literary historian Bonnie Zimmerman observes that lesbian romances in fiction often take place in nature and that nature imagery evokes the freshness that we associate with new love. Nature also represents a location existing outside of civilization, a place where the lovers can isolate themselves and explore their love but also experience transcendence through merging with each other and nature (Zimmerman 1990, 79–86). Krusenstjerna uses nature imagery in much the same way, evoking freshness and allowing Angela and Agda to become enclosed in each other and isolated from the outer world—they merge, and in this merging, nature images are intertwined.

The nature imagery also has political dimensions. Liv Saga Bergdahl argues that nature imagery in Swedish lesbian novels from the 1930s makes love between women come across as natural, thus challenging the contemporary legislation against homosexuality, which defined homosexuality as "against nature" (Bergdahl 2010, 85, 90, 106–7, 168). Thus the use of nature imagery can be read as a way to describe Angela and Agda's love as natural, a rejection of the 1930s sociopolitical discourse. Further, the allusion to the time of innocence in biblical Eden links their love to purity. Thus the erotic encounter between Angela and Agda both confirms and questions contemporary medicalized views on lesbianism; the imagery is connected to medical explanations of female homosexuality such as narcissism, but at the same time, this explanation is challenged since their love is described as natural and pure.

These opposing ideas about a single relationship can be better understood in the context of Jacques Rancière's theory on the relationship between literature and politics. According to Rancière ([2006] 2011), "there is an essential connection between politics as a specific form of collective practice and literature as a well-defined practice of the art of writing" (3). He defines politics not as an exercise of or struggle for power but as "the construction of a specific sphere of experience" (3), a shared world of objects, where human subjects are thought of as capable of arguing about these objects. This sphere is not fixed but open to change, and political activity thus changes the common world. For Rancière the politics of literature is not the same as the politics of writers and their engagements with or depictions of political struggles or structures of their time. Instead, literature is political in that it intervenes in the shared world and changes what is perceptible in it: people and objects and the relationship between them. Literature can make subjects and objects visible and thus changes the political arena. Read within Rancière's theoretical framework, Krusenstjerna's novels are political in that they make different perspectives on lesbianism visible and understandable. The books confirm and reinforce some contemporary discourses on lesbianism, such as the medical discourse, but they also show lesbianism from new angles that challenge the sociopolitical discourse of the 1930s. Since their love is depicted as natural and pure, Angela and Agda are represented as lesbian subjects rather than case studies in pathology. Applying Rancière's ideas to the context of these novels, the different portrayals of lesbianism can be seen as a political arena or scene that expands the range of ideas and attitudes, both positive and negative, that enter the discourse of the time; this changes the common world of experience, which hitherto has been dominated by medical explanations for female homosexuality.

The chapter depicting Angela and Agda's realization that they are in love ends with a detailed description of the sexual act between the two women, and the following chapter begins with the phrase: "Yes, during those times old Eka was like a greenhouse"[16] (*Av samma blod*, 248). The phrase refers to the fact that the three young women Angela, Agda, and Frideborg are pregnant, but given that the word "greenhouse" is also used as Angela and Agda come together, it also emphasizes the fruitfulness of their love, the ideal conditions for growth. At first glance this reference to fruitfulness in a lesbian couple might seem paradoxical since the two women cannot reproduce, at least not biologically. However, it can be read metaphorically, as if their relationship is based on premises that make it more likely to survive than the vast majority of the other relationships depicted in the book series. Besides, both women are already pregnant, so the procreation has already been taken care of; instead, the emphasis is on the growth of the women and the expected children under the best of conditions. These ideas can be read in light of Swedish politics in the 1930s. During this time Sweden had the world's lowest birth rate, and a population commission was appointed in 1935. Although some voices

arguing for a solution that would promote gender equality
were raised in the public debate, the population commission
recommended a different model in their final memorandum in
1938. In this document all population reforms were structured
in accordance with a model based on a (heterosexual) couple
with one (male) provider. Women in the workplace were even
framed a problem, and the commission wanted to strengthen
the position of women working at home (Hirdman [2001]
2003, 154–55; Lennerhed 2002, 88–91; Lindholm 1990, 69–
71). The status of the heterosexual couple as the key to raising
the birth rate was thus reinforced during the 1930s. However,
Fröknarna von Pahlen challenges heterosexuality as central to
population growth; an environment where women live together
without men is depicted as more suitable for raising children
than the heterosexual family. Here, too, literary representations
intervene in the specific sphere of experience that is generally defined by politics, according to Rancière. By depicting a
women's commune as a greenhouse and "a big and loving land
for children and women," Krusenstjerna's work contributes to
the political discourse on population growth with an alternative
solution that changes the understanding in the shared world.

Shortly after her erotic encounter with Angela, Agda starts
dressing in men's clothes, and the depictions of her relationship
with Angela shifts from sameness to difference. Angela as well
as the other women at Eka appreciate Agda's cross-dressing,
and Frideborg even starts flirting a little with her. Agda's new
image is connected to sexology's view on lesbianism as related
to masculinity, in line with contemporary medical discourse on
lesbians as belonging to a third sex. However, Agda is never
described as particularly masculine. She does dress in men's
clothes, but compared to lesbian characters in contemporary
literature, she stands out as feminine: many descriptions emphasize her curvy body and long dark hair. Both Stephen Gordon
in Radclyffe Hall's classic *The Well of Loneliness* (1928) and
Charlie in Margareta Suber's Swedish novel *Charlie* (1932)
borrow not only names but also some of the looks and qualities
from the opposite sex. The text never mentions exactly what
Agda's masculine role consists of, but the clothes and the way

Agda looks are presented as masculine. She also adopts a protective attitude toward Angela and the other women, the same
role male characters such as Thomas Meller take. In contrast,
the descriptions of Agda's body and the fact that she is good at
sewing, a traditional feminine occupation, suggest traditionally
female characteristics. Agda's gender does not seem to be limited to certain qualities; instead it is open and negotiable, linked
to pants and a protective attitude as well as to a curvy body and
sewing. As Anna Williams argues, Agda becomes a class of her
own, far from the terms *masculine* and *feminine*. Williams also
points out that Agda is pregnant; she is a pregnant woman in
men's clothes, an image that further plays with gender identities
(Williams 2004, 105–6). Hence Agda's masculinity does not
simply confirm contemporary medical discourse on lesbianism;
the character also challenges this discourse by performing masculinity as something open and negotiable—not rigidly defined.

Fröknarna von Pahlen challenges other contemporary ideas
in addition to the connection between child-rearing and the
heterosexual couple. In fact, the novels also defy the contemporary discourse that defines heterosexuality as the norm and
lesbianism as deviant. During their trip in the winter landscape
surrounding Eka, Angela and Agda discuss their love and worry
about not being "real women." While Agda's playful balance of
masculinity and femininity was previously highlighted, here the
emphasis is on likeness and mutuality again, not on difference:
"'It's really not the same as falling in love with a man,' [Agda]
said thoughtfully. 'A man is so different from us. We have to
search for a long time. We have to compare to ourselves. We
are simply on terra incognita. A woman quickly understands
another woman because they are so similar, have the same
points of departure. At least that is how Bell used to explain
things'"[17] (*Av samma blod*, 259). Agda uses Bell's ideas to sort
out how women and, specifically, the two of them relate to each
other. Angela objects and says that she never really understood
Bell despite the fact that they are both women. Agda answers
by saying that Bell might not be a real woman because she
has a twisted emotional life, but that she and Angela are "real
women, even if we don't have men and don't need them now,

either"[18] (*Av samma blod*, 259–60). This passage challenges contemporary medical discourse, specifically sexology's image of lesbians as a third sex: the two women love each other and thus should be viewed as lesbians, but they still define themselves as "real women." Furthermore, this passage challenges the assumption of heterosexuality as norm. Agda mentions that she and Angela do not need men "now," indicating that their love is as important and meaningful as the love between man and woman, since a male lover can be interchanged with a female. Moreover, they are both pregnant and do not need men for reproduction anymore. By juxtaposing same-sex and heterosexual love and finding them equal and interchangeable, Krusenstjerna's novel questions the 1930s view of heterosexuality as the norm and lesbianism as deviant and undesirable. When read in connection with the previously discussed imagery relating Angela and Agda's love to natural and innocent phenomena, the book series challenges contemporary sociopolitical discourse by portraying lesbianism as nondeviant and as "natural" as heterosexuality.

Viewing homosexuality and heterosexuality as equal expressions of human sexuality was rare in the 1930s. In 1933, one groundbreaking member of parliament, Vilhelm Lundstedt, was the first to suggest to the Swedish parliament that homosexuality should be decriminalized. Lena Lennerhed describes him as a radical: "Lundstedt not only worked for decriminalization; he also held homosexual and heterosexual connections as equals"[19] (Lennerhed 2002, 162).[20] Lennerhed points out that Lundstedt was criticized by his contemporaries, reflecting the contemporary political discourse norms (Lennerhed 2002, 163–64).

Lundstedt's controversial view of lesbianism as equal to heterosexuality is also expressed in Krusenstjerna's novels, as in the passages discussed before, and it is reinforced by the interchangeable genders of Angela's love objects; she falls in love with and is attracted to men and women equally. Moreover, the fact that lesbianism is continually connected to positive phenomena, such as closeness, mutuality, and growth, while love between men and women is usually represented as dysfunctional, suggests that love between women is an even better alternative than heterosexuality.

So far we have seen how Angela and Agda's relationship challenges some of the medicalized explanations of female homosexuality. However, the couple can also be said to challenge the Foucauldian approach to the history of sexuality, according to which homosexuality came to be viewed as connected to the identity of an individual as opposed to a behavior that could coexist with heterosexual behavior. In contrast to Bell von Wenden, who is defined by her sexuality, Angela and Agda can freely engage in homoerotic practices that never determine them as homosexual individuals. As such, their love is more similar to the way love between women was viewed prior to the rise of the science of sexuality, though with one important exception: Angela and Agda's love is not seen as morally wrong and as something that should be against the law. Despite the fact that homoerotic practices were criminalized in Sweden at the time when Krusenstjerna wrote *Fröknarna von Pahlen*, same-sex love is almost never described in the book series in illegal terms.[21]

Moreover, Angela and Agda's love challenges the two contemporary medical explanations for homosexuality as either innate or acquired. The congenital explanation dominated within sexology. Biologically determined homosexuality was thought of as incurable, and as previously mentioned, those suffering from it were usually described as inverts, belonging to a "third sex." The psychoanalytic approach saw homosexuality as acquired, due to disturbed psychological development, and thus curable. There was no consensus on the reasons behind the disorder, and various diffcrent and sometimes contradicting explanations for homosexuality existed side by side in the 1930s debate (Lennerhed 2002, 159–71). Bell von Wenden has been shown to represent both congenital and acquired homosexuality. Although not described as a mannish lesbian, some of her behavior could be read as a symptom of innate homosexuality. As she tries to seduce both Angela and Agda, Bell embodies the concern within medical science that congenital homosexuals would try to lure young "normal" women into homosexual

practices. Angela and Agda, however, are depicted as different from Bell. They do compare themselves to her but reach
the conclusion that they are different from her since they are
"real women," thus challenging sexology's view of lesbians as
a third sex. Also, both Angela and Agda fall in love with and
are attracted to men and women equally. However, their love
for each other does not fit neatly into the model of acquired
homosexuality either, since it is never explicitly medicalized.
Although imagery is borrowed from the medical discourse,
Angela and Agda's relationship is not portrayed in the same
pathologizing ways as Bell, whose sexuality is described partly
as a result of her difficult upbringing.

Angela and Agda's sexuality has more in common with an
attitude expressed in Austrian writer Sofie Lazarsfeld's advisory
book on marriage and sexuality from 1931, known and read in
Sweden during this period. When writing about female homosexuality, Lazarsfeld strives to stay out of the medical debate
on congenital and acquired homosexuality but still argues that
homosexuality often is acquired and thus curable. However,
she adds that many people do not wish to be cured from their
homosexuality; many women are happier in same-sex relationships than in relationships with men, since men tend to focus
on physical performance in love and forget about closeness and
tenderness. Lazarsfeld continues: "Only in rare cases of heterosexual love have I found the complete empathy and the tender
devotion that is found without exception in homosexual relationships between women"[22] (Lazarsfeld [1931] 1938, 219;
see also Laskar 1997, 196–201). In *Fröknarna von Pahlen* the
relationships between men and women are generally unequal
and distant, while the relationships between women are sources
of closeness and mutuality—Angela's relationship with Agda in
particular. In comparison, Angela's lover Thomas never seems
to intend to have a long-term relationship with Angela, and he
also leaves her to reunite with his wife when the war breaks out.
Agda is married to a man who is not attracted to women but to
other men, and she has casual sex with a married man.

As radical as Krusenstjerna's novels are in challenging 1930s
discourse on lesbianism, they also reinforce some of them. As

discussed before, the medical discourse is indeed questioned in Angela and Agda's relationship, but the imagery suggests medical explanations to female homosexuality such as narcissism and androgyny. It is even possible to trace another so-called *M*, the *mothering* explanation, in Angela and Agda's relationship, since both women lose their mothers early in life. Agda's mother returns later, but Agda never forms a close relationship with her, and their relationship becomes even more complicated when Agda as an adult comes to Berlin, newly wed to Count Gusten Sauss af Värnamo. Gusten, who is attracted to men rather than women, has hitherto been incapable of consummating his marriage, but in an orgy with incestuous elements he finally succeeds. Agda's half sister Lotty arouses Gusten by kissing and touching Agda, and eventually she leaves room for Gusten, who—with the assistance of Lotty and Rosita, who is Lotty and Agda's mother—is able to engage in intercourse with his wife (*Av samma blod*, 154–56). Agda's relationship with her mother can thus be described as complicated and distant in line with psychoanalytical explanations of female homosexuality as caused by a complicated relationship to the mother.

As previously mentioned, Angela and Agda's relationship can be read as a kind of political arena where a wide array of descriptions of lesbianism can be expressed. These descriptions are sometimes contradicting, but so were the attitudes toward homosexuality in the sociopolitical debate of the 1930s. Contemporary medical explanations of lesbianism are reinforced through imagery but also challenged, and the book implicitly places a high value on lesbianism, as equal to or even better that heterosexuality. The books present descriptions of lesbianism that were not accessible in the 1930s mainstream sociopolitical discourse. In line with Rancière's argument as discussed earlier, the representation of Angela and Agda's relationship is political; it makes lesbianism visible in new ways that are unrelated to pathology and thereby changes what is perceptible in the common world, influencing the discourse on the subject.

Angela and Agda: Freedom and Equality

The previous section explores how lesbianism is portrayed as equal to heterosexuality in the context of Angela and Agda's relationship, but the book series implicitly pushes this valuation further: lesbianism is even presented as a better alternative. The high status of women's same-sex sexuality is connected to feminism in the novels. In *Fröknarna von Pahlen*, femininity is regularly valued higher than masculinity, and some scholars have noted that the book series hardly contains any positive depictions of men (Backberger 1968, 159; Williams 2004, 112). While Angela and Agda's relationship is based on equality and mutual understanding, the heterosexual relationships depicted in *Fröknarna von Pahlen* are generally unequal. Angela's male lover, Thomas Meller, is older and more experienced and therefore dominates their relationship. Agda's husband Gusten is an aristocratic, older man, and she is inferior to him not only because of her age but also because of class and ethnicity—she is a working-class woman, and her grandfather was Romany. The imagery further highlights the inequality in these relationships. When they first meet, Angela and Thomas spend time together walking in a cemetery, and they always make love in enclosed spaces. Their first erotic encounter takes place in a boathouse that is dark and damp and filled with spider webs, and later they make love in a cottage that Thomas has rented over the summer and decorated with things he brought home from his journeys over the world, things that are alien and slightly frightening to Angela. Agda makes love to Angela's male cousin, Sven von Pahlen, a couple of times throughout *Fröknarna von Pahlen*, and the erotic encounters happen in an enclosed space, a hay barn, where the lovers are surrounded by dried hay. All these images convey negative feelings such as alienation, insecurity, infertility, claustrophobia, and even death; these ideas provide a stark contrast to the flower and greenhouse images that emphasize life, growth, and freedom in Angela and Agda's relationship.

While the novels portray same-sex relationships in a better light than heterosexual ones, this was clearly not in line with the mainstream sociopolitical discourse of the time. Women's emancipation had made progress in Sweden during the 1920s—for instance, women gained the right to vote and be elected in 1921—but in the process of industrialization and modernization that took place in the 1930s, women came to be viewed as part of a family rather than as individuals. When the Social Democrats came to power in 1932 and started building "the people's home," the new reforms were directed toward the heterosexual couple or family rather than at the individual. The welfare state was founded on a traditional ideology of men as providers and women as caregivers. All the reforms in the 1930s reinforced gender segregation; men were directed toward wage labor and politics in the public sphere while women were directed toward home and the private sphere. Several proposals in the parliament aimed at banning married women from the labor market in the 1930s, but these never were passed, and married women were able to enter the labor market. However, in reality most married women did not work in the public sphere; a highly segregated labor market where women had the most monotonous and the lowest paid jobs resulted in a situation where women who could afford it left their jobs for unpaid labor at home when they got married (Hirdman 1990, 84–87; Hirdman [2001] 2003, 131–34, 147–55; Lindholm 1990, 67–74; Wikander 1992, 49–56).

Krusenstjerna's representations of lesbianism challenge this women's role in society at the time. The portrait of Agda can be read as an alternative to the gender segregation in contemporary Swedish society. Agda is not placed squarely as either "masculine" or "feminine" but borrows qualities from both gender stereotypes. She becomes a category of her own, in Anna Williams's words, and thus questions and transgresses contemporary boundaries between genders. The change in Agda's way of dressing occurs after she makes love to Angela, and the love between Agda and Angela could thus be read as that which makes it possible for Agda to rebel against the boundaries of "female" and become something new. The depiction of Agda is another example of Rancière's argument that literature changes what is perceptible in the shared world by adding gender ambiguity to a sociopolitical context preoccupied with gender segregation.

Agda's gender ambiguity is depicted as an asset in her relationship with Angela. Her attempts to conform to the binary
gender system and take on the role of the man in relation to
Angela are unsuccessful. During their trip in the winter landscape, the two women get lost in the forest. Angela, who is
further into her pregnancy than Agda, becomes tired, and Agda
then realizes her own limitations; she is not strong enough to
carry Angela like a man would have done, and this leads to her
asking herself whether she is allowed to love Angela without
having the strength of a man. Soon after she hears the jingling
of bells and realizes that they are close to the road. She runs
ahead and stops a sleigh driven by Angela's cousin Edla. Eventually, Agda is able to help her beloved into the sleigh and make
sure she arrives safely at home. Her strong initiative when she
asks Edla for the reins of the sleigh suggests that she has once
again found her gender balance, and the interactions between
the two lovers reflects this. From Edla's perspective, the warmth
between them returns, and Edla likens them to a newlywed couple (*Av samma blod*, 261–66). Anna Williams reads this passage
in line with Judith Butler's theories as a manifestation of the
performative nature of gender and emphasizes the role of Edla
as observer who brings actions and practices into focus (Williams 2004, 108). However, the passage does more than just
assert gender as performative; by allowing Agda to take on the
protector role without using traditionally masculine traits such
as strength, it also dismisses heterosexuality as a role model.

Judith Butler argues that all human bodies become intelligible through the heterosexual matrix, "a hegemonic discursive/
epistemic model of gender intelligibility that assumes that
for bodies to cohere and make sense there must be a stable
sex expressed through a stable gender (masculine expresses
male, feminine expresses female) that is oppositionally and
hierarchically defined through the compulsory practice of heterosexuality" (Butler [1990] 1999, 194). Butler describes the
heterosexual matrix as a binary gender system that defines us
as men and women only if we follow an imaginary straight line
between sex, gender, and desire: A woman is someone with a
female body and female gender who desires men, and a man

is someone with a male body and male gender who desires women. People who do not fall neatly into these categories are not even culturally intelligible, and the heterosexual matrix thus illustrates a cultural need to define the framework for each gender and keep up a sharp boundary between them.

Agda's reflections on her love for Angela can be read in the light of the heterosexual matrix. Since the two women are in love with each other and not with men, they stray away from the path the heterosexual matrix stipulates for women. Desire for women is defined as masculine within the heterosexual matrix, but Angela's and Agda's bodies and genders are female. Their conversation about Bell and their worry about not being real women show awareness of the fact that loving another woman might lead to a questioning of their femininity. Agda's cross-dressing could be read as a way for her to adjust to the heterosexual matrix by performing the male gender. At the same time her body expresses femininity with its soft curves and progressing pregnancy. Agda's attempts to perform a male gender show how the heterosexual matrix governs the definitions of masculinity and femininity—visible also in contemporary society's strong emphasis on gender segregation and heterosexuality. However, the book series demonstrates clearly that the heterosexual matrix is not a productive model for gender and love. Looking at the passage discussed previously through the framework of this matrix, Agda initially feels humiliated because she lacks the strength of a man and therefore cannot carry Angela. According to 1930s heterosexual standards, Agda stands out as a nonman, and her limitations are highlighted. When she stops the sleigh so that Angela can get a ride home, Agda does take on an active role that could be described as masculine. However, Agda does not save Angela with masculine strength but by being observant and resourceful, qualities usually belonging to a feminine, or at least a gender-neutral, sphere. Instead of conforming to the heterosexual matrix and trying to become a man, Agda keeps her gender ambiguity and is able to solve the problem.

Thus the same-sex love relationship seems to be the most functional when it becomes a class of its own instead of being created with the heterosexual love relationship as a role model. This assertion applies to all same-sex love relationships in *Fröknarna von Pahlen*, including Angela and Petra's (Björklund 2009). Petra is Angela's aunt, so they are relatively closely related, but in spite of that their relationship sometimes bears resemblance to a romantic relationship (Bergdahl 2010, 102– 10; Björklund 2009). This becomes more obvious when Angela is pregnant and Petra believes herself to be a stand-in father who should be able to protect Angela. However, it is only when Petra refrains from the masculine role as a father that the two women become close and intimate: "just two women and a child that they were expecting, a child that they both would care for and protect when it arrived. They would be a family. A little holy family consisting of two women and a child, sure to be a woman, too"[23] (*Bröllop på Ekered*, 66–67). The word "just" is exclusive, indicating that the man is not part of this family constellation. The fact that both Petra and Angela will take on the traditionally female role of caring and the tradition- ally male role of protecting suggests that they will both perform conventional masculinity as well as conventional femininity, like Agda. Petra and Angela's alternative family is even idealized by being referred to as a "holy family," an allusion to the biblical holy family.

Petra and Angela's family differs from contemporary stan- dards but is still referred to as a family, again challenging the heterosexual nuclear family ideology that dominated Sweden in the 1930s. In line with the politics of the population crisis at the time, the woman's role as a mother in Krusenstjerna's book series is strongly emphasized, but her role as wife in a family consisting of a man, a woman, and children is rejected entirely. Anna Williams points out that traditional marriage is not depicted as particularly desirable in the book series. None of the protagonists marry, and the marriages portrayed in the novels are without exception unhappy. Also, the wedding itself is ridiculed and criticized in a long scene that parodies the tradi- tion (Williams 2013, 316). By depicting and idealizing a family consisting of two women and a child, *Fröknarna von Pahlen* questions the 1930s parameters.

This challenge to contemporary family ideology escalates in the final novel when Petra and Angela start a women's commune, which places a high value on female relationships that range from platonic to sexual. This haven for women at Eka alludes to ideas that will enter the sociopolitical sphere during the second wave of feminism almost half a century later.

In her book *Sexual Politics*, radical feminist Kate Millett argues that sex is political. She defines politics as "power-structured relationships, arrangements whereby one group of persons is controlled by another" (Millett [1970] 2000, 23). All known societies are patriarchies according to Millett, and she argues that patriarchy, which infiltrates all parts of society, is based on two principles—the power of men over women and the power of older men over younger men. Furthermore, she views the family as the most important institution of patriarchy: "It is both a mirror of and a connection with the larger society; a patriarchal unit within a patriarchal whole. Mediating between the individual and the social structure, the family effects control and conformity where political and other authorities are insufficient. [. . .] As the fundamental instrument and the foundation unit of patriarchal society the family and its roles are prototypical" (Millett [1970] 2000, 33). Krusenstjerna's novels give women control over reproduction and create an alternative family constellation where same-sex love is an option. This starkly contrasts Krusenstjerna's 1930s society, which promoted heterosexual marriage and valued women primarily as wives and mothers. Krusenstjerna's novels dismiss men, heterosexuality, and the traditional family and present a women's commune, a place where men are banned, as the ideal place to raise children. The depiction of the commune as "a big and loving land for children and women" seems to suggest that the population crisis in the 1930s can be solved in other ways than through reforms that strengthen heterosexual marriage.

Another radical feminist, Adrienne Rich, argues that compulsory heterosexuality, the idea that heterosexuality is women's natural choice, contributes to the oppression of women. She wants women to see the potential in the bonds between women, a lesbian continuum, which does not only include erotic relationships between women. This idea embraces a broad spectrum of women-identified experiences, such as close friendships between women as well as different groups where women support each other emotionally or politically (Rich 1980). Krusenstjerna's women's commune can be viewed as a place grounded in the lesbian continuum as Rich described it almost half a century after *Fröknarna von Pahlen* was published: the women share each other's lives and support each other, and Angela and Agda have an erotic relationship. To define relationships as erotic or nonerotic becomes secondary, as in Rich's view; the focus is on the political dimension of love between women—lesbianism becomes a way of leading a life without men, outside a male-dominated society.

This attitude toward love contrasts with the romantic love ideal in 1930s discourse. This heterosexual ideal grew out of the emerging bourgeois middle class during the nineteenth century and was still prevalent during the 1930s. In this paradigm, love is seen as a fundamental force that makes possible for the individual to develop his or her personality and become fulfilled as a human being. Moreover, love is viewed as something that can give the world meaning and coherence by uniting important opposites such as masculine/feminine and spiritual/sensual. A woman is thought of as having a unique position because she can unite the opposites of the world to a greater extent than man (Sanner 2003, 44–48). The strong emphasis on heterosexuality and the family in Sweden in the 1930s rests in part on the idea of the romantic love ideal: man and woman are seen as two opposite but necessary parts of a unit, and thus welfare measures are directed toward that unit rather than toward individuals.

At Krusenstjerna's Eka, love does not rest on the romantic love ideal. Love between man and woman is not celebrated, and love's ability to unite opposites is not the focus. Instead the boundaries between opposites are blurred; love is not limited to man and woman—it does not even have to be limited to two people, as shown by Angela's relationships to Agda and Petra: she is said to love them both but in different ways. The boundary between the spiritual and sensual does not exist. The women love each other in both spiritual and sensual ways, as the case of Angela shows. Opposites are not united, and the blurring of boundaries (e.g., gender and family) becomes a prerequisite for ideal love in *Fröknarna von Pahlen*. A woman does have a unique position at Eka, not because she has a special ability to unite opposites, but because she, in contrast to the men depicted in the book series, can give love and engage in relationships on equal terms.

The lesbian continuum in the women's commune at Eka also transgresses the 1930s boundaries of class and ethnicity. Angela belongs to the aristocratic upper class, while Agda is working class. In the last novel Petra finds out that Agda and her half-sister Frideborg—who used to be a maid but later becomes part of the women's commune at Eka—are related to Petra and Angela: Petra's aunt once had a secret love affair with a Romany man from Spain, an affair that resulted in a child, Agda and Frideborg's grandmother. Thus Angela and Agda's love crosses class boundaries as well as ethnic boundaries.

Fröknarna von Pahlen offers alternatives to Krusenstjerna's society, thus highlighting the shortcomings of the norms of the time. These novels are not the first to make connections between lesbianism and feminism. Lillian Faderman points out that Havelock Ellis directly connects female homosexuality and women's emancipation, showing how the threat of women's increasing independence contributed to the stigmatization of lesbianism at the turn of the twentieth century (Faderman [1981] 2001, 233–53). A similar connection between lesbianism and feminism can be found in Swedish discourse in the beginning of the twentieth century (Järvstad 2008, 141). However, there is a difference between the connections made in 1930s sociopolitical discourse and those found in Krusenstjerna's novels: While sociopolitical discourse generally describes lesbianism as an unwanted and negatively charged effect of women's emancipation, the connection between feminism and lesbianism is depicted as intrinsically good in *Fröknarna von Pahlen*. Lesbianism is intertwined with a feminist project, similar to that of radical feminism almost half a century later. Through presenting an alternative family constellation, thereby suggesting that changes in society should be anchored on a private level, the book series shows us what radical feminists would later point out: that the personal is political. The emphasis put on the connections between women as a way to escape male oppression brings to mind another radical feminism slogan: sisterhood is power. Once again, Krusenstjerna's novels contribute different perspectives from those in 1930s society by rejecting the medical discourse that acknowledged a connection between women's emancipation and lesbianism but portrayed it as negative. The happy ending of *Fröknarna von Pahlen* adds a new perspective in the construction of the sphere of experience that Rancière defines as politics and fills the connection between lesbianism and feminism with a different meaning. By bringing new subjects and objects into the shared world, Krusenstjerna's novels challenge normative heterosexuality and women's subordinate status in 1930s Swedish society, changing that world.

Most Krusenstjerna scholars acknowledge that Bell's homosexuality is related to the medical discourse. Many of them also define Angela and Agda's relationship as the most positive and beautiful love story depicted in the book series. It is tempting to dichotomize Krusenstjerna's portrayal of lesbianism: Either it is medicalized and threatening, as in the case of Bell, or it is something good, an empowering source for women, as in Angela and Agda's relationship. However, as this study shows, the divide between positive and negative lesbian characters is not completely clear, and even the "good" lesbianism can contain traces of the medical discourse of the time that defines love between women as deviant and pathologized. Krusenstjerna's complex characters that embody different and contradictory views on lesbianism add depth and nuance to the sociopolitical discourse on gender and sexuality.

On the one hand, Krusenstjerna's work represents lesbianism as empowering for women and challenges normative heterosexuality and contemporary negative attitudes toward lesbianism. On the other hand, it represents love between women with the aid of images from the same medical discourse that is being questioned in the text, which contributes to reinforcing the image of the lesbian woman as deviant and medicalized. In the political scene that literature constitutes, these views on lesbianism coexist and create an ambiguous discourse on lesbianism. The fact that the explanations of lesbianism within the parameters of turn-of-the-twentieth-century sexology and psychoanalysis are visible in the text through imagery and symbolic language suggests that the medical discourse is part of the discourse on lesbianism itself, so that it becomes impossible to even talk about lesbianism without connecting to these images.

OTHER STORIES: AGNES VON KRUSENSTJERNA AND LITERATURE OF THE 1930S

Agnes von Krusenstjerna is the Swedish writer who writes the most and also the most articulately about love between women in the 1930s. However, there are a few other literary works that touch on the same subject matter as well. In 1932, Margareta Suber's *Charlie* was published, and two years later Karin Boye's *Kris* came out. Both novels have lesbian themes, although neither of them depicts sexuality as explicitly as in Krusenstjerna's novels, and love remains unrequited in both novels. This section focuses on the representations of lesbianism in *Charlie* and *Kris* when compared to the representations in *Fröknarna von Pahlen*. Instead of looking for new lesbian themes in Suber's and Boye's novels, I draw on previous scholarship and focus on connecting the novels to each other, to Krusenstjerna's novels, and to the sociopolitical context in order to gain a more nuanced understanding of the Swedish discourse on lesbianism in the 1930s.

Margareta Suber's *Charlie* takes place at a vacation resort by the ocean where protagonist Charlie spends the summer. Charlie is a young woman depicted as a tomboy who dresses in men's clothes, drives a sports car, and sends roses to the object of her love, the young widow Sara. At first, neither Charlie nor Sara is aware of the fact that Charlie is in love with Sara, and both Sara and her children enjoy spending time with her. Charlie is well liked at the resort; she is funny, playful, and easygoing. Eventually she realizes that she is in love with Sara after someone leaves a book on homosexuality in her chair. She reads the book and tells Sara, who comforts her but later decides to leave the resort. In the last chapter, fall has arrived, and a conversation with a friend reminds Charlie of Sara. The novel ends with the following passage:

> Charlie went to bed early and flipped through a small album with amateur photographs. They were all of Sara. She put it under her pillow, turned off the light and fell into a deep, sound sleep. The lace of the sheet rose and fell with her long, even, breaths. She found new strength in the wholehearted, unbroken rest of youth, which completed what is growing.
> Now her body was mature and ready to start leading the life for which our Lord had chosen to create her.[24] (Suber 1932, 148–49)

Although the ending is ambiguous, previous scholarship has emphasized that the novel still depicts lesbianism in a more appealing way than, for instance, Radclyffe Hall's *The Well of Loneliness*, which came out just four years prior to *Charlie*.

Karin Lindeqvist compares Suber's novel to Hall's novel and argues that *Charlie* can, in fact, be read as a response to *The Well of Loneliness*. Hall's novel describes sexuality as congenital and determining of the individual, and it portrays the protagonist Stephen Gordon as deviant and tormented. In Suber's novel, on the other hand, same-sex desire as such is never defined, and the protagonist Charlie is a lively tomboy, surrounded by friends and family who like her. Also, heterosexuality as such is not established as the norm in *Charlie*, as it is in *The Well of Loneliness*; Charlie's love object Sara is a widow who does not mourn, and patriarchal masculinity is undermined in several ways. There are also very few positive portrayals of men in the novel. Moreover, Lindeqvist's discussion of the endings of the two novels supports her reading of *Charlie* as a challenge to ideas presented in Hall's novel. In the end of *The Well of Loneliness*, Stephen Gordon is lonely and prays to God to acknowledge her and her fellow homosexuals and give them the right to live. Lindeqvist reads the ending of Suber's novel as an encouragement for Charlie to lead her life as the person she is, and she also emphasizes Charlie's youth and God's intentions, both positive references, in contrast to Stephen's "abnormality." Lindeqvist comes to the conclusion that both novels refer to the 1930s medical discourse on homosexuality but that Hall's novel accepts this discourse while Suber's novel contradicts and undermines it. Thus *Charlie* can be seen as a commentary on the older novel, which was a focal point in the 1930s Western literary discourse on homosexuality (Lindeqvist 2006).

Birgitta Svanberg, too, notices the differences between Charlie and Stephen Gordon. She assumes that Radclyffe Hall's novel inspired Margareta Suber's subject matter but argues that Charlie, who is lively and playful, has little in common with Stephen Gordon, who is characterized by heavy bitterness and tormented heroism. Svanberg also mentions the different endings. She does not establish one reading as more preferable to the other but instead acknowledges the ambiguity in Suber's novel that contrasts with Stephen Gordon's exhausted questioning of God (Svanberg 1996, 433–34).

Kristina Fjelkestam discusses the connection between Charlie and contemporary medical theories about lesbianism and shows how the novel draws on the three *M*s: *masculinity, mothering,* and *mirrors.* Moreover, she compares Suber's novel to *The Well of Loneliness* as well. Fjelkestam argues that Stephen Gordon is unambiguously connected to a medical discourse and described as a female invert, reflecting a traditional gender system where masculinity and femininity are seen as opposite and complementary. Charlie, on the other hand, is never placed in a category and conveys a more ambiguous image of female sexuality that challenges and transgresses the traditional view (Fjelkestam 2002, 112–30; Fjelkestam 2005). Liv Saga Bergdahl acknowledges that the medical discourse is present in the novel but argues that Charlie defies it by refusing to label or name her love for Sara. As previously mentioned, Bergdahl emphasizes the connection between lesbianism and nature in the 1930s novels, and she finds this connection in *Charlie* as well (Bergdahl 2010, 73–96). Eva Kuhlefelt reads Charlie as a case of female masculinity and argues that she becomes a gender transgressor who challenges heteronormativity (Kuhlefelt 2009).

As we have seen, several scholars compare *Charlie* to *The Well of Loneliness* and reach the conclusion that lesbianism is not medicalized to the same extent in the Swedish novel. The medical discourse is alluded to, but at the same time it is undermined by the character Charlie, who is represented as youthful, healthy, and well liked. The contrast between Hall's Stephen Gordon and Suber's Charlie that most scholars identify is similar to the contrast between Bell von Wenden and Angela and Agda's relationship in *Fröknarna von Pahlen*. The contemporary medical discourse on lesbianism is mainly represented in Bell von Wenden. Even if she is described as outwardly feminine most of the time, Bell could be said to colonize masculinity, mainly because she is competing with men for young women. Since she becomes a serious threat to the male-dominated society, it is not surprising that her lesbianism is medicalized in the novels: she becomes a literary stereotype that borrows traits from contemporary medical handbooks. This is also how previous scholarship describes Stephen Gordon. On the other hand, the portrayal of Charlie has more in common with that of Angela and Agda, who are never medicalized to the same extent in Krusenstjerna's novels; their love is presented as a contrast to Bell, who is medicalized early in the book series and becomes more and more pathologized. However, it is impossible to ignore the fact that Angela and Agda's relationship also contributes to reinforcing 1930s views on lesbianism as deviance and disorder. And as with Angela and Agda, even if Charlie defies the medical discourse to some extent, the very same discourse is continually referred to in the novel, and several scholars emphasize the ambiguity that this creates.

Moreover, Lindeqvist and Kuhlefelt discuss how heterosexuality and heteronormativity are being challenged in *Charlie*, and Lindeqvist argues that patriarchal masculinity is undermined, partly because of the negative portrayals of men. Men are portrayed negatively in Krusenstjerna's novels, too, and the fact that the women at Eka give up men and start a women's commune contrasts sharply with the 1930s model of the married heterosexual couple as the basic unit of the welfare state. Bergdahl finds a connection between lesbianism and nature in

Charlie as well as in other 1930s novels, much in the same way that we have seen the love of *Fröknarna von Pahlen*'s Agda and Angela associated with life, growth, and naturalness, coming across as the ideal form of love. The analyses of *Charlie* in previous scholarship thus seem to support the conclusion that, along with Krusenstjerna's book series, this book also contributes to a 1930s Swedish literary discourse that both confirms and challenges the medical discourse on lesbianism.

Karin Boye's autobiographical novel *Kris* (1934) depicts a young woman, Malin Forst, who is twenty years old and in the middle of the first year at a teacher's college. Up until now she has been a good Christian girl, but when the spring semester starts she enters into an identity crisis and has existential doubts. She questions the will of God—which parallels with the word of her own patriarchal father. Malin is sent to a psychiatrist, and she seeks support in her teacher, but the turning point comes when Malin falls in love with her female classmate, Siv. She admires her classmate from a distance but also identifies with Siv and finds her own identity through her. One day Malin finds out that Siv has a boyfriend, and consequently Malin's love never grows into a lesbian relationship with Siv. However, Malin does develop as a person; she finds herself in the process and learns to trust her own instincts and accept who she is, including her sexual identity.

Previous scholarship highlights the positive aspects of lesbianism in the novel. Gunilla Domellöf argues that *Kris* breaks down and changes patriarchal structures. The novel depicts a young woman developing into an independent subject, and the protagonist reaches independence through identifying with and loving another woman. By falling in love with Siv, Malin creates herself. She wants to be like Siv, who grows according to her own innate possibilities (Domellöf 1986, 213–86). Birgitta Svanberg emphasizes the joy of life in *Kris*. Malin's feelings for Siv are expressed in terms of nature, health, light, and joy—qualities that contrast against the contemporary view of lesbianism as connected to criminality and deviance. Malin does not start a lesbian relationship but wins new inner strength, which gives her self-confidence and an ability to trust her own moral judgments. She is able to accept the truth about herself, which, among other things, includes erotic desire for women (Svanberg 1983, 220–34; Svanberg 1996, 434–35). Kristina Fjelkestam notices the lack of terms from sexology and psycho-analysis in *Kris*. No terms are needed to describe Malin's desire for Siv, which instead takes physical shape in her blood and her eyes. Malin thus rebels against the Word, the world of signs, and the male norm (Fjelkestam 2002, 111–12). Liv Saga Berg-dahl reads lesbianism in *Kris* in a positive way. Malin is reborn through her love for Siv and wins her life back (Bergdahl 2010, 161–85).

Like in *Fröknarna von Pahlen*, lesbianism in *Kris* is con-nected to nature, health, and light. The book is also connected to self-growth and independence, and patriarchal structures are challenged in the novel. Lesbianism thus seems to be inter-twined with a feminist project, although it is not as spelled out or actualized as in Krusenstjerna's novels, where the women start a women's commune. Still, like Krusenstjerna's book series, *Kris* presents lesbianism in a positive light and challenges contemporary society's ideology of heterosexuality.

Critical looks at both *Charlie* and *Kris* show that Krusenstjer-na's work is no exception in the way it depicts lesbianism. The connections between lesbianism and the turn-of-the-century medical discourse are acknowledged, especially in *Charlie*, but scholars emphasize how this discourse is challenged and undermined in the novels. Like in Krusenstjerna's book series, lesbianism is depicted as a possible lifestyle. Suber's Charlie reads a sexological book on homosexuality, but she is not por-trayed as deviant, and the ending opens up for a reading where Charlie is young, strong, and ready to begin her life as a lesbian. Boye's Malin Forst is tormented, but not because of her homo-sexuality. The character goes through an existential crisis, but lesbianism neither has caused the crisis nor is described as part of it. Instead, Malin's love for Siv helps her out of the crisis and to grow as a person.

Read together, Krusenstjerna's, Suber's, and Boye's texts suggest that Swedish novels of the 1930s seem to represent lesbianism in an ambiguous and often contradictory light.

On the one hand, lesbianism is presented as empowering for women and is connected to radical feminist theory almost a half century before radical feminism. It can also be a means of working through a life crisis and gaining selfhood, as in Boye, or it can be a part of a new, playful identity, as in Suber's novel. On the other hand, lesbianism is represented with images that refer to the largely negative medical discourse on homosexuality established at the turn of the twentieth century, a discourse connected to the sociopolitical debates and the political reforms in 1930s Sweden. As we have seen, various and sometimes contradictory explanations and attitudes toward homosexuality existed at the same time in the sociopolitical discourse, but they all had elements of medicalization in common. However, literature, as part of the discourses in a given cultural context, tells us a more complex story about the Swedish discourse on lesbianism in the 1930s: the literature not only confirms medicalized ideas about female homosexuality but also represents it in a more positive light. These representations challenge contemporary ideologies—those that medicalize lesbianism as well as those that promote gender segregation and assume heterosexuality as the norm.

CHAPTER 2

SEXUAL REVOLUTION?

ANNAKARIN SVEDBERG AND THE 1960S

Like the 1930s, the 1960s was a decade of discursive change in Sweden in terms of sexuality. In some ways the 1960s sexual revolution can be seen as a continuation of the changes that took place in the 1930s, when a discourse that connected sexuality and reproduction was replaced by one that emphasized sexuality as pleasure. But while the discourse of the 1930s focused on sociopolitical and collective aspects of sexuality—increasing happiness in the population as a whole, solving the population crisis, and so on—the debate of the 1960s focused on the individual and was aimed at increasing individual freedom of sexuality. Sweden had become known abroad as sexually liberated in the 1950s, partly due to its status as the first country in the world to make sex education in schools compulsory in 1955. When the sexual revolution took place in the Western world in the 1960s, Sweden was already famous as "the country of sin" but was also—together with Denmark and Holland—thought of as the source of sexual enlightenment (Lennerhed 1994).

The debate was the most intense in Sweden during the first part of the 1960s. Young people, radicals, writers, and journalists challenged existing sexual norms and asked for sexual reforms that would increase individual freedom, such as free abortion, abolition of censorship, and better sex education in schools. Liberal voices argued that sexual differences should be tolerated; as long as other people were not hurt or had their freedoms limited, everyone should be allowed to do what they wanted sexually. This revolution was largely successful in Sweden; the liberals' claims were acknowledged and met with several governmental initiatives that examined issues such as abortion, censorship, pornography, and sex education. Homosexuality, too, was debated in the Swedish sexual revolution, and many liberals argued for a more progressive attitude toward it, but homosexuals themselves were strikingly absent from the debate. Both the RFSU (the Swedish association for sexual education) and the recently founded RFSL (the Swedish Federation for Gay and Lesbian Rights) kept low profiles, and nobody entered the debate as openly gay or lesbian. The invisibility of homosexuals suggests that the situation for the LGBTQ population in the 1960s was still difficult and that the 1960s sexual revolution was primarily heterosexual (Lennerhed 1994; Norrhem, Rydström, and Winkvist 2008, 152–53).

Considering the success of this revolution, which resulted in a new openness, surprisingly few novels with lesbian themes were published in Sweden in the 1960s. Although a few novels by other writers include lesbian themes, the two writers that usually represent this period in overviews of lesbian literature are Eva Alexanderson and Annakarin Svedberg. Alexanderson published only one novel primarily focusing on lesbianism and one with a minor lesbian theme, while all Svedberg's novels from the 1960s have more prominent lesbian themes. For that reason, this chapter is devoted to Svedberg's work, although Alexanderson's and a few other 1960s novels with lesbian themes are discussed at the end of the chapter.

Annakarin Svedberg (1934–) has published around twenty books since she made her debut in 1957 with *Vårvinterdagbok* (*Journal of Early Spring*). Her first novel on the topic of lesbianism was *Vingklippta* (1962; *Clipped Wings*), and this book was quickly followed by three more lesbian-themed novels: *Det goda livet* (1963; *The Good Life*), *Se upp för trollen! eller: Äntligen en bok om livet sådant det är* (1963; *Watch Out for the Trolls! or: Finally a Book on Life as It Is*), and *Din egen* (1966; *Your Own*). Svedberg has not received much scholarly attention,[1] and most people are not familiar with her work today, but in the

1960s she became famous for a pornographic short story—a parody of the fairy tale "Little Red Riding Hood"—published in a 14-volume collection of pornographic short stories by high-quality writers. The novel *Vingklippta* also placed her as a Swedish Beat writer (Holm and Schottenius 1997).

This study looks at the representations of lesbianism in Svedberg's four novels from the 1960s, read in light of historical research on sexuality and gender to examine the ways these fictional representations relate to the sociopolitical discourse on sexuality of the time. These ideas will also be compared to the previous chapter on the 1930s in order to understand the development and change that the literary discourse on lesbianism underwent in Sweden during the twentieth century. However, this chapter will suggest the 1960s literary discourse on lesbianism does not change much from that of the 1930s. The medical discourse on lesbianism is still present in Svedberg's novels; in fact, it has an even stronger presence in her work than in Krusenstjerna's, since it is expressed not only through imagery but also through direct and indirect references to Freud and psychoanalysis. But like in Krusenstjerna's novels, lesbianism is still depicted as a better alternative than heterosexuality. Svedberg's novels describe men as erotically and emotionally incapable or as misogynists, while lesbianism offers intimacy and equality. Lesbianism is connected to a feminist project, since it is depicted as the only way for women to have fulfilling relationships in a world dominated by men. Svedberg's novels deal with sexual-political issues as well, and they contain various strategies to depict lesbianism in a positive way, highlighting and challenging contemporary prejudices. Writing is an important theme in the novels, and it becomes a means of changing the common world in order to reach gender equality and gain acceptance for homosexuality. The representations of lesbianism in Svedberg's novels thus show remarkable continuity with those in Krusenstjerna's from the 1930s.

THE MEDICAL DISCOURSE: REINFORCING AND CHALLENGING THE THREE *M*s

The medical discourse on lesbianism, established at the turn of the twentieth century, has a strong presence in Svedberg's work, particularly in the two novels dealing the most with lesbianism, *Vingklippta* and *Din egen*. The novel *Vingklippta* depicts a group of young people in Stockholm in the 1960s from the perspective of an unidentified first-person narrator. She describes her bohemian life among friends and lovers and their strivings to find their place in the world. She has erotic relationships with both men and women, but her love affairs with women come to dominate as the narrative progresses. However, as lesbianism becomes more present, so do its connections to medicalization. The following quote from *Vingklippta* can be seen as a key passage for how the medical discourse is presented in Svedberg's work: "I couldn't possibly be in love with Carola. Everything in me resisted. Carola was so different from me in every possible way. Carina was like me, so I could love her. Inga was a mother figure, so I could love her. But Carola? A tomboy. A girl who wanted too much to be a man, to act like a man, to be seen as a man. I didn't want to"[2] (*Vingklippta*, 141–42). In this passage the narrator considers three of her love objects, each of which reflect one of the medical discourse's explanations for female homosexuality. Carina is said to be similar to the narrator, suggesting the medicalized *mirrors*/narcissism explanation. Inga is a mother figure, indicating that the narrator is looking for a mother substitute when choosing an object for love, another *M*. Last, Carola is a tomboy, an androgyne with a male soul in a female body. Thus in this short quote the three *M*s— *mirrors*, *mothering*, and *masculinity*—all appear within just a few lines. This key passage summarizes the way the medical discourse is dealt with both in the novel as a whole and in the other novels by Svedberg: The medical discourse, represented mainly by the three *M*s, are often referred to explicitly, like in Krusenstjerna's depictions of Bell von Wenden, and not only through imagery, as was usually the case in the representations of Angela and Agda.

The *mothering* explanation of female homosexuality is most explicitly referred to in Svedberg's work. The narrator rarely makes direct cause-and-effect connections between absent mothers and lesbianism, but such connections are still implicitly established in the novels. The characters' relationships with their mothers are often discussed at length and viewed as a cause of psychological instability, and the mental suffering caused by childhood trauma is sometimes healed through a lesbian relationship. For instance, the narrator of *Vingklippta* has a complicated relationship with both of her parents, but with her mother in particular, and she struggles with it through the entire novel. The narrator describes her mother's inability to love her and seems to view her as the cause of her dysfunctional childhood: "There's something wrong with my mother. A lack of something. A fatal flaw which made her almost as useless in life, almost as resistanceless as a—as someone with weak nerves, well, but isn't that what she is—isn't it . . . ?"[3] (*Vingklippta*, 5).

A clear connection between absent mothers and lesbianism is presented in the novel when the narrator accidentally bumps into her parents in a bar. The narrator feels upset, almost traumatized, by the encounter and leaves the bar immediately with her girlfriend at the time, Carola. However, Carola is not able to comfort her, and the narrator instead tries to get hold of Inga, the mother character referred to in the first quote (*Vingklippta*, 162–63). It is no coincidence that Inga is the one the narrator wants to talk to: Fat and with a big bosom, Inga is continually depicted as a mother figure in the novel. She is one of the most one-dimensional characters, with an almost stereotypical role of redeeming and liberating others. Many times she is explicitly defined as such: "Who is Inga? A mother is anonymous. Like the earth. A mother does not have a face. Only plentiful, giving breasts that never dry up"[4] (*Vingklippta*, 82). By making love to her, the characters hope to solve their childhood traumas. When the narrator and Inga make love, the present merges with the narrator's fantasy of a redeemed mother-child relationship:

Mother, my mother. Who are you? I'm searching for someone. I'm searching for a mother. Mother Cosmos surrounds me, like the pregnant mother surrounds the unborn fetus. Here I rest in a velvet night under twinkling stars and await the time to be born. Here. I. Rest.

There was another woman. There was another mother. Was she like these deep oceans? Was she like this warm wind and earth and sky? Somewhere there was a miscalculation. Her destiny was crushed against mercilessness. It is she who hurts so much in me, like broken glass in my veins. It is she. Mother. My mother. I lay in her arms once, maybe. Mother, my mother. Your crystals were broken a long time before my time. Can't you understand that?

I felt Inga's hard nipple against the tip of my tongue, and found between enormous thighs a dripping vagina.[5] (*Vingklippta*, 55)

In this quote, the mother of the past, the narrator's biological mother, is juxtaposed with the loving mother figure Inga in the present. The pain caused by the biological mother is conveyed through an image of destruction and death: it is not blood running in the narrator's veins but broken glass. But through the erotic encounter with Inga the narrator is reborn. Inga is the original mother—she is referred to as "Mother Cosmos"—and through her the narrator encounters the four elements: water in the shape of deep oceans, earth, air (the sky), and fire through the passion the two women experience in the act of love. Inga is not only a mother substitute but a love object as well, which becomes clear in the last sentence of the quote. The narrator feels Inga's nipple with her tongue, like a baby being nursed, and she moves "between enormous thighs," like a baby being born. But at the same time the encounter is erotic—the nipple is hard from lust and the vagina is dripping from desire. The merging of these two functions—mother and lover—together with the fact that the narrator wants to see Inga after her traumatic encounter with her parents confirms an acceptance of the *mothering* explanation for female homosexuality; the narrator is able to heal from her traumatic childhood through the love for another woman, who becomes a mother substitute.

The *mothering* explanation can be traced back to Freud, and, overall, Freudian ideas tend to be more common than sexological ones in Svedberg. The narrator of *Vingklippta* and her friends reflect on themselves and their psychological developments, and they do it in Freudian terms, often with explicit references to Freud himself. Since Freud's theories became part of the medical discourse on homosexuality in the twentieth century, the references to Freud in the novel thus reinforce these ideas.

However, the novels also challenge this same medical discourse. In the last chapter of *Vingklippta* the narrator gives birth to a child, whom she loves and protects. It is unclear whether this actually takes place in the fictional world of the novel or in the narrator's dreams, but the passage can nevertheless be read as if the narrator sees and takes care of the small child in herself. Shortly after this occasion she dreams that her biological mother saves, embraces, and comforts her. The narrator thus seems to be liberated from her traumatic childhood memories, but contrary to psychoanalytical models she is not "cured" from her homosexuality; in the end, she lives happily with Carola in a lesbian relationship.

The *mothering* explanation for female homosexuality is present in the novel *Din egen* as well. This book portrays the love between two young women, Rebecca and Helena, and takes place mainly in Greece, where the two women travel because Rebecca is ill and needs to rest. Like the narrator in *Vingklippta*, Rebecca has grown up with an absent mother, but Rebecca's mother was physically, not emotionally, distant; she spent long periods of time away from home to be treated for her tuberculosis and eventually died. The connection between the absent mother and same-sex love is established early in the novel. Rebecca is in charge of a theatre group on tour, and when leaving Stockholm with the tour bus she cries when leaving Helena: "Never before had she felt such grief over having to part with somebody. Well, yes, as a child, when her mother had to leave because of her illness, and later, even worse, when her mother irrevocably died"[6] (*Din egen*, 12). A similar passage occurs a few pages later, where Rebecca describes her strong feelings for Helena: "Never before in her life had she even come close to such a feeling.—The only person for whom she ever had had similar feelings was her late mother"[7] (*Din egen*, 19). In both quotes, Rebecca's bond to and feelings for Helena are compared to the connections she had to her mother in the past, and Helena thus comes across as a mother substitute, in line with psychoanalytical models for understanding female homosexuality.

The connection between the loss of a mother and a lesbian love object is more strongly emphasized in passages referring to one of Rebecca's past love relationships with a woman whom she turned to after her mother died. Rebecca describes this relationship as based not on love but on her need for company and emotional support (*Din egen*, 19, 105–10). Furthermore, the trauma caused by her mother's death is brought out by references to the unusually strong bond between Rebecca and her mother; Rebecca even describes it as perhaps too strong, indicating a dysfunctional dimension of her childhood (*Din egen*, 117–18). The medicalization of Rebecca is further reinforced by her psychological instability. One of her friends describes her as "incurably hysterical"[8] (*Din egen*, 25), and later in the novel she tries to kill herself after a fight with Helena (*Din egen*, 165–90).

Mirrors or narcissism is not as explicitly present in Svedberg's work. However, this explanation is presented through imagery. For instance, lesbian relationships are characterized by the same closeness as they are in Krusenstjerna's novels, while heterosexual relationships are portrayed as dysfunctional. When the narrator makes love to Carola, the lovers' bodies become entangled: "Moist pubic hairs become entangled with each other and breasts are pressed together. A hand reaches for a breast. A mouth looks for a nipple"[9] (*Vingklippta*, 138). Lacking pronouns, this quote describes the love encounter as an exchange between body parts acting on their own; the individualities of the lovers seem to have dissolved, which suggests that merging has taken place. Generally, similarity is emphasized throughout the chapter that depicts this love encounter. The narrator claims that she loves Carola's femininity and that she does not want her to be masculine. The familiarity of female softness is the focus, which the narrator prefers over male difference: "I recognize a woman's body in your body. Your cheek is soft against mine and not rough"[10] (*Vingklippta*, 138). In this case, the pronouns reinforce closeness; though this passage is internal narrative, the narrator refers to Carola in second person and addresses her directly. This creates distance from the reader and closeness between the two lovers.

The images of closeness and similarity suggest the *mirrors* explanation for lesbianism but are also connected to psychoanalytic theories positing that lesbian couples have a stronger tendency to merge than other couples. In her critical examination of psychological research on the role of fusion in female homosexual relationships, Julie Mencher shows that previous scholarship defines fusion as a problem. Fusion is defined as a state of unity in which ego boundaries are crossed and identification and intimacy are prioritized over independence and self-development. According to Mencher, traditional psychodynamic theory has pathologized the idea of fusion based on three assumptions: "First, life begins in a state of symbiotic merger with mother. Second, development consists of a series of progressive disengagements from this (and subsequent) relationships [. . .] Third, fusion in adulthood represents regression to an infantile stage of merger and must therefore be held at bay" (Mencher 1997, 320). However, Mencher challenges the idea of fusion as pathology by arguing that it rests on a male and heteronormative view of self-development. Instead she suggests that fusion might actually be a better way of self-development for women, and lesbians in particular (Mencher 1997, 311–30).

While Mencher is critical of the medicalization of fusion, her article still shows that the legacy of the medical discourse has been dominant in the field of psychology. A similar observation is made by Sara Ahmed, who suggests that the psychoanalytic approaches to the idea of lesbian merger rest on an assumption that women are "the same" and that lesbian relationships are narcissistic and deny difference. She refers to Beverly Burch, who argues that the psychoanalytic explanation of lesbian merger is based on the idea of homosexuality as resulting from various early childhood deficits and thus as pathology (Ahmed 2006, 96–97). The closeness that the narrator of *Vingklippta* experiences with other women could be read in line with a medicalized understanding of lesbian relationships. Furthermore, the merger or symbiotic dimensions of lesbian love are at times portrayed as problematic. When the narrator considers getting a mistress, Carina cautions her: "Then she will fall in love with you, and you'll never get rid of her"[11] (*Vingklippta*, 48). Carina herself is hesitant to having a relationship with the narrator because she is afraid it will become too serious: "No, I don't dare because then I'll never get rid of you. I know how girls are. They suck you in"[12] (*Vingklippta*, 147). In these quotes, Carina puts into words the idea of female same-sex partners as more clingy in love than men, the same idea that can be found in other depictions of love between women in the novel. For instance, Carola is extremely demanding in her love relationship with the narrator, and she is often jealous, which makes the narrator feel limited (*Vingklippta*, 164–66).

The love between Rebecca and Helena in *Din egen* is continually described in a way that highlights closeness and merging. Although one passage in the novel explicitly mentions "the *false* belief in the stronger emotional commitment of homosexual love"[13] (*Din egen*, 133, emphasis mine), thus challenging this idea, the novel as a whole can be read as an argument for this stronger emotional commitment of lesbian love. A recurring symbol for the strength of Helena and Rebecca's love is the double bed, as opposed to twin beds that are often found in European hotels. Everywhere they go, both in Sweden and in Greece, they want to sleep in a double bed, and they are willing to go through much effort to avoid sleeping apart. The double bed is said to make closeness possible: "And no matter how close the mattresses are to each other, a tiny gap is still a gap, preventing the lovers from crawling into each other and falling asleep as closely entangled as they wish"[14] (*Din egen*, 69). This quote puts a high value on closeness but also fusion: the gap is said to prevent the lovers from crawling *into* each other.

While the closeness that the women in Svedberg's novels experience in relationships with other women is generally a positive feeling and a source of strength and happiness, it also connects lesbianism to the medical discourse by suggesting both the *mirrors* explanation to female homosexuality and the psychological theory of lesbian merger. The representations of the *mothering* explanation are direct and thus more explicitly medicalized. However, the allusions to *mirrors* and fusion have more in common with the subtle medicalization of lesbianism in Krusenstjerna's portrayal of Angela and Agda's relationship: the relationship is explicitly depicted as a source of empowerment, but the imagery still suggests medicalization.

The *masculinity* explanation to female homosexuality is also referred to in Svedberg's work, and like the *mothering M*, representations of masculinity are more explicitly connected to the medical discourse. With a few exceptions the main characters are usually not referred to in terms of masculinity; instead masculinity works as a foil, as if the narrator were rejecting that model for lesbianism. When the narrator of *Vingklippta* attends a party with a group of lesbians, one of them is described as follows: "She did not really make any deeper impression on me; rather, she seemed a little boring, charmless and dull.—Typical dyke, I thought and looked at her pants, dark-blue sweater, short hair and graceless movements"[15] (*Vingklippta*, 132). This woman is depicted as unfeminine, dressed in men's clothes and with short hair. She contrasts sharply with one of the narrator's lovers, Carina, who is described a few lines later: "Carina was very beautiful in her chair, wearing high heels and a straight, fitted dress, and she looked at me with her green eyes"[16] (*Vingklippta*, 132). She comes across as feminine in her dress and high heels, and is evaluated as beautiful, in opposition to the "typical dyke's" boring and charmless appearance.

In this passage, Carina is depicted as something else than the typical dyke; she is feminine despite being attracted to women. A similar idea is presented in *Din egen*, where the male actor in Rebecca's theatre group, Rickard Assarsson, talks about Rebecca and Helena's relationship: "'She is no regular girl-friend,' he said to his female colleague in a sour voice. 'I've seen this before.—But it's strange, I don't understand. Both of them are so feminine'"[17] (*Din egen*, 15). Overall, Rickard is depicted as an unsympathetic and misogynist male, and this passage can be read as an expression of his lack of understanding. However, it also reflects a stereotype of lesbians as masculine, which can be traced back to sexological understandings of lesbians as a third sex. Rickard's statement reinforces the medical discourse by suggesting the connection to masculinity, but at the same time, this discourse is challenged since the person who makes the reference is unsympathetic. The discourse is also challenged by the fact that the main characters in Svedberg's novels are generally defined in opposition to masculinity. However, despite these challenges, the *masculinity* explanation is present in the novels, and the way the main characters are distanced from it could in fact be seen as a reinforcement of the medical discourse, since the mannish lesbians depicted come across as even more stigmatized. Thus the positive portrayals of lesbianism in Svedberg's novel are in a way at the expense of certain kinds of lesbianism, represented by masculine lesbians. The acceptance of lesbianism that is being promoted in the novels is not an inclusive acceptance, and the rejection of masculinity reinforces the medicalization of (certain kinds of) lesbianism.

However, even if the main characters in *Vingklippta* are usually described as feminine, contrasting the mannish lesbians, they still challenge contemporary normative femininity. Although many women entered the labor market during this time, the normative woman in the early 1960s was still a housewife. The majority of married women did not work in the public sphere, and if they did, they were still responsible for housework and children. Women's salaries were about 40 percent lower than men's, and women usually had the most boring and low-status jobs. Also, the tax system, which counted husband and wife as a unit, did not encourage married women to work (Hirdman 1990, 87–89; Hirdman [1992] 2004, 212–14; Wikander 1992, 57–58). In contrast, the narrator of *Vingklippta* and her female friends are neither loyal wives nor nurturing mothers. They lead their lives as bohemians, just like their male friends. The narrator does not even have her own apartment and moves in and out with various friends. It is not entirely clear what they all do for a living, but the narrator seems to be a writer. These women drink plenty of alcohol and have love affairs with both men and women—sometimes with more than one person at the same time. By depicting an alternative lifestyle for women who do not identify as masculine, *Vingklippta* could be seen as a way of challenging normative femininity, the housewife ideal of the early 1960s.

Overall, the presence of the medical discourse on lesbianism is stronger in Svedberg's novels than in Krusenstjerna's. Although Bell von Wenden was explicitly medicalized, represented as a "lesbian evil" character, Angela and Agda's relationship was depicted as one of the most beautiful love relationships in the book series and as a source of strength and empowerment. However, the medicalization of their relationship can be seen in imagery. In Svedberg's work, on the other hand, only the *mirrors* explanation connected with the theory of fusion is limited mostly to imagery. The other *M*s of the medical discourse on lesbianism, the *mothering* and the *masculinity* explanations, are more explicitly visible in the text, and the many references to Freud and psychology, particularly those of distant mothers, further contribute to reinforcing the medical discourse's influence on the understanding of lesbianism.

In general, Svedberg's texts have an ambiguous relationship to the medical discourse, a discourse that is simultaneously reinforced and challenged. For instance, the narrator of *Vingklippta* reads a book titled *Kvinnlig homosexualitet* (*Vingklippta*, 133; *Female Homosexuality*), which might be Frank S. Caprio's book with the same title that was translated into Swedish in 1958, four years before Svedberg's novel was published. Caprio is a doctor with a psychoanalytical perspective on homosexuality and views lesbianism as a symptom of a neurosis, usually of narcissistic character, which could be successfully cured (Caprio [1954] 1958). In this example the medical discourse is reinforced through the presence of Caprio's book but also challenged since the narrator is never "cured" and is in a happy lesbian relationship when the novel ends.

As in the 1930s, the tendencies to medicalize lesbianism in 1960s literature correspond with the sociopolitical discourse of the day. Surprisingly, the decriminalization of homosexuality in 1944 did not lead to a more liberal attitude, and 1950s Sweden, like the rest of the Western world, went through a period of homophobia. Two different scandals involving male homosexuality took place in Sweden in the early 1950s and might have contributed to the harsh climate: the Kejne and Haijby affairs.

Karl-Erik Kejne was a pastor who worked for *Stockholms Stadsmission*, a Christian organization dedicated to social outreach and charity work. In 1949 Kejne reported to the police that one of his colleagues, Gösta Malmberg, had harassed him and spread rumors about him being homosexual. In the police investigation and media debate that followed, Kejne and Malmberg accused each other of homosexuality, but both denied being attracted to men. The police investigation was delayed, and Kejne accused them of intentionally dragging their feet because the state and the legal system were, according to him, infiltrated by homosexuals who were protecting each other. One of those he believed was in need of protection was church minister Nils Quensel. During the 1930s Quensel had been in contact with several young men and had been helping them financially. One of these men died in a fire in 1936, and the circumstances around his death were suspicious. In the 1950s Kejne claimed that a document confirming Quensel's contact with the young man had disappeared from the police files. The media debate surrounding Kejne put pressure on the government to start an investigation into whether the police had acted unlawfully. Finally, in 1951 Quensel left his government position, not because he was found guilty of any crime but because his private life had been exposed in the media.

At the same time another affair connected to homosexuality was uncovered in Sweden, and this incident involved King Gustav V (1858–1950). Kurt Haijby had been extorting money from the Royal Court during the 1930s and 1940s, claiming that he had been involved in sexual acts with the king, and in 1948 he published a novel, a roman à clef, detailing the alleged affair. In 1952 Haijby was sued for blackmailing and sentenced to six years of labor, and in 1965 he committed suicide. The Kejne and Haijby affairs and the long media debate that followed the Kejne affair are more complicated than these brief summaries suggest,[18] but the main outcome of the affairs was that homosexuality came to be seen as a threat to society. People with power (a government official and the king) were involved in both affairs, both with messy endings, and the public court system came to be seen as corrupt due to homosexuality. Homosexuals were thought to be part of an organized network, similar to the Freemasons, with the purpose of helping its members to more powerful positions in society. This development was viewed as the end of the civilized and democratic society. Surprisingly, left-wing media and writers were the most homophobic in this debate, setting Sweden apart from many other countries where conservative groups have tended to be more homophobic (Lennerhed 1994, 70–88; Norrhem, Rydström, and Winkvist 2008, 149–52; Söderström 2000).

The legacy of the discourse on homosexuality as a threat to society was reflected in the different legal ages for opposite-sex and same-sex sexual relations, an inequality in the law that was still in effect in the 1960s in Sweden. Justification for the higher legal age for homosexual relations was based on the so-called seduction theory: a young person might "contract" homosexuality if seduced by a same-sex partner. Only one homosexual experience was thought to be enough to "disturb" a young person's development as heterosexual (Andreasson 2000, 38–43; Lennerhed 1994, 159–60). This legislation, in place in Sweden until 1978, highlights the belief during that period in homosexuality as a disease that could be contracted, something that had to be prevented from spreading. This attitude in the 1960s sociopolitical discourse might explain the more direct references to the medicalized discourse on lesbianism in Svedberg's novels compared to Krusenstjerna's. However, the negative attitude toward homosexuality of that period might have also prompted a more outspoken challenge to this attitude in Svedberg's novels.

DYSFUNCTIONAL MASCULINITY AND HETEROSEXUALITY AS PERFORMANCE

As we have seen in the previous section, Svedberg's main characters reject and are distanced from the *masculinity* theory of female homosexuality. Liv Saga Bergdahl suggests that the *Vingklippta* characters' tendencies to contrast themselves with masculine lesbians could be read in the light of 1970s lesbian feminism.

During this second wave of feminism, lesbians generally rejected masculinity and its connection to lesbianism and focused on an identification with women instead. Bergdahl argues that Svedberg might have had a similar goal in mind: to create new images of lesbians by rejecting old ones (Bergdahl 2010, 215). Taking Bergdahl's argument further, the distance these books take from masculinity can be seen as part of a feminist project in Svedberg's work, a project that depicts heterosexuality as a prison for women and thus impossible to engage in.

Overall, Svedberg's novels demonstrate a lack of faith in men and their abilities. In *Vingklippta*, three men have more prominent roles, and only one of them is able to have erotic relationships. Tomas is physically impotent, and Holger is in psychoanalysis and has decided not to sleep with a woman again until he knows he wants to marry her, which psychoanalysis is supposed to help him determine (*Vingklippta*, 46–47). The only man who can perform intercourse is Ingvar, an older man with whom the narrator has a relationship in the beginning of the novel. He, on the other hand, is unable to connect to the narrator on an emotional level, and the narrator describes him as "no more sensitive than an old tractor"[19] (*Vingklippta*, 27). Besides being incapable of having relationships with the female characters, men live in a world of their own and are sometimes even misogynistic. The relationship the narrator has with Holger is depicted as unequal. He talks for hours about the state of the world while she quietly listens, even if she does not agree with him: "I didn't say anything. I listened and knew that I did not want to agree with him. I knew I wanted to say entirely different things but said nothing"[20] (*Vingklippta*, 40).

However, Holger's authority is also challenged in the novel, usually when he is portrayed as ridiculous and self-important. The narrator sometimes lets her mind wander while Holger is talking, not paying attention to what he says, which makes his speech come across as an eternal flow of words. She also distances herself from what he says by repeatedly using the expression "he says" when describing Holger's monologues, emphasizing that the words are his and not hers. As the narrative unfolds, Holger becomes more misogynistic. In the beginning of the novel he represents a softer masculinity compared to, for instance, the older and more conservative Ingvar. However, later, when Holger talks about women in his monologues, it becomes clear that he views them as either virgins or witches and as subordinate and passive beings who need to be guided by men. The narrator's encounters with men in the novel result in repeated disappointments. The men are self-centered and incapable of loving, either emotionally or physically. At one point in the novel they are dismissed in a way that implies that they cannot be counted on; referring to Tomas, who has been struggling with his impotence and his anxiety, and Holger with his refusal to have intercourse with the narrator, Inga laughs: "'Look at the men we are surrounded by!' she says and shakes her head"[21] (*Vingklippta*, 92). Inga's dismissal indicates that the men in the novel are not to be taken seriously. A few pages later the narrator ends her relationship with Holger and devotes herself entirely to relationships with women.

In her book on lesbian feminism in Sweden, Hanna Hallgren argues that female homosexuals *became* women in the 1970s. Prior to the second wave of feminism, female homosexuality had primarily been connected to sexology's definitions of the homosexual as a third sex, but during the 1970s lesbianism became associated with the feminist movement and was seen partly as a choice or a political statement: the lesbian was a woman-identified woman who dismissed men on all levels, including as sexual partners (Hallgren 2008). In *Vingklippta* the narrator's change in love partners—she goes from having relationships with men only, through relationships with both sexes, to relationships with women exclusively—runs parallel to another development in the narrator: her feminist awareness is growing. The depiction of masculinity as incomplete in *Vingklippta* can be read in light of this feminist consciousness: lesbianism became a way of challenging the traditional 1960s sociopolitical models emphasizing the man as provider. In the story, women are not portrayed as perfect either, but compared to the dysfunctional men, lesbianism seems to be the only option for women who want to be in relationships based on

love. Dysfunctional men, feminist consciousness, and lesbianism thus seem to be intertwined in *Vingklippta*.

The way Svedberg's characters distance themselves from
mannish lesbians can also be read in connection with the 1970s
woman-identified women that Hallgren describes. While Bergdahl (2010), who also refers to Hallgren's study, focuses on this
distancing as a way of creating new images of lesbians (215),
Hallgren also argues that lesbian feminists distanced themselves
from masculinity also because they rejected all male identification. Generally, the second wave of feminism saw masculinity as
destructive, no matter if it was expressed by a man or a mannish lesbian, and therefore lesbians should identify with women
instead (Hallgren 2008, 161–62, 203). The narrator's critique
of mannish lesbians in *Vingklippta* and her efforts to depict her
friends and lovers as feminine can be read as an embracing of
the budding feminist discourse of this time, especially since her
feminist awareness grows during the course of the novel and
because men are depicted as dysfunctional in various ways.

Dysfunctional masculinity is a recurring theme in Svedberg's
novels, and it is often contrasted with happy lesbian relationships; *Det goda livet* (1963) is no exception. This novel portrays
two Swedish women and a child on retreat on the Spanish
island Ibiza. The relationship between the two women is never
explicitly referred to as lesbian, but their sexuality is still clear
from the description of their life: they sleep in the same bed,
argue, and give each other compliments and affection. Men are
not very present in the novel and generally appear as minor
characters or, like in this quote, in a book:

> In a book we found a picture of a man, drawn by a prostitute.
> "A penis with a human head!" Brita said.
> "And what a flaccid one," I said. "It must be impotent."
> "Yes, it's not worth much. So now we know."[22] (*Det goda
> livet*, 49)

Brita's words can be seen as a kind of validation of something
the reader of *Vingklippta* has already suspected: the characters
believe men cannot be counted on, and the women are happier on their own. The two women's lifestyle also confirms

this: In the Ibiza house they lead their everyday life with each other and the child, far away from men. They do not seem to miss anything and are happy, an idea reflected in the title, *The Good Life.*

The novel *Din egen* portrays a different kind of dysfunction than the impotent masculinity found in *Vingklippta* and *Det goda livet.* In *Din egen* men have a prominent position, not as potential lovers but as persistent admirers who refuse to leave the two women alone. In Greece, Rebecca and Helena meet a man who is married to the Swedish tour guide and who follows them for more than an hour to show them the town's medieval castle—even if his company is obviously unwanted by the two women and his wife is waiting for him in the hotel lobby (*Din egen*, 49–50). They accept a dinner invitation from the Greek men Kosta and Georgos in a move to get rid of them, but this leads up to more evenings with the two men, who will not take no for an answer (*Din egen*, 50–56). On another occasion they are forced to stop buying groceries at a store because the owner is so solicitous (*Din egen*, 124–25). The narrative presents the persistence of these men in universal terms: all women are said to suffer from unwanted male attention, and the characters' experiences are thus connected to women's situation in general (*Din egen*, 50–51). The unwanted attention is also explicitly tied to a gendered power relationship with a long history: "Centuries-old ideas of women as subordinate to men were forced upon them. In front of any man they were suddenly without will and choice and without the right to decide their own actions. It was not only their love that reacted. There was a deeper and more fundamentally human sounding board of muttering unwillingness. There was a strong feeling of irritation with the fact that these men viewed their own company as something so obviously attractive that every woman, if not happy at least flattered, was expected to respond to their handclasps and embraces"[23] (*Din egen*, 60–61). This quote expresses an underlying theme throughout the book that the gendered power relationship results in a belief that men have the right to women and their bodies. Women are subordinate to men and have to adapt to men's wills. However, the novel makes it clear that the gender roles are not thought to be based on biology: "There was something ceremonial over the way in which the Greek men hoped to make contact with a woman—the man played his part, which he had identified with since childhood, and he expected that the women would act their parts with the same matter of course as an actor expects his fellow actors to follow the script"[24] (*Din egen*, 100). This quote presents gender roles—particularly those relating to courting—as a social construct: Men's efforts to approach women are like acting. Theatre is a recurring theme in the novel—Rebecca works as a tour leader of a theatre group—and theatre and acting can be seen as metaphors for social constructions, particularly in terms of gender.

Rickard Assarsson, who is the male leading actor in the play Rebecca works with, is more than sixty years old but still hits on the young women in the theatre group: "He caused all three female tour members lots of trouble, not only by continuously seeking their company, but even more so through his physical advances. Despite their repeated rejections, he began new attacks every evening, full of hope. But nobody was interested"[25] (*Din egen*, 16). This passage contains several words that describe repetition; Rickard's approaches are repeated every night, just like a theatre show, and the approaches are continually rejected. The theatre context highlights the dimension of performance, which makes gender roles come across as a performance of roles in a play. Judith Butler suggests the parallel: Gender is performative, she asserts—a stylized repetition of acts (Butler [1990] 1999, 173–80). Through the theatre references, gender is depicted as lacking core essence; rather, gender is acted out and reinforced though endless repetition. Rickard performs masculinity by approaching the female actors over and over again, and the female actors perform femininity rejecting him.

With few exceptions, men in *Din egen* are portrayed as unsympathetic individuals who are only interested in women as sex objects and will not leave them alone. This masculinity differs from the inadequate masculinity depicted in *Vingklippta*, but the two kinds of masculinity have a common link: they are unwanted. In *Din egen* the men's performances of hetero-sexuality are rejected with a performance of femininity, while Rebecca and Helena's love is depicted as happy and strong—and it comes across as natural and easy in opposition to the heterosexual ritual. For this reason, lesbian love seems to be presented as a better alternative than heterosexuality. In the heterosexual "play" women have everything to lose, since it is essentially a power play where women are subordinate to men. For Rebecca and Helena lesbianism is not a choice but a strong force that brings them together. However, since their love is continually presented as a foil for the heterosexual power play, it still has feminist implications; lesbian love seems to be the only real love option for women in a society dominated by men.

While *Vingklippta* and *Din egen* mainly depict lesbian rela-tionships or casual heterosexual relationships, the novel *Se upp för trollen!* also presents heterosexual marriage. This novel por-trays several different characters and is written in a dreamlike way with no clear main plot. It takes place in 1960s Sweden as well as in a fairy-tale world, and the characters move freely between the two worlds. The depictions of heterosexual mar-riage can be read in light of the sociopolitical discourse of the time. For instance, the marriage between Mary and Edvin fol-lows contemporary ideals; he is the provider, working in the public sphere, and as a housewife Mary does unpaid labor in the private sphere. But the novel does not reinforce 1960s gender stereotypes; by depicting the marriage from Mary's perspective, the novel offers insight into the life of a housewife, and this insight questions the 1960s gender roles.

When the book opens, Mary and Edvin's marriage has reached the point of stagnation. They hardly speak to each other about important things but instead have polite conversa-tions about the weather and Edvin's job. Mary is worried that her husband has stopped loving her, and this thought leads to further concerns, "because no matter what, she was dependent on his love. If it were to disappear—well, where would she go in life?"[26] (*Se upp för trollen!*, 22). Mary does not mention why she is dependent on Edvin's love, but from the descriptions of Mary's life, the reader can conclude that she is economically dependent on Edvin. For instance, when Mary wants to buy things, she has to ask Edvin, but she does not always ask him for money in fear of making him angry and contributing to "a bad atmosphere at home"[27] (*Se upp för trollen!*, 16). This economic imbalance results in a power relationship where Mary is subordinated to Edvin, a power structure that corresponds to the life many Swedish women led in the 1960s. By highlighting Mary's unhealthy dependence on and subordination to Edvin, Svedberg's novel questions this model.

Furthermore, the marriage makes heterosexuality seem performative rather than natural. Neither Mary nor Edvin seems to be happy; Edvin has fallen in love with another woman, and Mary is bored with her life as a housewife and wants children:

> Mary leaned over Edvin and kissed him.
> "Now my love," she said, "I want a baby. I don't want to wait any longer. What are we waiting for? We have everything we need—apartment, bathroom, modern kitchen with an electric stove, two rooms—that will be enough, at least during the first years—plenty of cabinets and closets, nice furniture, refrigerator, a nice pantry, good kitchenware, twenty sets of sheets, sixty pillow cases, four dozen hand towels and four dozen kitchen towels, two dozen terry cloth and four excellent bath towels."[28] (*Se upp för trollen!*, 32)

Again, Mary's dependency on and subordination to Edvin is highlighted, since a child is yet another thing she needs to ask Edvin for, in the same way she asks for a new dresser. But what stands out in this quote is the long list of the couple's belongings, which continues for another ten lines after this quote ends. The measure of a heterosexual marriage comes across as dependent on the accumulation of things, and the child Mary wants seems to be just another thing that will make the perfect home and heterosexual marriage complete. The heterosexual dynamic is tied to material consumption and the staging of the perfect home, and is thus described as something that needs to be done or a standard that must be upheld rather than as something we desire as humans. Like gender in *Din egen*, heterosexual marriage in *Se upp för trollen!* is presented as a performance, a set of practiced behaviors Mary and Edvin hold to despite their mutual dissatisfaction.

Reinforcing the idea that marital roles are social constructs and not innate behaviors, Mary is described as a well-educated housewife whose skills are learned. She picks up ideas from women's magazines: "The idea to 'sew your own bedroom curtains' she had picked up from *The House Wife*. 'In lovely blue, sheer pink, or white'"[29] (*Se upp för trollen!*, 15–16). She also gains relationship advice from listening to the radio and reading women's magazines: "But confidence cannot be forced—that was something she has read in *The Ladies World* and often heard on the radio"[30] (*Se upp för trollen!*, 22). The role of women's magazines in the education of housewives was part of the mainstream discourse of the time. For instance, in a study of representations of gender in women's magazines from the 1960s, Barbro Backberger argues that all different parts of the woman's magazine—articles about famous people, beauty advice, short stories, advice on sex and psychological problems and much more—contribute to creating a feminine ideal: The perfect woman prioritizes her family over her own career, devotes time and energy to her looks in order to please men, avoids promiscuity, and aims for marriage. The magazines might be presented as innocent entertainment, but Backberger points out that many women read nothing except magazines and hence got all their knowledge about femininity and gender from them; thus the magazines contributed to maintaining female subordination (Backberger [1966] 2003). Central to Backberger's argument is repetition; the same feminine ideal recurs in all different parts of the woman's magazine. Svedberg's novel cleverly uses this same strategy to a different end: Repetition is crucial in the depictions of Mary's life as well, although the effect can be read as critique or even a satire of the feminine and also the heterosexual ideal. Her role as a housewife is played in relation to the role of the male provider. In this marriage, heterosexuality comes across as disconnected from love; instead, it is a performance of opposite gender roles, which are reinforced through repetition.

Adding depth to the novel's portrayal of the construct of marriage, the novel also explores the life of Edith. She seems to belong to an older generation than Mary, which brings the novel's depiction of the gender system out of the specific time period and ties it to a more universal condition for women. Edith used to have her own career as a nurse but was forced to leave her job when she got married because her husband did not want his wife to work outside of home; in his words, "Don't you think I'm man enough to support my wife and children?"[31] (*Se upp för trollen!*, 18). In his statement, masculinity is tied to the ability to provide for a family, in line with twentieth-century gender ideals. Edith's husband also makes this decision about Edith's career, which emphasizes the power dimension of this gender system. Without a job outside the home, Edith devotes all her time to her son, Svante, who grows up to become a spoiled young man.

The depiction of Svante as spoiled and unsympathetic can be read as a way of challenging the results of a gender-segregated society, mirroring Betty Friedan's critique of the American housewife ideal from her now-classic book *The Feminine Mystique*, published in 1963. Friedan argues that the housewife ideal has left women with feelings of emptiness and dissatisfaction, since the role keeps them from devoting their lives to something more meaningful than housework. Women become incapable of developing their own identities and instead lead their lives through their husbands and children. This, in turn, has severe consequences for the children, who grow up to become passive, since they have been spoiled by their mothers and are not used to taking responsibility for their own lives. Friedan mainly focuses on American housewives of the 1950s, but her theories still apply to the women in Svedberg's novels. Like the women Friedan describes, Svedberg's female characters are defined in relation to their husbands. They lead empty lives in the private sphere, with no opportunities for self-fulfillment except through their children (Friedan 1963). By portraying these same roles, Svedberg's novels suggest that a rigid, dependent, and limiting ideal has far-reaching implications, not just for these women, but for society as a whole. Edith's son Svante has turned into a spoiled, passive young man after being raised as the object of his mother's self-fulfillment—just like the children Friedan describes in her book. The husbands are not happy either—both Edvin and Edith's husband leave their wives. Svedberg's novels seem to suggest that if women are not allowed to seek fulfillment outside of home, the family falls apart: the kids become dysfunctional and marriages deteriorate; love cannot thrive when husbands and wives lead their lives in separate spheres, the public and the private.

In addition to the bored and subordinated housewife, the female characters in *Se upp för trollen!* have another option: the role of mistress or dangerous woman. This role is played by Agneta, the woman Edvin falls in love with. When an admirer says that Agneta's soft white hand reminds him of the hand of a good fairy, she responds playfully by saying she has the claws of a witch, drawing on the stereotype of the beautiful but dangerous woman, the femme fatale. Agneta gets plenty of male attention and leads a more adventurous life than the average housewife, but her role is still defined in relation to men: she is reduced to an object for men's desire. As either housewives or femme fatales, most of the female characters in *Se upp för trollen!* are limited by the traditional representations of women, which could be summed up as either the Madonna or the whore.

While the femme fatale might seem more independent than the housewife, she is still limited by the heterosexual script. Through the character Mona, Svedberg's novel suggests both the origins and the conflicting desires represented by the feminine ideal. Mona is a young woman who works in a shop but daydreams of a fairy-tale prince who would enter the store, shower her with gifts, and take her away in his black limousine to his castle (*Se upp för trollen!*, 77). Eventually the prince appears, and because of the experimental and dreamlike character of the novel, it is impossible to determine whether their encounter takes place in Mona's fantasies or in the fictional world of the narrative. Regardless, Mona's story can shed light on the feminine ideals represented in the novel. Mona's modern version of her fairy-tale prince drives a limousine, but their relationship still rests on a traditional gender model where he is active and she is passive. She wants to be saved from a boring life as shop assistant and dreams of fulfilling herself through a man. However, when she later settles down with her prince in his castle, they do not live happily ever after. One night Mona leaves the prince and enters the world on her own, but she quickly meets a new man who wants her to come with him to *his* castle. At first he tries to convince her to come with him voluntarily by offering her valuable gifts in return, but when she refuses, he kidnaps her: "And he sat her down on the pommel of his saddle, wrapped her in his cloak and galloped off. A cloud of dust whirled around them and the horse was frothing at the mouth.—In the cloak Mona struggled, screamed and went completely wild, beating with her fists, biting whatever she could find in anger. 'I don't want to I don't want to!' But *he* wanted it, and at this moment that was the determining factor"[32] (*Se upp för trollen!*, 140). The gendered power dimension of the traditional fairy-tale theme in this quote is central. The romantic implications of the fairy tale—the prince on his horse who saves the princess and brings her to his castle where the two of them live happily ever after—is instead described as an act of violation in Svedberg's novel. The persistent prince bears resemblance with the men who courted Rebecca and Helena in *Din egen*, although those men never used physical violence. The power relationship is more explicit in Mona's case, but both novels depict the same gendered relationship: Rebecca and Helena are as unable to resist the wills of their admirers as Mona is.

Mona remains unhappily in the new castle, but one night she is able to escape with the aid of an eagle that lets her ride on his back. The narrative of Mona can be read as a critique of the feminine ideal, the woman who sees marriage as a path to self-realization, the same ideal promoted in the women's magazines in Backberger's study. This paradigm is challenged by representing heterosexual marriage as a prison for Mona. The eagle is a conventional symbol of freedom, here leading Mona to a life without men. However, gradually she starts missing love. The eagle says that he can take her to the man she loves, but she must then leave her life with the eagle for good—she thus has to choose between freedom and love. Mona chooses love and is reunited with one of the men, but the other one is looking for her, and when he eventually finds her she feels torn. In the end of Mona's narrative, the two men flip a coin for her, but since, for some reason, nobody wins, she splits in two halves (*Se upp för trollen!*, 219–20). This resolution can be read as Mona breaking with convention by wanting to live with two men, challenging the ideals of the nuclear family and monogamy. But this decision implies a cost: she splits herself in order to satisfy two men who both want her, thus going to destructive lengths to uphold the role of the woman who adjust to the will of men and the normative status of the heterosexual couple.

The status of the heterosexual woman in public life did not significantly change between 1930 and 1960 in Sweden. While women's influences on Swedish politics slowly increased during the decades following women's suffrage in 1921, women still had a marginalized position in the public sphere for many decades; only 10 percent of the members of the parliament were women in the beginning of the 1960s. About 40 percent of all women (28 percent of the married women) between 15 and 64 worked outside of home, but the labor market was gender segregated, and women's jobs had lower status and less pay. However, the 1960s marked the first rumblings of change. While the second wave of feminism did not start until around 1970 in Sweden, the media began to take up the discussion on women's liberation almost a decade earlier, as was the case with the debate that followed the 1961 publication of Eva Moberg's article "Kvinnans villkorliga frigivning" ("Women on Parole"), which criticized the limitations of women's liberation so far. According to Moberg, women were on parole—many of them had entered the workforce, but the feminine ideal promoted by society was still connected to the roles of wife and mother (Hirdman 1990, 87–89; Hirdman [1992] 2004, 212–14; Lennerhed 1994, 112–18; Ohlander and Strömberg 2008, 203–6, 219–21, 224–25; Wikander 1992, 57–58). The fact that women's situations were debated to a certain extent at that time might explain the difference between Svedberg's and Krusenstjerna's novels. Like in Krusenstjerna's book series, masculinity and heterosexuality are dismissed in Svedberg's novels. However, Krusenstjerna's novels are less preoccupied with the everyday aspects of heterosexual relationships, while Svedberg's describe inequalities and gendered power dimensions in detail. Svedberg's novels thus come across as more outspoken when it comes to feminist politics and more critical of women's roles than Krusenstjerna's, likely due to the fact that the private sphere was discussed to a greater extent in the 1960s feminist politics.

Like Krusenstjerna's novels, Svedberg's also portrays lesbianism as a better alternative for women than heterosexuality. They suggest that freedom and love are impossible to combine in a heterosexual relationship. In *Se upp för trollen!* Mary and Edith give up the power of their own lives to men who eventually leave them, and Mona learns that she cannot be free while loving a man. However, the portrayals of lesbian relationships imply that love and freedom can coexist in this model, and lesbianism is thus tied to the rejection and critique of heterosexuality. When Mary and Agneta meet and start a relationship, they are very happy together. Their relationship is connected to life and growing—Mary and Agneta's happiness in love is described in connection to nature, much like the imagery connected to Angela and Agda in Krusenstjerna's novels. The two plant onions and seeds and later look "for tiny green seedlings in the black dirt that they had sewn"[33] (*Se upp för trollen!*, 130). Moreover, their apartment is located near a yard that "was overgrown with flowers and greens: ivy, marigolds, roses, tulips, narcissus—all kinds of growing greenery climbed along walls and sprouted in flower beds"[34] (*Se upp för trollen!*, 132). Like the connection between lesbianism and natural growth found in Krusenstjerna's novels, Svedberg's novel suggests the fruitfulness of same-sex love and makes it come across as natural.

In line with most of Svedberg's representations of erotic encounters between women, Mary and Agneta's lovemaking is characterized by closeness. In one depiction the pronouns change, and the characters blend together, just like in the description of the love encounter between the narrator and Carola in *Vingklippta*. Initially Mary and Agneta are referred to in third person, but later they are referred to in first and second person, as "me" and "you," again creating a distance from the reader and closeness between the lovers. It is not clear which of the characters is first and which is second person, emphasizing the moment of merging in love. Out of the closeness between the women, a distance from men grows. Edvin becomes more and more distant in relation to Mary; she meets him in her dreams but hardly recognizes him (*Se upp för trollen!*, 107, 110–11). Agneta recalls her past life: "Once she had been the tempting siren with irresistible attractiveness. She had made every man that looked at her crazy. What a hassle! How annoying to keep enough distance without making them lose interest!"[35] (*Se upp för trollen!*, 174). Agneta's interactions with men are described as a struggle to maintain the right level of admiration, and the effort this required contrasts with her easy life with Mary in the present.

The only thing Mary and Agneta miss in their life together is the ability to have children. They want their happiness to extend to the world outside as well, to reach another person. Against all odds, Mary becomes pregnant; possibly a man is involved, but this is not relevant anymore—the child is Mary and Agneta's now. Mary gives birth to the child on a day when "the flower beds flourished, the trees were in bloom"[36] (*Se upp för trollen!*, 211). Earlier themes connecting life and growth become even stronger when the fruit of their love, the child, arrives on a spring day when nature has been wakened after the winter. The use of (spring) nature imagery mirrors Krusenstjerna's depictions of Angela and Agda's love, both of whom are pregnant in spring as well. Both Svedberg's and Krusenstjerna's novels idealize the unconventional families, connecting them with church references. In *Fröknarna von Pahlen*, Petra and Angela's family is referred to as a holy family; in *Se upp för trollen!*, Mary shares her name with Virgin Mary, and the father of her baby is not to be found on earth.

Metaphors for life and growth are connected to lesbianism, portraying it as fruitful, natural, life enhancing, and even sacred. *Se upp för trollen!* makes it clear that a woman cannot have both love and freedom in relationships with men, a fact that seems to be tied to the 1960s sociopolitical context as well, where the most common career for women was housewife, a dependent of and subordinate to the husband, the provider. Like in Krusenstjerna's time, 1960s Swedish welfare measures were aimed at the traditional family, and like *Fröknarna von Pahlen*, Svedberg's novels can be said to challenge the sociopolitical ideal of the nuclear family as the institution on which society should rest. Svedberg's work shows how normative relationships between women and men are based on male power and thus at odds with maintaining freedom for women. The novels suggest that the only way for women to combine love and freedom is lesbianism, where love is based on closeness and equality. Furthermore, as in Krusenstjerna's novels, lesbian relationships are depicted as better suited for raising children. This environment contrasts sharply with that of the heterosexual relationship, where children like Svante grow up to become spoiled and egotistical since they are part of their mothers' self-fulfillment rather than an extension of love, like the child in Agneta and Mary's relationship. Mary never becomes pregnant with Edvin, who would be more suited as procreator according to the heterosexual ideology. Not until she is in a loving relationship with a woman is she able to give birth to a child.

When looking at the portrayal of lesbianism from a sociopolitical context, Svedberg's novels are similar to Krusenstjerna's in that their negative portrayals of heterosexuality and men are connected to a feminist project. But they also differ from Krusenstjerna's in at least one important way that reflects a growing change in the larger societal discourse climate in Sweden: The critiques of normative heterosexuality are more direct. As such they reflect discussions about women's liberation that were part of the sociopolitical discourse of the early 1960s, but only to a certain extent. With its woman-identified lesbianism and rejection of masculinity, Svedberg's work anticipates the radical feminist movement, which emerged in Sweden in the 1970s, and especially the movement's lesbian feminism as described in Hallgren's study. Emma Isaksson dates the birth of second-wave feminism in Sweden to 1970, and Hallgren shows that the lesbian feminists began to formulate their ideas in the first half of the 1970s (Isaksson 2007, 49; Hallgren 2008, 118). As this study shows, ideas that bear resemblance to radical feminist thinking could be found already in Krusenstjerna's work from the 1930s, where the women reject men and start a women's commune and where lesbianism is connected to empowerment. However, in Svedberg's novels the critique of male domination and heterosexual marriage is more outspoken and thus more similar to radical feminist thought. Moreover, by connecting heterosexuality to performance with the aid of imagery from theater and acting, the critique of normative heterosexuality is more direct.

SEXUAL POLITICS: HIGHLIGHTING THE MARGINALIZATION OF LESBIANISM AND TELLING NEW STORIES

The 1960s and 1970s in Sweden brought about a change in feminist discourse in Sweden, and Svedberg's novels can be seen as a bellwether of the connections between lesbianism and a larger feminist project. The texts, depicting masculinity as dysfunctional and heterosexuality as a prison for women, contribute to changing the shared space by offering alternative descriptions of the ways heterosexuality and homosexuality are perceived in this world. As discussed in the chapter on Agnes von Krusenstjerna, Jacques Rancière argues that literature is political precisely because it intervenes in the specific sphere of experience; it makes subjects and objects and the relation between them visible in new ways. Svedberg's novels intervene in the 1960s shared world, a world that constructs heterosexuality as the norm, by showing that heterosexual marriage can be harmful to women. Reflecting changes in the larger discursive tone in Sweden, Svedberg's texts are more openly critical of the subordination of women than Krusenstjerna's work is. But her novels differ from Krusenstjerna's in another important way as well; they are more concerned with lesbians' positions in society. This section explores the different strategies used in Svedberg's novels to draw attention to the marginalization of lesbians, strategies that are political in that they contribute to change the shared space.

When the narrator of *Vingklippta* first enters into relationships with women, she is inexperienced in this area. Still she
reflects surprisingly little on what her new same-sex desire means
in terms of her sexual identity, which makes same-sex love come
across as not different enough to mention and thus nondeviant. Since the narrator and her fellow characters rarely refer to
love between women as different or deviant in any way, it is
represented as no less "normal" than heterosexual love. However, a few passages address the narrator's desire for women as
nonnormative:

> There it is again. Can women love women? And if so, how?
> It's hard to get over. Sometimes you think that you have,
> but then doubt appears again as a nail through your heart. As
> if homosexual feelings were not real feelings. As if homosexual-
> ity was not real sexuality. But it is real; I know that. As full of
> nuances, as important, as intense and as heartfelt as other sexual-
> ity.[37] (*Vingklippta*, 140–41)

In this quote the narrator questions her love for women, but
she also reaches the conclusion that same-sex love is right—and
no different from other forms of sexuality. Her doubt seems to
come from the outside, since it is more theoretical and in line
with 1960s understandings of homosexuality as lesser than heterosexuality to some extent. However, the narrator's conclusion is based on her own experiences, something that indicates
authenticity and could be seen as a truth claim. In this quote,
homosexuality and heterosexuality are described as interchangeable, as equally real, just like in Krusenstjerna's novels, although
in Svedberg's work this attitude is expressed explicitly and not
only implied through imagery, for example.

As we have seen in previous sections, lesbianism is often
depicted as a better alternative to heterosexuality in Svedberg's
novels. However, another strategy to validate lesbianism can be
found in the novels: Lesbianism is often portrayed as similar
and equally legitimate as heterosexuality and thus as something
that does not need special attention. In *Se upp för trollen!* Mary
and Agneta enter into a lesbian relationship after they have been
romantically involved with different men. Their relationship is

never discussed as deviant from their previous heterosexual relationships; instead it is depicted as better because it is based on
closeness and equality, the same qualities and values generally
used to assess heterosexual marriage. In *Det goda livet* lesbianism is not even referred to directly; instead, Svedberg presents
the relationship with the same normative assumptions that heterosexual relationships are often presented with. The reader can
conclude from the circumstances that the two women have a
love relationship, but this is never discussed, and their relationship thus comes across as any other relationship, not a different
type. By depicting the two women's everyday life and showing
it to be no different from the everyday life led by a straight
couple, Svedberg contributes to changing the understanding of
lesbianism in the common world; thus making the text political
in Rancière's sense.

In the 1960s, depictions of lesbians' everyday lives did not
belong to the common world, since homosexuality was marginalized and seen as deviant. The everyday, even mundane,
descriptions in *Det goda livet* add an understanding of lesbian
experiences to the shared world, which, in turn, change what
can be perceived in it. As discussed in the introduction, both
Sherrie A. Inness and Niall Richardson argue that cultural
representations of homosexuality take on unusual importance
precisely because they constitute the reality of homosexuality
for many people. Considering the marginalization and stigmatization of lesbianism in the 1960s, Svedberg's depiction of
lesbianism as nondeviant and not any different than heterosexuality can be seen as an important political strategy.

Din egen uses a similar strategy to validate female homosexuality. The love between Rebecca and Helena is portrayed
as unusually strong, but despite the strength of their love,
the characters find themselves in several situations where they
have to hide behind the seats on a train or in dark alleys in
order to be affectionate (*Din egen*, 42, 47–49). The novel
also depicts other characters' reactions to their love. The actor
Rickard describe the two women as "two twisted individuals"[38] (*Din egen*, 207), and the reader learns that Rebecca's
father and brother have reacted negatively to her relationship

with Helena (*Din egen*, 207–8). During their trip to Greece, Rebecca and Helena meet a Swedish couple who express hostility toward homosexuality without knowing that the two women are in a relationship (*Din egen*, s. 205–6). Some passages in the novel refer to the different and unequal rights and conditions for heterosexual and homosexual couples; Rebecca and Helena try on rings together and talk about the fact that they would never be able to get married despite the strength of their love (*Din egen*, 15).

These passages, together with the portrayal of Rebecca and Helena's love as unusually strong, draw attention to the fact that same-sex lovers cannot express their love in the same way as heterosexuals. This inequity contrasts with the portrayal of a love based on true emotional connection—the kind of love heterosexual norms also celebrate. The novel is primarily a love story, a beautiful depiction of the strong and overwhelming love between the two people, and this makes the hostility same-sex love is met with seem even more unfair. The portrayal of Rebecca and Helena's love can be read as a challenge of contemporary sociopolitical understandings of homosexuality as deviant.

In the Swedish sex debate at the beginning of the 1960s, some voices argued for a more liberal understanding of homosexuality. Henning Pallesen and Lars Ullerstam, for instance, influenced by the Kinsey reports, argued that homosexuality was just one way among others of reaching orgasm, and thus as normal as any other way of expressing sexuality. They saw homosexuality as a minority problem rather than a medical problem—homosexuality is repressed by the majority, who do not want to share their recently gained sexual liberty. However, despite these efforts, homosexuality remained marginalized in the 1960s, and the gay liberation movement did not begin until the 1970s. Furthermore, lesbianism was fairly invisible in the debate—when homosexuality was discussed, the focus was on male homosexuality (Lennerhed 1994, 153–69; Lennerhed 2000; Pallesen 1964; Ullerstam 1964). In this sociopolitical climate, Svedberg's *Din egen* contributes with new perspectives on lesbianism; it acknowledges the prejudice against lesbians in society and, at the same time, depicts a lesbian relationship from within, showing it to be based not on deviance and perversion but on "the multifaceted concept referred to with one single name: love"[39] (*Din egen*, 203). Her novel depicts Rebecca and Helena as subjects driven not by pathology but by a strong love for each other, and this love is represented as no different in kind from love between a man and a woman.

Sometimes minor characters in *Vingklippta* express prejudice against homosexuality, but prejudice is always met with counterarguments by the main characters. For instance, when someone at a social gathering indicates that homosexuality might be perverted, Carina and the narrator quickly contradict them (*Vingklippta*, 141). Characters who do not belong to the narrator's circle of friends are sometimes depicted as ignorant on the subject. Carina describes her male lover Staffan as ignorant since he does not understand that Carina and the narrator are in love and does not even know the name for love between women, presenting another discursive challenge faced by lesbians' struggle for equitable treatment. The ability to name things is an important dimension of discourse, in the Foucauldian sense; knowledge production requires language. In other words, in order to discuss and make sense of a topic, we need a specific, mutually understandable vocabulary. Rancière emphasizes the ability of literature to change the common world by telling new stories and explaining in detail the relationships between people and things. Literature can thus be said to contribute to the knowledge production in the common world, and this includes the production of a common vocabulary. By depicting some characters as ignorant, Svedberg's novel suggests the need for knowledge; if people do not even know how to name love between women, lesbianism will not be part of the discourse.

Lack of knowledge can also be understood in the context of contemporary sexual discourse. In *Se upp för trollen!* the narrator comments on Mary and Agneta's longing for children and the impossibility of them procreating together in a biological sense: "Perhaps is this why these relationships are viewed as slightly inappropriate by certain groups. In this context they usually talk about 'pleasure without purpose,' whatever that means. It makes me wonder what experiences lie behind such a statement"[40] (*Se upp för trollen!*, 179–80). In this quote, prejudice against homosexuality is connected to hostility toward nonreproductive sexuality in general. As discussed in the chapter on Krusenstjerna, the attitude to sexuality as exclusively connected to reproduction belonged to an older discourse that had already lost its impact in the 1930s. By connecting hostility toward homosexuality to this discourse, *Se upp för trollen!* depicts this attitude as reactionary in a broader sense.

As we have seen, Svedberg's novels contribute to the knowledge production of the common world by depicting lesbianism in ways that go beyond 1960s sociopolitical understandings. At the same time, the focus on knowledge and information is ridiculed in another passage in the novel when the narrator and Carola visit a gay club. When Carola tells the narrator that there is a gay club for women only, run by the Federation of Gay and Lesbian Rights, the narrator laughs so much so that she almost chokes on her beer:

> "Now we have to go there! It seems hilarious! What are they doing there? Sitting around discussing how to influence the public opinion with brochures and meetings and campaigns . . ." And again I start laughing irreverently at these unfortunate people.
>
> "Oh, but it is serious," Carola says and is now serious herself and a little embarrassed by my cheerfulness and her own complexes. "Of course they want to be like everybody else."
>
> "But they can't be! Not in the same way! So they want to legitimize homosexual relationships then, like marriages?"[41] (*Vingklippta*, 173)

What stands out in this quote is that the narrator and Carola—who are in a lesbian relationship—define themselves in opposition to other gay people by referring to the others as "them" or as "these unfortunate people." This could be read as a way of adding diversity to the society's ideas of, and thus the discourse on, lesbianism. In line with such a reading, lesbians are not a homogeneous group, but different people with different ideas and needs. This seemingly contradicting attitude toward homosexuality could also be read in the light of the medical discourse's understanding of homosexuality as either congenital or acquired, as discussed in Chapter 1. As we have seen, the medical discourse has a strong presence in Svedberg's work, and the narrator firmly rejects characters that embody these standards. Several minor characters can be understood in connection with the congenital understanding of homosexuality: the lesbians at the club, the stereotypical mannish dyke at the party discussed earlier, and two dykes that the narrator sees in a park: "They looked pathetic in the overcast daylight. Rugged, lonely—two under the trees. With pale hands sticking together in the raw and chilly air. Further away a man and a woman approached. Soft and easy they embraced each other, smiled, talked. Happy"[42] (*Vingklippta*, 211). In contrast to the happy heterosexual couple, the narrator views the lesbian couple as almost diseased—their hands are pale and sticky and the air around them raw and chilly. Despite being together, they are described as lonely and pathetic.

The narrator distances herself and her friends from these characters that embody a medicalized view of lesbianism, but she also pities them. Her pity can be seen as connected to the arguments for decriminalization of homosexuality in the 1930s emphasizing medical understandings of homosexuality as a deviance that the individual could not help suffering from. While the depiction of the unfortunate lesbians in *Vingklippta* could thus be seen as a strategy to evoke pity in the reader, the narrator is clear that she does not belong to the same category.

The distancing from mannish lesbians can also be read in light of Liv Saga Bergdahl's previously mentioned argument: It is a way of creating new images of lesbianism that contrast with and create distance from previous, diseased images of homosexuality. Hanna Hallgren argues that the lesbian feminists of the 1970s used this rejection as a strategy of resistance. By emphasizing their similarities with heterosexuals in terms of sex/gender, they wanted to avoid being defined as diseased and deviant (Hallgren 2008, 162). The way the narrator distances herself from the deviant lesbians in *Vingklippta* is similar to the way Angela and Agda were depicted as different from Bell von Wenden in Krusenstjerna's novels. Like Angela and Agda, the narrator thus comes across as "normal" in line with the novel's attempt to depict homosexuality and heterosexuality as equal expressions of sexuality.

However, like Bell von Wenden, the lesbians at the club are not simply dismissed as deviant and pathetic by the narrator. There is something in their lifestyle that attracts her, and she enjoys seeing girls dance with girls and boys with boys. The club is said to be different from the regular world "where men and women still have their identities"[43] (*Vingklippta*, 169); men and women at the club are said to have "come apart"[44] (*Vingklippta*, 172), and gender is no longer rigidly defined. These reflections can be read as a critique of heterosexuality and a male-dominated society often expressed in Svedberg's novels. As we have seen, Svedberg portrays the interaction between women and men as a performance or theater where the women and men play different parts, thereby emphasizing the gender roles as socially and culturally constructed. At the gay club these gender roles are deconstructed, and it is here that the potential for change lies: gender is troubled at the gay club, to paraphrase Judith Butler. Feminism and lesbian politics are intertwined; through lesbianism, traditional gender roles can be deconstructed, allowing for something new to emerge.

Svedberg's novels draw attention to the marginalization of lesbianism in the sociopolitical discourse in several different ways. The main characters of all her novels continually encounter prejudice and injustices in their interactions with the surrounding world. The novels thus change the shared space by making the reader aware of these injustices. At the same time the novels contribute with new knowledge on lesbianism by telling stories that challenge contemporary understandings of lesbianism as deviant and medicalized. These stories can be said to normalize lesbianism by depicting same-sex love as no different than heterosexual love, by portraying love relationships between women in a beautiful way, by describing prejudice as grounded in ignorance or reactionary attitudes in general, and by distancing main characters from deviant lesbianism. But Svedberg's work also suggests a hope for change. The lesbian club offers a glimpse of an environment that has moved beyond gender. As opposed to Krusenstjerna's novels where gender diversity (cross-dressing) requires moving away to a closed-off commune for women, a community beyond gender already exists in the middle of Stockholm in Svedberg's novel. These stories add a new dimension to the way lesbianism is perceived in the shared world and become political in Rancière's sense. Since knowledge about homosexuality—and lesbianism in particular—was limited in 1960s society, these cultural representations of lesbianism take on unusual importance and can contribute to opening up discursive space for a more tolerant attitude to lesbianism.

"I Want to Write, Write, Write": Writing as a Political Strategy

Literary representations in both Krusenstjerna's and Svedberg's novels present new aspects of lesbianism to the common world, opening up new discursive space for lesbianism. Svedberg specifically presents the reoccurring theme of writing as a tool for changing the world and making it a better place for lesbians and for women in general. Rancière connects writing to politics in his previously quoted statement: "there is an essential connection between politics as a specific form of collective practice and literature as a well-defined practice of the art of writing" (Rancière [2006] 2011, 3). As already mentioned, Rancière argues that the politics of literature is not the same as the politics of writers. Connected to this idea, the theme of writing in Svedberg's novels draws attention to literature as political, and the art of writing is represented in a variety of ways as a political strategy in Svedberg's novels.

The narrator of *Vingklippta* seems to be a writer, as she sometimes refers to articles she is writing and describes it as "work." Writing is not a major theme in this novel, but it is sometimes depicted as a way for the narrator to process things in life, thus seeming to have a therapeutic function: "I want to write, write, write. Let all the shit gush out of me. Everything, shit, happiness, scum and the shimmering blessed moments— the shimmering blessed life, growing, hope, faith, love and death"[45] (*Vingklippta*, 213). Writing seems to be truth evoking for the narrator; she writes about everything in her life, both good and bad. With its connections to life and truth, writing in this quote seems to do what Rancière suggests: It contributes with new perspectives on the shared world. This quote does not refer to lesbianism but is a reminder of what writing in general can accomplish, and since the novel itself is so preoccupied with portraying lesbianism in new and more positive ways, we can read the narrator's stories as something that does change the common world.

Writing is a more prominent theme in *Det goda livet*. The first-person narrator is a writer, and she writes all the time, usually in the present tense so that the narrative seems to unfold simultaneously with the writing process. The text is studded with the word "now,"[46] giving the impression that the narrative is ongoing, as in the following passage: "Now Stella is sitting on my lap. A little hard to write, but it works"[47] (*Det goda livet*, 45). When the narrator does write in past tense, it is usually to describe something that is supposed to have already happened. For instance, she might write about how she took a walk in the morning. The narrator also describes herself writing, and the short and incomplete sentences make the writing look like notes in a journal. The narrator's partner, Brita, sometimes comments on how the narrator portrays her: "I say such silly things in your writing. It's a caricature of me. Why don't you say how charming I am? Why don't you write: *Now Brita walks beautifully down to the pine tree*, for example"[48] (*Det goda livet*, 67). Brita's commenting on the writing further emphasizes the book's presentation as a work in progress. Here, too, writing has a connection to life and truth, and the work-in-progress character of the novel adds authenticity and makes the narrative seem "more real." The focus on writing becomes a reminder of the potential of writing in this novel, too: By depicting the everyday life of a lesbian couple, the novel adds lesbian experience to a sociopolitical context that lacks similar stories.

The narrative in *Se upp för trollen!* does not address the topic of writing, but the novel begins with a sort of preface signed by the author and with the inscription "Ett gott råd" (Good advice) in which writing is brought to the fore. The narrator encourages the reader to read what is in the text instead of trying to trace influences or make comparisons. The writer is said to write in order to be read. The preface can be read as a critique of literary scholars who look for hidden or underlying meanings in texts instead of focusing on what is actually in the text. The message suggests a faith in writing as communication: the text is thought to have a meaning that can be conveyed to the reader (and the common world) without the interference of literary scholars. The text is not a riddle waiting to be solved but delivers a message. As such, texts contribute with meaning to the shared world, and as we have seen, what the novel *Se upp för trollen!* contributes are positive representations of lesbianism.

Din egen is more preoccupied with theater as a topic than with writing; as we have seen, theater becomes a metaphor for the performative nature of gender. However, theater is based on a script, and the relation between the textual character of the script and the art of acting is discussed in the novel. The script is said to be limiting as well as liberating, and it provides security. This discussion follows upon and is connected to the passage portraying men's courting of women as a play, as previously discussed. The script represents the rigid gender roles, but the text allows the actor a certain amount of flexibility, which contains the potential for change (*Din egen*, 100–101). Directing has a similar potential. Rebecca dreams of becoming a director in order to be able to create a new world that would have impact on the audience (*Din egen*, 8), and the two women talk about Helena writing a play for Rebecca to direct (*Din egen*, 42). It seems like the script is portrayed as a web of rigidity, while acting and directing allow for flexibility and change. However, it is in fact the stability of the text that allows the actors and the director to improvise and create new worlds. Acting and directing are tied to creation in *Din egen*, but it is a creation that rests firmly on the script, which has an elasticity that allows for interpretation and change. Though scripts, theater, and performance are generally associated with gender roles in the novel, they also contain a potential for change. Scripts are not as rigid as they might seem, and with the aid of actors and directors, they can be used in the creation of a world where gender is acted out differently.

In all Svedberg's novels, writing is associated with truth and authenticity. It is a way of processing life experiences, large or insignificant, and a means to communicate "the truth" (the reader is encouraged to focus on the written word) holding the possibility to create one's own truth. Svedberg takes the element of truth one step further: writing is at times semiautobiographical in her texts. For instance, in *Det goda livet* the narrator receives the reviews of *Vingklippta*, the author's own work, implying a direct connection between the book and her "real" life. The novels break down the boundaries between life and art, truth and fiction, intertwining life with writing and making it part of the sociopolitical discourse that sets the boundaries for how different objects and people in the common world are defined. Svedberg's novels challenge the way lesbianism is understood in the 1960s sociopolitical discourse by providing other stories of lesbianism in a form that validates the authenticity of the experiences in the narratives. But rather than focusing solely on homosexuality, her novels also display the shortcomings of the entire gender system of the time. Svedberg's work thus illustrates Rancière's point that politics is something literature does simply by being literature. The art of writing—the way literature depicts subjects and objects and the relation between them—changes the political landscape. But Svedberg's theme of writing as a tool to communicate the truth highlights the function of literature as politics; it draws the reader's attention to the ability of literature to change the common world.

OTHER STORIES: ANNAKARIN SVEDBERG AND LITERATURE OF THE 1960S

While the tone of and voice in literature changed significantly through the middle of the twentieth century, literary representations of lesbianism in Svedberg's novels are strikingly similar to those found in literature from the 1930s; lesbianism is often depicted in contrary ways. The medical discourse on lesbianism is both reinforced and challenged, and lesbianism is medicalized but also portrayed as a better option than heterosexuality. This contrast is articulated even more strongly in Svedberg's novels than in those of the 1930s, since both the medical discourse and feminist/lesbian politics are more explicit at the time she wrote. Although few novels with lesbian themes were published in the 1960s, Svedberg was not alone. Eva Alexanderson was the most famous lesbian writer of the 1960s next to Svedberg, but she only published one novel with lesbianism in focus, although she did publish another novel in the 1960s with minor lesbian themes. Subtle lesbian themes can also be found in Finland-Swedish writer Disa Lindholm's novel *Ficklampsljus* (1961; *Flashlight*), and Nils Hallbeck's pornographic novel *En kvinnas älskarinna* (1969; *A Woman's Mistress*) is primarily concerned with lesbian eroticism. These novels have much in common with the discourse on lesbianism that is represented in Svedberg's work.

Eva Alexanderson's novel *Fyrtio dagar i öknen* (1964; *Forty Days in the Desert*) depicts a woman who spends forty days in the Norwegian mountains in order to recover from an unspecified disease. During this time she goes through a religious crisis and in the ending she converts to Catholicism. Lesbianism is a minor theme; the reader learns that the woman has had erotic relationships with women, but the subject is not discussed to any larger extent, and her love for women is never depicted as a problem. Her same-sex desire is not explicitly medicalized in the novel, but the medical discourse is still present, mainly through references to the three *M*s. The *mothering* explanation for lesbianism is implied in the woman's difficult childhood—her mother also seems have died early, and the protagonist is looking for mother substitutes. Mirrors and double exposures are recurring in the novel, suggesting the *mirrors* explanation. While the *mothering* and *mirrors* explanations are present in imagery or referred to in passing, *masculinity* is developed more explicitly; when the protagonist grew up, she wanted to be a man so that she could love women. Disease is also a topic in the novel as a whole since the protagonist is recovering from an illness. While this illness is physical in kind, the woman also suffers from psychological instability, and she is said to be suicidal. The protagonist's health problems are not explicitly connected to lesbianism, but this topic nevertheless connects the narrator to medicalization.

Lesbianism is at the center of Alexanderson's novel *Kontradans* (1969; *Contra Dance*), which depicts a woman, Eva, who falls in love with a younger woman, Claudia. They meet in a convent, probably in Italy, and the novel describes their struggle with personal faith and the possibility of combining faith and same-sex love. The novel is narrated in first person, and she speaks to Claudia in second person. As in Svedberg, this narrative technique establishes closeness; the "I" and the "you" become a bond that shuts the reader out, and a secluded space is established around the two lovers. Like in *Fyrtio dagar i öknen*, the medical discourse is present in this novel through frequent references to mirrors. The book begins with the narrator looking into a mirror, and the book cover portrays a person framed by something that looks like a mirror. Furthermore, Eva often watches Claudia in different mirrors. Although the other two *M*s are never referred to in the novel, the medical discourse is still strongly implied in *Kontradans* since Claudia is in psychoanalysis, with the explicit aim to become "normal" in order to marry a man and have children. In the end, the two women do not end up together, and Eva continues to miss Claudia for a long time.

With its bleak ending, *Kontradans* draws a darker picture of lesbianism than most other novels discussed in this study. On the surface, the medical discourse seems to win; the two lovers do not end up together. However, the portrayal of lesbianism is still ambiguous: As Liv Saga Bergdahl points out, Eva comes to the conclusion that love can never be wrong, not even same-sex love (Bergdahl 2010, 221–22). This is similar to the previously quoted conclusion reached by the narrator in Svedberg's *Vingklippta*: despite her doubts, she knows from experience that love between women cannot be wrong. Jan Magnusson mentions that Eva tries to forget her beloved

Claudia by writing a book (Magnusson 2000, 66–67). Thus their love leads to the creation of something. The first-person narrator is a writer, and her book project together with her conclusion that same-sex love is not wrong once again presents writing as a way to communicate a reality. The novel also has an autobiographical theme—the narrator is a writer named Eva, who writes a book about a lesbian relationship, strongly paralleling Annakarin Svedberg's work. In Svedberg's novels the autobiographical aspect contributes to the idea of writing as politics, and the same can be said of *Kontradans*. In comparison to Svedberg's novels, Alexanderson's are less outspoken in their challenging of the medical discourse on lesbianism. However, with their subtle challenges the two novels still belong to the same category of ambiguous literary representations of lesbianism as Svedberg's; they reinforce the medical discourse through references to its explanations of lesbianism, but at the same time, this discourse is challenged through depictions of love between women as nondeviant (*Fyrtio dagar i öknen*) or based on closeness (*Kontradans*) and through the conclusion reached in *Kontradans* that lesbianism is not wrong.

While subtle, the lesbian themes in Disa Lindholm's *Ficklamps-ljus* (1961; *Flashlight*) are depicted in the same ambiguous way. The novel depicts the schoolgirl Ruth who grows up in Helsinki, Finland, during the interwar period. Ruth is romantically interested in women and has a passion for her teacher, Ström. She also has a strong friendship with another girl, Inga-Lill, who shares her passion for Ström, and their friendship in turn has romantic overtones. Homosexuality is referred to a few times in the novel, but Ruth's romantic interest for women is never questioned and seems to be accepted by everyone around her. This might be due to the fact that her love is never expressed in erotic terms; it could be interpreted as a phase that will pass, in accordance with theories from the first part of the twentieth century that romantic friendships between girls are preparations for heterosexual love (Beauvoir [1949] 2010, 355–59, 420, 428; Key 1903, 63–64). However, it could also be read in light of Svedberg's novels as a strategy to "normalize" lesbianism by portraying same-sex love as no different in kind from heterosexuality, like in *Det goda livet*, where homosexuality is never mentioned although it is obvious that the narrator and Brita are in a relationship.

Ruth is a writer, and sometimes her writing becomes therapeutic, like when she processes Inga-Lill's death. This can be connected to writing in Svedberg's novels, which is connected to life and truth and becomes a reminder of the political nature of literature: it can contribute with stories of lesbian experiences to a sociopolitical world where no such stories exist. Furthermore, Ruth's father dominates her mother and the rest of her family, and Ruth's love for her teacher might be read as a search for a mother substitute. The *mirrors* explanation is not present, but once Ruth dreams about being a man, suggesting the *masculinity* explanation. Like in Svedberg's and Alexanderson's novels, the medical discourse on lesbianism is reinforced, although more subtly. Men do not have prominent roles in the novel, which mostly takes place in a girls' school and depicts Ruth, her schoolmates, and her teachers. Some of the teachers are male, but in general they are weak, like some of Svedberg's male characters, and the women seem to be in charge. This women-dominated universe becomes a refuge for Ruth, where she can develop and grow without being intimidated by her father. This parallels the idealized world of Krusentjerna's last novel, where the women's commune at Eka offers a similar refuge from male domination. In the end of the novel Ruth converts to Catholicism, like Alexanderson's protagonist, but her sexual orientation is never seen as a problem in her religious development, which might be due to the fact that it is depicted as fairly innocent. Thus same-sex romance in Lindholm's novel is represented in the same ambiguous way as in the other 1960s novels; the medical discourse is present, but love between women also has positive implications as a source of empowerment for women. Like in Svedberg's novels, the medical discourse is also challenged by the depiction of lesbianism as nondeviant.

Both critically acclaimed and popular cultural representations contribute to and are at work in the creation of discourses, and both of these categories are represented in this study. Pornography was a subject of debate during the sexual revolution in the 1960s, and as mentioned, Annakarin Svedberg contributed with a pornographic short story to an anthology where several famous Swedish writers published so-called high-quality pornography. Nils Hallbeck's pornographic novel, *En kvinnas älskarinna* (1969; *A Woman's Mistress*), is an interesting example of the intersection of lesbianism as politics and popular culture in the form of genre fiction. Hallbeck's Viola moves to New York to become a model. Erotic depictions are obviously the primary focus of the novel, but in these descriptions, lesbianism is, in fact, represented in a way that has much in common with the other 1960s novels discussed. The medical discourse is strongly present in the text, particularly the *masculinity* explanation; Viola's first lover, Elizabeth, looks like a boy or a man, and so do many of the other lesbian women Viola meets. Viola is treated badly by both men and women throughout the novel, and love between women is not presented as a better alternative than heterosexuality as in many other novels discussed in this book. However, Viola acknowledges that making love with women is softer and better since women are not focused on their own orgasms like men are. She also ends up with a woman, Angela, in the end of the novel, although the two women discuss whether they should invite Angela's husband to their relationship as well. While Viola still wants to sleep with men once in a while, the foundation of this relationship are the two women. Thus the medical discourse is reinforced in Hallbeck's novel but also challenged, since love between women is depicted as nondeviant and even as a source to happiness and pleasure. Furthermore, the heterosexual norm is challenged, since the two women consider an unconventional relationship consisting of two women and a man.

The Swedish novels of the 1960s thus represent lesbianism in the same ambiguous and often contradictory way as the 1930s novels. The medical discourse established at the turn of the century is present in the novels, even more so than in the 1930s since it is often referred to in more explicit terms. Despite the more liberal attitude to homosexuality advocated in the 1960s sexual debate, literature suggests that the situation was still difficult for homosexuals. However, this same literature challenges the medical discourse. Although Eva in Alexander-son's *Kontradans* ends up alone, she reaches the conclusion that lesbianism is not wrong. Ruth in Lindholm's *Ficklampsljus* draws strength from the women-dominated environment at school. Even Viola in Hallbeck's pornographic novels prefers to make love with women because they are softer and not as self-centered. In Svedberg's novels, men and heterosexuality are dismissed, and lesbianism is tied to larger feminist ambi-tions. Furthermore, the novels depict lesbianism as nondeviant, and the focus on writing draws attention to literature as politics. Considering the decades that had passed since the 1930s and the sexual debate that took place in the 1960s, which brought forward a more liberal attitude to homosexuality, one could have expected the literary representations of lesbianism to be less influenced by the medical discourse. Instead, this discourse is even more explicit in the literature of the 1960s, which sug-gests a lasting and pervasive legacy of medicalization. However, as this chapter has shown, the negative literary discourse on lesbianism of the 1960s also had other, more positive and empowering dimensions, just like the discourse of the 1930s.

The 1960s novels challenge contemporary sociopolitical attitudes toward lesbianism and gender equality more explic-itly than the 1930s literature does. As discussed, this could be due to the fact that sexuality and gender were debated to a larger extent at that time, due to the sexual revolution and the debate on women's situations that led up to the second wave of feminism in the 1970s. At the same time, the lived experi-ences of homosexuals in general and lesbians in particular were fairly invisible in the sexual debates; the RFSL kept a low pro-file, and nobody came out as homosexual in the debate. In this context the 1960s novels can be seen as a contribution to a sexual debate that primarily focused on heterosexuality. They represent the Swedish sexual revolution as a *hetero*sexual revolu-tion by highlighting the marginalization of lesbianism in 1960s society. But they also challenge the focus on heterosexuality by offering a lesbian perspective, and the novels contain a faith in writing as a way of changing the common world. Writing is a prominent theme, and the novels bring to the fore what Rancière describes as the essential connection between politics and literature; by depicting the world in new ways, literature adds a dimension that contributes to changing the way we perceive the shared world.

CHAPTER 3

CHALLENGING THE IMAGE OF SWEDEN

LOUISE BOIJE AF GENNÄS, MIAN LODALEN, AND THE TURN OF THE MILLENNIUM

During the last few decades, Sweden has undergone many social and political changes that have benefited and boosted gay and lesbian rights. Homosexuality was removed from National Board of Health and Welfare's manual of psychological disorders in 1979 and has gradually gained acceptance in Sweden. Parliament has taken several measures to strengthen the status of LGBTQ people, mainly through legislation. Discrimination against homosexuals has been illegal since 1987, and that same year a law passed that gave cohabiting same-sex partners many of the same rights as cohabiting opposite-sex partners. Further legislation on domestic partnership was enacted in 1995, giving same-sex couples the same rights as married heterosexual couples, with the exception of the right to marry in the church and reproductive rights such as the right to fertility treatments and to be considered as adoptive parents. Same-sex couples have gradually gained rights in these areas since 1995, though Swedish laws have not yet granted total equality. Same-sex couples gained the right to be considered as adoptive parents in 2003, and since 2005 lesbian women have been eligible for assisted reproduction in the tax-funded Swedish hospitals. After the Swedish parliament changed the marriage laws in 2009, making marriage gender-neutral, the Church of Sweden started wedding same-sex couples. Several Swedish celebrities have come out as gay or lesbian during the last twenty years, also indicating a new openness toward homosexuality among the Swedes (Andreasson 2000, 36–58; Norrhem, Rydström, and Winkvist 2008, 130–57; Rosenberg 2002, 103–6; Rydström 2005, 308–35; Rydström 2011).

Considering the move toward progressive laws for the LGBTQ community (though transgender laws, for example, still have a long way to go) and the open attitude to homosexuality in general, Sweden can be seen as representing the changing Western perspective on homosexuality, as discussed in the introduction. According to this theory of progress, the Western world has gradually abandoned its previous prejudice toward homosexuality and now recognizes same-sex sexuality as an orientation equal to heterosexuality; homosexuals should thus have the same rights as all other citizens. With LGBTQ laws that are generally more progressive than most Western countries, Sweden can even be seen as a pioneer for Western attitudes to homosexuality. However, despite its pioneer status, Sweden is not a paradise for gays and lesbians. Recent studies show that compared with heterosexuals, the LGBTQ community suffers from poorer health—particularly mental—due to discrimination, and these statistics hold true specifically for lesbians. The health problems can be seen in connection with a recent increase in hate crimes against homosexuals in Sweden (Andreasson 2000, 57; Swedish National Institute of Public Health 2005; Tiby 1999, 251–54; Tiby and Sörberg 2006, 13).

Lesbianism is not an unusual theme in Swedish literature at the turn of the millennium. Several novels with lesbian themes have been published, and lesbian characters and lesbian subthemes can be found in even more novels, including children's and young adult literature.[1] This chapter focuses on three novels by two writers, chosen for this study because of these books' wide readerships. In 1996, Louise Boije af Gennäs (1961–) published her novel *Stjärnor utan svindel* (1996; *Stars without Vertigo*) depicting a thirtysomething woman who breaks up from her heterosexual marriage to pursue a lesbian relationship. This novel became a bestseller, reaching an audience outside of the lesbian community. Mian Lodalen's

(1962–) novels *Smulklubbens skamlösa systrar* (2003; *The Shameless Sisters of the Scraps Club*) and *Trekant* (2005; *Threesome*), depicting lesbian journalist My and her friends in Stockholm, have also reached a broad readership. Both Boije af Gennäs's *Stjärnor utan svindel* and Lodalen's *Smuklubbens skamlösa systrar* have been translated into other Nordic languages as well as German. Due to their wide audiences, Boije af Gennäs's and Lodalen's novels can be said to be part of the contemporary discourse on lesbianism to a certain degree, probably more so than those lesbian-themed novels discussed at the end of the chapter that have reached a more narrow circle of readers.

Louise Boije af Gennäs is a journalist, television script writer, and author, and her first novel, *Ta vad man vill ha* (*Take What You Want*), came out in 1991. *Stjärnor utan svindel* is her fourth novel and the only one with a major lesbian theme. Mian Lodalen is a journalist and lesbian activist who made her debut as an author with *Smulklubbens skamlösa systrar*. Neither Boije af Gennäs nor Lodalen have received much academic attention,[2] but they have a certain celebrity status in Sweden, due in part to their romantic relationship in the 1990s.

By examining the representations of lesbianism in Boije af Gennäs's and Lodalen's novels in light of the turn-of-the-millennium sociopolitical context, this chapter looks at the literary discourse on lesbianism in Sweden at this time. Together with the chapters on the 1930s and the 1960s, the literature from the 1990s and early 2000s makes it clear that this discourse has not changed much during the twentieth century. While the literary tone and norms have changed, lesbianism is depicted in the same ambiguous way in the turn-of-the-millennium literature as it was in the literature from the 1930s and the 1960s. On the one hand, lesbianism is intertwined with feminist politics and is therefore often presented as a better alternative than heterosexuality. Love between women is liberating and allows for diversity in various contexts; it transgresses traditional class, gender, and family boundaries and leads to a new kind of intimacy. Lesbianism is also connected to freedom and equality in various ways.

Writing is a crucial theme in the novels, and as in Svedberg's novels writing becomes political, since it provides a way to open up new discursive spaces that can change the common world into a better place for lesbians as well as for women in general. On the other hand, the medical discourse on lesbianism established at the turn of the century is still present in the novels. It is not as visible as in Krusenstjerna's and Svedberg's novels, but medical references occur in imagery, for instance, suggesting the persistence of the medical discourse established in the early 1900s.

HETEROSEXUALITY VERSUS LESBIANISM: SUBORDINATION OR EMPOWERMENT

Louise Boije af Gennäs's *Stjärnor utan svindel* takes place in Stockholm in the 1990s and portrays Sophie, an upper-class, aristocratic woman in her early thirties. She is happily married, has a promising career as a writer, and lives in a beautiful house in a wealthy suburb. One day Sophie meets lesbian radical feminist Kaja, and despite their different lifestyles and backgrounds the two women instantly like each other and become friends. Aside from being committed feminists, their perspectives are as opposite as they can get—Kaja is a socialist who sympathizes with the struggles of the working class, while Sophie votes to the right and goes to parties with her friends in the upper class. Their friendship eventually evolves into love, and Sophie, who has always thought of herself as a straight woman, breaks up her marriage and moves in with Kaja to start a new life.

Sophie's social context has two foundations: upper class and heterosexuality. Class is an issue continually discussed throughout the novel, but Sophie never entirely rejects the upper class she was born into. However, heterosexuality is dismissed and works as a foil for lesbianism. The main problem with heterosexuality, according to Sophie, is male domination. Male dominance can be traced to seemingly innocuous situations like dinner parties, for example, where the upper-class women adjust to their husbands' food preferences; they choose steak and heavy red wines in the presence of men and eat salads and shellfish at a dinner for only women. These kinds of decisions imply that women's loyalties lie with men rather than with other women.

However, Sophie does not blame women for their loyalty to men, and she acknowledges how she herself went through the same process of giving up her independence in a relationship with a man (*Stjärnor utan svindel*, 309). Instead Sophie sees socialization as the cause of women's subordination: "This happened because we women, slowly but surely, from *Cinderella* as kids to *Pretty Woman* as adults, have been convinced that a man in a heterosexual romantic relationship is the foundation of our existence and that we would never become happy without one. Without a man we would remain hired slaves or whores; that is the moral of these stories"[3] (*Stjärnor utan svindel*, 310). This quote suggests that the role of a woman and her place in a heterosexual relationship is learned through a process that starts early with childhood fairy tales, an idea connected to cultural criticism at the end of the twentieth century. In the 1990s feminist theories of gender as socially constructed were challenged in Swedish media debate, which caused many feminists to examine and criticize essentialist positions (see for instance Björk 1996; Lindén and Milles 1995). Sophie's statement can be read in this context as a claim for gender as socially constructed, not derived from biology or genes. But Sophie also connects this position on gender to heterosexuality, suggesting that heterosexuality is also learned behavior, in line with a social constructionist perspective. Her description of herself as independent and strong when single but dependent and weak when in a heterosexual relationship further suggests that female independence cannot be achieved in a heterosexual relationship.

Women's subordination in contemporary society is a recurring theme in Boije af Gennäs's novel. Sophie is aware of this subordination and wants to change the world. However, there is not a place for these ideas in her marriage. On one occasion Sophie runs into an old friend from college at a café who is dying from late-stage anorexia. The encounter upsets Sophie, and she calls her husband, Lukas, who is at work, too busy to talk to her—her priorities are subordinate to his. Instead she calls Kaja, who is able to meet her right away, and she listens to

Sophie's story and gives her the attention she needs. Kaja stands out as understanding and full of sympathy compared to Lukas, who doesn't make the time to listen to his wife.

Sophie's friendship with Kaja is also connected to politics—the two women want to make this world a better place for women and discuss strategies to achieve that goal. However, it becomes clear that political activism is not compatible with heterosexuality in the novel. That same night Sophie and Lukas watch television and Sophie cuddles up next to Lukas: "He was cute and his hair was curly, and I did not need to take on everyone else's problems. We were in our cocoon, in our secure place. The newscaster was talking about the war in Bosnia, but I closed my eyes and focused intensely on just breathing"[4] (*Stjärnor utan svindel*, 118). In this quote, heterosexuality stands for security—but also, and primarily, for escapism and a lack of political awareness. Sophie literally closes her eyes to the television, the outer world, the war in Bosnia. More generally, heterosexual relationships in the book are also associated with images of being closed in or limited: "As a token this ring encloses us, like a band of metal. From golden ring to iron grip"[5] (*Stjärnor utan svindel*, 159). The ring, the symbol of marriage, made of precious gold, transforms to a symbol of captivity. Like in Svedberg's novels, heterosexual marriage is described as a prison.

Heterosexuality and the society that promotes it are Sophie's main enemies in the novel. But she also blames men for contributing to gender inequality. The novel contains several passages where Sophie—usually together with Kaja—reflects on men and the trouble they cause in society. Kaja argues that hating men is easy: "Women are beautiful, wise, intelligent and competent. Men are ugly, stupid, meaningless and incompetent. It's always the same. Wherever you look. In families, in relationships, at work, in politics. Every time something meaningful is done—health care, taking care of the old and the poor, helping refugees and victims of war—it's the work of women. And always when some kind of shit happens—budget cuts, starting war, rape, domestic violence, child abuse, unprovoked violence on the streets—men are the cause of it. All the time. Without exception"[6] (*Stjärnor utan svindel,* 116). Here, men are described as the cause of all the evil in the world, while women are depicted as the heroes. Similar passages polarizing men and women recur throughout the novel, and gender inequality in contemporary society is continually discussed by Sophie and Kaja.

In the turn-of-the-millennium sociopolitical discourse, Sweden is viewed as one of the most gender-equitable countries in the world. Women's political representation is strong; after having increased slowly during the twentieth century, the political parties scrambled to appoint more women in the 1980s, and since 1994 the number of women in the parliament and the government has been close to 50 percent. Furthermore, the Swedish welfare system, with paid parental leave and state-funded preschools, has made it increasingly possible for both women and men to combine family and professional life. Sweden also has strong laws protecting women from violence by men, including a special law for domestic violence (Ohlander and Strömberg 2008, 203–27).

From a perspective focusing on rights and opportunities, Sweden does indeed come across as one of the most gender-equitable countries in the world. However, Sophie and Kaja's conversations on gender equality in *Stjärnor utan svindel* can be seen as a way of challenging this image on a broader level. While the characters in Krusenstjerna's and Svedberg's novels struggle against a society where women are visibly marginalized and subordinated, the characters in *Stjärnor utan svindel* inhabit a society where men and women seem to have equal opportunities. However, as pointed out in the novel, women still suffer from marginalization. Sophie and Kaja discuss different and less visible and quantifiable aspects of gender inequality, such as men's access to women's bodies, eating disorders, and power asymmetries in individual relationships between men and women. Taken together these different aspects contribute to the structural subordination of women. Many of the ideas that Sofie and Kaja discuss relate directly to the real situation for women in Sweden at the turn of the millennium.

Statistics Sweden, a government agency that looks at various aspects of Swedish society, confirms that Swedish women are

still subordinated on a structural level. According to their num-
bers, the job market is still segregated by gender, and women's
work is less valued than men's. Female-dominated professions
are paid less than male-dominated ones, and even when working in the same professions, women's salaries are generally lower
than men's. Women do more unpaid (house) work and take
on a greater responsibility for children than men. Women fear
being subjected to crime to a larger extent than men and often
choose different routes or means of transportation because of
their fears (Statistics Sweden 2012). These statistics confirm
Sophie and Kaja's critique of contemporary society, challenging
the idea of a "gender equitable Sweden." By presenting numer-
ous examples of how women are valued less in society and are
forced to stand back and adapt to the needs of men, Boije af
Gennäs's novel illustrates the reality of the structural subordination of women. It tells stories about women who spend their
lives struggling against societal norms that value them less than
men. These stories intervene in the shared world, challenging
the sociopolitical discourse on gender in Sweden and thus contributing to changing our understanding of women's status in
this supposedly equitable society. As such, this book is political
according to Jacques Rancière's theories, as discussed in previous chapters.

While focusing on lesbianism, Boije af Gennäs's novel also
presents a look at friendship between women. Throughout the
novel women are a source of security and strength to Sophie,
regardless of her love for Kaja. In a conversation with her best
friend Baby, Sophie states that men and women do not understand each other and asks, "why can't we live together, you
and me and a few other girls in a house full of happy women?"[7]
(*Stjärnor utan svindel*, 301). Sophie says this half-jokingly, and
similarly Baby does not take her question seriously. However,
the idea of living in a house full of women suggests the solution Agnes von Krusenstjerna presented more than sixty years
before: While Eka, described as "a big and loving land for children and women," becomes a (fictional) reality in *Fröknarna
von Pahlen*, neither Sophie nor Baby is really serious about
living in a women's commune together, and the idea is never

directly brought up again in the novel. However, Kaja shares an apartment with a female friend, Ankan, and their home is sometimes depicted as a refuge for lesbians and other women, echoing this same idea. But when Sophie divorces her husband and moves in with Kaja, Ankan moves out, which suggests that a commune-like home is a temporary idea, only possible as long as none of its members wants to live with a partner. What was possible in Krusenstjerna's *Fröknarna von Pahlen* in the 1930s is thus depicted as a fantasy in a novel from the 1990s. While Boije af Gennäs's novel is more explicitly concerned with feminist politics, since the characters have ongoing discussions on feminist topics, Krusenstjerna's novels are, in fact, more radical when it comes to the characters' possibilities to choose nontraditional ways of leading their lives.

The closest Sophie comes to a women's commune in *Stjärnor utan svindel* is through the lesbian community, which represents a temporary refuge from the male-dominated society. Ultimately, it is Sophie's love for Kaja that makes her leave her marriage and start a lesbian life, but being a lesbian is, to Sophie, also a part of a continuum of women-identified experiences. When her friends ask her about her relationship with Kaja, she stresses that she is in love with her, but she also mentions that men are difficult to deal with: "But it also feels like Kaja redeems me in a different way, after years of difficult relationships with men. And I think that if more women realized that we could be with each other, a VERY big part of the female, heterosexual supply would disappear from the market"[8] (*Stjärnor utan svindel*, 396–97).

The lesbian community in *Stjärnor utan svindel* can thus be read in the light of Adrienne Rich's theories of compulsory heterosexuality and the lesbian continuum, discussed in Chapter 1. The women share each other's lives and support each other, and they have erotic relationships with women. In line with Rich's lesbian continuum, the emphasis is on the political dimension of love between women—lesbianism becomes a way of leading a life without men, outside of male-dominated society. Furthermore, Rich argues that the lesbian existence can be understood as resistance against patriarchy: "a direct or indirect attack on male right of access to women" (Rich 1980, 649). This idea corresponds to Sophie's theory that many heterosexual females would choose lesbianism if more women realized that lesbianism was a choice: according to Rich, the ideology of compulsory heterosexuality forces women to become loyal to men instead of focusing on women-identified values (Rich 1980, 637–38). Thus it is compulsory heterosexuality that Sophie identifies at the dinner parties she attends, where women are loyal to their own values and food preferences only when their husbands are not present.

Lesbianism is frequently contrasted with heterosexuality in the novel; female homosexual experiences are associated with closeness and equality while heterosexual intercourse is described as repressing and humiliating: "This was not a man who wanted to suppress me, dominate me, humiliate me, spout his semen into me. This was a woman who was horny together with me, who loved me and therefore wanted to make me happy"[9] (*Stjärnor utan svindel*, 315). Heterosexual intercourse is depicted as an act of power, almost an invasion— the male conquest of the female body—while lesbian sexuality develops out of love and mutuality. These ideas are in line with radical feminist Andrea Dworkin's depiction of intercourse as male dominance, as the possession and occupation of a woman's body: "Intercourse is a particular reality for women as an inferior class; and it has in it, as part of it, violation of boundaries, taking over, occupation, destruction of privacy, all of which are construed to be normal and also fundamental to continuing human existence" (Dworkin [1987] 2007, 156). Boije af Gennäs's protagonist Sophie rejects this invasion, rebelling against the patriarchy by choosing Kaja, a woman, as her partner in love. This perspective—lesbian sexuality as mutual and based on community and heterosexual intercourse as based on power—can be found also among Swedish lesbian feminists in the 1970s (Hallgren 2008, 172–76). Lesbianism is thus connected to the radical feminist ideas that flourished both in Sweden and abroad in the 1970s. In this way Boije af Gennäs's novel parallels those of Krusenstjerna and Svedberg, which, as we have seen, portray lesbianism in ways that are based on ideas of women's empowerment that would later be found within radical feminist thinking.

Stjärnor utan svindel portrays love between women as a better and more equitable choice; lesbian love is described as mutual, close, and empowering, and the imagery plays an important role in conveying those impressions. For instance, when Sophie and Kaja kiss for the first time, it is described with imagery from nature: Sophie's body turns toward Kaja like a flower in bloom, and Kaja reminds her of a bunch of wild flowers (*Stjärnor utan svindel*, 209). As in Krusenstjerna's and Svedberg's novels, nature imagery suggests life and growth, implying that lesbianism is natural. Love between men and women, on the other hand, is less equitable and not as close or connected to life and growing. For instance, in the second chapter when Sophie makes love to Lukas, she is not present in the act but keeps thinking about a thank-you note she needs to send, and she notices that Lukas, too, is distant: "Lukas was turned on, but I felt that he was far away"[10] (*Stjärnor utan svindel*, 49). They are also interrupted at one point because Sophie is bothered by one of the dogs' bones that she finds in the bed. The polarization of lesbian and heterosexual love dominates Boije af Gennäs's novel; Sophie continually reflects on the differences and reaches the conclusion that heterosexual love is suppressing. As we have seen, Sophie's attitude toward lesbianism can be understood within a radical (lesbian) feminist framework: lesbianism becomes a politicized choice because it is, in part, in response to an invasive attack—Sophie chooses a woman as a way to have an equal relationship where she can get love and closeness but still keep her freedom as an individual. Radical feminist thinking is also the foundation of Sophie and Kaja's discussions about the structural aspects of gender inequality in contemporary society. The strong presence of radical feminism in the novel's representations of lesbianism might be due to the relative success of these ideas in Sweden, but as Chapter 1 has shown, the connections between lesbianism and radical feminist thinking has a longer history in the Swedish literary discourse on lesbianism. In Krusenstjerna's novel, lesbianism was connected to a feminist project that we might call radical feminist before radical feminism was established as a political movement. Furthermore, the rejection of men and heterosexuality in Svedberg's novels and the way these choices are tied to lesbianism could also be termed radical feminist. This continuity in thought suggests that radical feminist thinking is part of the Swedish discourse on lesbianism during the entire twentieth century, well before the rise of the radical feminist movement in the early 1970s.

Mian Lodalen's novels give a different perspective on lesbianism in the narratives of journalist My and her friends. Set at the turn of the millennium in Stockholm's lesbian community, the novels have several things in common with *Stjärnor utan svindel*. Like in Boije af Gennäs's novel, friendship between women plays a crucial role, and My and her friends also tend to engage in the same kind of activities as the characters in *Stjärnor utan svindel*; they attend demonstrations, discuss politics, go out to girls' clubs, and attend the annual Pride Festival. However, taking place almost entirely in the lesbian community, they initially seem to have a different attitude about lesbianism and its relation to men, heterosexual relationships, and feminist politics.

With the exception of My's friend Mackan—who is heterosexual but part of the lesbian community and thus comes across as nonnormative—heterosexual people are almost invisible in the novel. On a few occasions My encounters women who define themselves as straight but still dream of having a love affair with a lesbian. In this context, heterosexuality comes across as oppressive, since the straight women are depicted as too conventional or scared to give up their heterosexual marriages in order to associate themselves with lesbianism. In a scene further explored in this chapter, when My meets two heterosexual women at a dinner party, she quickly reads them as straight, based on the way they are dressed: in skirts, tall boots, push-up bras, and heavy makeup. My then reflects on the difference between lesbians and straight women: "No dyke would ever deck herself out like that. I feel a sudden empathy for all the straight women in the world. Is this what it takes to be viable on today's market? Why else would they waste so much time, energy and cash on their appearance?"[11] (*Trekant*, 108–9). My studies these women closely and with fascination, almost like an anthropologist observing a new and foreign culture. She realizes that she is different from the women, but she does not feel deviant. Like an anthropologist, she instead sees herself and her friends as the norm, and since what the straight girls do in order to seem attractive to men is described as a waste of time and money, they are the ones that come across as unnatural and strange.

The dichotomy presented in these novels—normative lesbianism and deviant heterosexuality—is tied to the books' lesbian perspective; they hardly have any straight characters. Even the few nonlesbian characters portrayed are described from My's perspective, and their appearances and actions are filtered through My's mind, since she is the first-person narrator of both novels. The reader only has access to their actions and speech and never to their inner thoughts or wishes. The first-person narrator can thus be seen as a narrative political strategy to present the underlying assumption that lesbians are the norm and the nonlesbians are deviant.

The same narrative strategy is used in the depiction of male characters; they are rarely portrayed, and when they are, they are described from My's perspective. Straight men are generally depicted as disrespectful and violent. On International Women's Day, My and her friends celebrate in a restaurant but are interrupted by rude comments from a group of straight men. One of the lesbians, Karlsson, is later harassed by one of them, who grabs her ass and feels her up her legs. She surprises them by fighting back; she quickly turns around and knocks the man down, and the women leave the restaurant with quiet applause from the staff (*Smulklubbens skamlösa systrar*, 41–44). On the one hand, the women could be said to have won the fight: Karlsson defeats the man, and the other people at the restaurant seem to side with the women. On the other hand, the women are the ones who leave, and no one tries to stop the men from harassing the women, which indicates that both patrons and workers assume men still are in power even if some women, like Karlsson, are able to fight back.

Overall, men play an unusually insignificant role in Lodalen's novels; the characters do not pay much attention to them since their lives do not revolve around men. In this way Lodalen's novels differ from *Stjärnor utan svindel*, where men and heterosexual relationships, as we have seen, serve as foils for lesbianism, which becomes intertwined with feminism and allows for freedom and a new kind of intimacy. This image of lesbianism is challenged in Lodalen's novels. For instance, My is not interested in a serious relationship, at least not initially; in *Smulklubbens skamlösa systrar* she is primarily looking for casual sex. My pokes fun at the belief that lesbian relationships are more intimate and symbiotic than others, and she presents herself as a counterexample:

> Lesbians only need to have sex once before they start fumbling with engagement rings.
>   But I am the exception that proves the rule. I actually don't have to identify with the entire dyke community. I can make my own decisions about my own life. I will defy the norm and try to meet a Mistress.[12] (*Smulklubbens skamlösa systrar*, 70)

Like Sophie in Boije af Gennäs's novel, My acknowledges the intimacy between lesbians, but unlike Sophie, she doesn't want to be part of it. My wants sex, not a relationship, and she is not that interested in intimacy and female solidarity; she even emphasizes that she does not like all women (*Smulklubbens skamlösa systrar*, 132–33). She is a lesbian because she is sexually attracted to women and not to men, not because she wants to escape a male-dominated society. Moreover, My's account of the lesbian community differs from Sophie's idea of the community as a lesbian continuum. Several passages in Lodalen's novels describe how small and sometimes acrimonious the Swedish lesbian community is; everyone has slept with each other, and lesbian club nights always end with scenes of jealousy since old and new lovers gather in the same place. For example, when My and her friends leave a lesbian club night they watch a fight, Mackan says that she is not at all surprised: "Here four hundred chicks are packed into the very same place, and almost everybody has slept with one or more person or has been in relationships with each other and at least thirty of them are still into their exes, who are already coming onto somebody new, who, on top of that, happen to be someone else's old ex and so on and so on in a big mess"[13] (*Smulklubbens skamlösa systrar*, 137).

While lesbianism and feminism are intertwined in Boije af Gennäs's novel, feminism does not seem central in Lodalen's books, at least not at first glance. My prefers to discuss sex over "tedious radical feminism"[14] (*Smulklubbens skamlösa systrar*, 39), and she misses the International Women's Day demonstration because she is hung over and goes to the wrong meeting spot (*Smulklubbens skamlösa systrar*, 39–40). However, a closer reading suggests that Lodalen's books are just as preoccupied with feminist issues as Boije af Gennäs's. Like in *Stjärnor utan svindel*, men are dismissed as inferior compared to women. For instance, when jokingly comparing men to dildos, My and her friends reach the conclusion that dildos have far more advantages (*Smulklubbens skamlösa systrar*, 128–29). In general, men are depicted as unable to sexually satisfy women, and My jokes about the possibility of making money as an advisor to straight men who want to learn how to make their women happy (*Smulklubbens skamlösa systrar*, 72).

But the depictions of gender inequalities also have a serious side, as seen in the previously discussed passage depicting how My and her friends are harassed by men at a restaurant on International Women's Day. Furthermore, like Svedberg's novels, Lodalen's novels deal with the subject of persistent men; My discusses the rudeness of men who join strange women in a restaurant without asking and who will not leave even if it is obvious that their company is unwanted (*Smulklubbens skamlösa systrar*, 60–61). She also brings up a story about a woman who was told to wear a shorter skirt while working as a maid at a hotel so that the guests would have something to look at (*Smulklubbens skamlösa systrar*, 82). These passages clearly display the gender roles and inequalities at the turn of the millennium: women are still thought of as sex objects who should be available to men.

Despite My's apparent rejection of the idea, lesbianism is sometimes depicted as a refuge from male-dominated society. My's straight friend Mackan constantly complains about her sexual identity, and she wants to be a lesbian. When her boyfriend breaks up with her she cries on My's shoulder: "Do you understand how horrible it is having to deal with the enemy all the time? Do you think it's possible to teach myself to become a dyke?"[15] (*Smulklubbens skamlösa systrar*, 73). Mackan wants to be a lesbian because men are difficult to deal with, as she makes clear when referring to them as "the enemy." This attitude toward men is, in fact, similar to Sophie's in *Stjärnor utan svindel*. However, while radical feminist ideas are at the center of lesbianism in Boije af Gennäs's novel, in Lodalen's books, lesbianism is motivated by a desire for women and not by politics, and gender equality is discussed to a more limited extent. However, whenever men and feminist issues *are* discussed, the attitude is much the same as in *Stjärnor utan svindel*; compared to what relationships with men have to offer—subordination, lack of power, and lack of subjectivity—lesbianism is preferable.

SEXUAL POLITICS: HIGHLIGHTING THE MARGINALIZATION OF LESBIANISM AND CHALLENGING HETERONORMATIVITY

The main political focus in Lodalen's books is sexual politics, and the novels continually depict injustices and prejudice that lesbians encounter in contemporary society. Boije af Gennäs's novel is less explicitly concerned with sexual politics than Lodalen's novels, which offer plenty of detailed depictions of the stigmatization of lesbians, such as homophobia and hate crimes. For instance, My writes an article about two girls who were thrown out of a restaurant after kissing each other (*Smulklubbens skamlösa systrar*, 56–60). My worries about hate crimes against gays and lesbians, and she becomes a victim of one in *Smulklubbens skamlösa systrar*: when she comes home one night, someone has scratched "Fucking bitch—foul dyke"[16] on her door (*Smulklubbens skamlösa systrar*, 92).

Navigating homophobic parents is a recurring topic in Lodalen's novels. My's friend Hedda invites friends to celebrate

Christmas at her place, and some of the lesbians attend because they are not welcome at their homophobic parents' homes (*Smulklubbens skamlösa systrar*, 23–24). The novel *Trekant* describes how My's girlfriend Bob's mother had a breakdown when Bob came out as a 17-year-old and tried to force Bob to go to therapy in order to be "cured" (*Trekant*, 28). When two of My's lesbian friends, Clara and Linn, have a ceremony to register their partnership, their parents do not attend, and one of their mothers call during the celebration dinner that follows to tell her daughter not to publish the news in the paper because she does not want her neighbors to know that her daughter is a lesbian (*Smulklubbens skamlösa systrar*, 158–64).

Lodalen's novels also describe everyday situations where lesbians and lesbian sexuality are neglected, not on purpose, but because heterosexuality is the norm in contemporary society. For instance, when telling her gynecologist that she does not use any kind of birth control, the gynecologist asks My if she is trying to get pregnant. When My comes out to the gynecologist and says that she does not sleep with men, the gynecologist is embarrassed. This event makes My think about a study she has read about lesbians and gynecologists: according to this study, 70 percent of the lesbians never told their gynecologists about their sexual orientation, and many of them left the doctor's office with prescriptions of birth control pills (*Smulklubbens skamlösa systrar*, 105–7). The doctors assumed that all these women were straight, and these women did not feel comfortable challenging this assumption. When My is asked when she came out as a lesbian, she is annoyed: "As if you did it once and then it is over. I come out every day"[17] (*Smulklubbens skamlösa systrar*, 107). In the beginning of My's relationship with Bob, My calls the doctor for Bob, who has severe back ache. She talks about Bob as "my girl" in a form that usually refers to "girlfriend" (*min tjej*), but the doctor asks how old her daughter is, assuming that "her girl" had to be her child: "People assume that you can't be gay. Not even when you tell them right to their faces"[18] (*Trekant*, 83).

These passages give evidence that contemporary society is guided by heteronormativity—that is, the assumption that

everyone is heterosexual and that heterosexuality is the orientation that is natural or normal (Rosenberg 2002; Warner 1991).
In a heteronormative society, lesbianism comes across as deviant, as in these examples; My has to "come out" as someone
who is different from what is considered normal. Furthermore,
Lodalen's novels highlight the idea that sociopolitical legislation
usually rests on heteronormative principles, resulting in lesbians
being treated as second-class citizens. For instance, My reads
about a lesbian whose life insurance was paid to her parents
after her death instead of to her partner of 25 years (*Smulklubbens skamlösa systrar*, 98–99). Lesbians who long for children
are present in both novels; in *Smulklubbens skamlösa systrar*,
My writes an article on this topic, and in *Trekant*, My's friends
Hedda and Karlsson try to have a baby. When My starts doing
research for her article, she doesn't know much about the laws
that govern reproductive assistance for lesbians, which makes
it easier for a reader to identify with My and her dismay as she
discovers that lesbians cannot get any assistance from the Swedish health-care system.[19] She speaks to a lesbian who questions
these laws: "I pay as much taxes as anybody else, but I don't
have access to the same rights"[20] (*Smulklubbens skamlösa systrar*,
31). The book follows My's work on her article, uncovering for
My as well as for the reader different examples of how lesbians
are not treated as equal citizens in contemporary society.

Sweden's progressive laws for the gay and lesbian community
rest on years of long and difficult struggles for equality. During the 1970s, several proposals that would have strengthened
the rights of homosexuals in various ways were brought forth
but turned down in parliament. However, in 1973 one of them
was rejected with an official statement saying that "homosexual
cohabitation was a life form fully acceptable to society" (Rydström 2011, 41; see also Andersson 2011, 134–35; Norrhem,
Rydström, and Winkvist 2008, 139). This self-contradictory
move—on one hand, to define homosexuality as a fully acceptable form of existence and speak for legal recognition, and on
the other hand, to imply secondary status by turning down
proposals that would strengthen the standing of homosexuality—is characteristic of the way the Swedish state has dealt with

gay and lesbian rights. Often the rejections referred to a belief that homosexuality is different than heterosexuality and thus should be treated differently. For instance, the 1988 law on cohabitation (*sambolagen*) consisted, in fact, of two laws: one that regulated heterosexual cohabitation (1987: 232) and one that regulated homosexual cohabitation (1987: 813). The laws on cohabitation gave legal recognition and protection to those who lived together as a family without being legally married, a group that grew bigger in Sweden in the 1960s and the 1970s. While most of the two laws were the same, the law on homosexual cohabitation lacked the language that regulated children. Since the law on homosexual cohabitation was an addition to the law on heterosexual cohabitation, legally it was possible to ignore parts of the main law, applying rights selectively. Furthermore, other laws that had bearings on cohabitation, such as laws on rental housing, sometimes only referred to the law on heterosexual cohabitation, and homosexual cohabitation was thereby left out. These differences were acknowledged by the government commission investigating new cohabitation legislation in 1999, and the new legislation based on this commission's report that took effect in 2003 became gender neutral and regulate both heterosexual and homosexual cohabitation (Andersson 2011, 133–35, 148–49). Jens Rydström acknowledges a similar hesitancy in the law. The Homosexuality Commission (*Homosexutredningen*) was appointed by the government in 1978 and came to be the largest investigation of homosexual life in Scandinavia. The group worked for six years and the report presented in 1984 was rather radical and included several proposals that would have strengthened the status of gays and lesbians in Sweden. However, only two out of the report's four proposals resulted in legislation: the law on homosexual cohabitation and the law against discrimination (Rydström 2011, 50–51).

While the laws on cohabitation had given homosexual partners who lived together certain legal protections, neither the one from 1987 nor the one from 2003 are as far-reaching as the legislation on marriage, especially regarding the right to inheritance. The cohabitation laws applied to both same-sex and opposite-sex couples, but these laws did not provide very strong protections for any couple. However, opposite-sex couples had the opportunity to get married in order to gain further rights, an option that same-sex couples didn't have until 2009. The idea of gay marriage was discussed among activists from the 1970s onward, but gays and lesbians were divided on this issue. Many activists, especially lesbian feminists, were opposed to marriage because of its heterosexual and patriarchal foundations, and those who argued for marriage rights wanted the same rights as heterosexuals and not a special law for gays and lesbians. The established gay and lesbian organizations supported a law on domestic partnership, and they were well organized and were able to enter the discussion with policy makers. Furthermore, when the Danish law took effect in 1989, the resistance among Swedish gays and lesbians vanished. This was the first time ever that the state recognized same-sex couples as legitimate. In 1995, Sweden became the third Scandinavian country to introduce a domestic partnership law, after Norway in 1993 (Rydström 2011).

In some ways the Scandinavian laws on domestic partnership were a victory for gay and lesbian rights. The possibility to register partnership meant that gays and lesbians had access to most of the same rights as heterosexual married couples. At the same time, domestic partnership was different from heterosexual marriage, and the law contained three major exceptions: at least one of the same-sex partners had to be a Swedish citizen, they were not allowed to marry in the church, and they did not have the same rights in regards to children and reproduction as heterosexual couples. Catrine Andersson highlights an interesting contradiction in the Swedish state-policy documents concerning homosexuality from groups such as the Homosexuality Commission and the domestic partnership commission. In these documents, homosexuality is described as similar to and different from heterosexuality at the same time. It is similar because both homosexuality and heterosexuality are based on love, according to both commissions. But homosexuality is also defined as different; the partnership commission from 1993 states that there is a lack of knowledge on how homosexual couples organize their daily lives. Similar statements on the lack of knowledge in regards to homosexual couples can be found in other policy documents, while there is no corresponding lack of knowledge in regards to heterosexual couples (Andersson 2011, 146–53, 160–63). The contradiction found in the policy documents is mirrored in the domestic partnership law, with its similarities to and differences from heterosexual marriage. Moreover, the law met with resistance, within both parliament and the political parties and in the media, and the implementation of the law was met with some obstruction, in particular since some municipalities refused to appoint partnership registrars (Rydström 2011).

Resistance against reproductive rights for gays and lesbians has been strong in Sweden. When the legislation for domestic partnership was proposed, its opponents argued that this was only the first step, one that would be followed by marriage in the church, adoption, and assisted reproduction. The chair of the Standing Law Committee tried to calm the opponents by saying that this was the only change and that no such adjustments of the law would follow. She was wrong. The strong resistance against reproductive rights for gays and lesbians in Sweden faded quickly, and less than ten years after the law on domestic partnership passed, homosexual couples gained the right to adopt (2003) and lesbian couples could get fertility treatments in state-funded Swedish hospitals (2005). These laws, especially regarding adoption, were more than anything a result of an adjustment to reality. Gay and lesbian couples had already found their own ways to start families. In the 1980s it became common for male and female couples to cooperate to have children, which resulted in the so-called four-leaf-clover family. The 1990s saw a lesbian baby boom as new reproductive technologies made it possible for lesbian couples to have children without involving men. This new reality called for legislation that regulated and protected the rights of these children and their parents. The adoption law that took effect in 2003 was preceded by a long debate in the parliament but resulted in granting homosexual couples the same rights as heterosexual couples to be considered as adoptive parents. This meant that same-sex couples received the right not only to internal adoption, to adopt the child of a partner, but also to external adoption. However, most adoption agencies have been unwilling to consider same-sex couples, thus in practice eliminating, or at least limiting, their access to external adoption. The commission's report leading to the law on adoption also proposed that lesbians should be given access to assisted reproduction services in Swedish hospitals, but this proposal was rejected until the 2005 legislation made it possible (Barr 2009; Rydström 2011, 145–65).

While the debates on adoption and assisted reproduction both took the child's best interests as their point of departure, the debate on adoption affected children that already existed. The debate on assisted reproduction was aimed at children that did not yet exist, which opened the door to a more philosophical debate about defining a "normal" family in the era of biotechnology. Still, both laws were constructed with the heterosexual family as a norm. In the commission's report on adoption, same-sex couples were said to be equally good at taking the child's interest into account as heterosexual parents, thus reinforcing heterosexuality as a model. While recognizing two women as legal parents, the law on assisted fertilization still takes the biological father into account. Swedish sperm donors cannot be anonymous, and the child has the right to find out about his or her biological origin at the age of 18. This applies to heterosexual couples as well, and they are encouraged to tell their children about their origin. However, unlike lesbian couples who cannot hide the fact that they need a sperm donor, heterosexual parents can decide not to reveal that a sperm donor is involved, and studies have shown that heterosexual couples often choose not to tell their children about it (Barr 2009; see also Edenheim 2005).

Reproductive rights for gays and lesbians seem to have been a more difficult issue to solve than marriage. Once these two topics were regulated in separate laws, a law on gender-neutral marriage passed in the parliament by a large majority and without much debate. The same year, 2009, the Church of Sweden decided to allow same-sex couples to get married in the church (Rydström 2011, 145–65).

As this summary of events makes clear, the struggle for legal recognition of same-sex couples and their families has been hard earned, despite Sweden's reputation as one of the most gay-friendly countries in the world. Many proposals suggested by government-appointed commissions were rejected before turning into legislation, and most that did become legislation were met with resistance and long debates, both in the parliament and in the media, before they eventually passed. As pointed out by Andersson and discussed previously, many state policy documents from the 1980s and 1990s seem to struggle with two opposing ideas: that homosexuality is indeed similar to heterosexuality but at the same time different, and the hesitancy toward granting equal rights for homosexual relationships is justified by policy makers' lack of knowledge in the area. This contradiction can be read in the light of Jens Rydström's explanation of why Scandinavian societies were the first to give legal recognition to same-sex relationships. He argues that the structure of the welfare state is based on the agreements between farmers' parties and the social democratic parties in the 1930s, which created a strong base for social reform, consensus, and willingness to compromise. In these societies the needs of the weak were met, but the demands for assimilation were strong and the individuals had to accept certain limitations of their freedom: "In such a society, an 'anomaly' like homosexuality could be handled in two ways: by utter rejection, as in the 1950s, or by incorporation and assimilation, as in the 1980s and 1990s" (Rydström 2011, 68). Furthermore, Rydström argues that assimilation could be seen as a manifestation of the majority's tolerance; the assimilated gay couple becomes a symbol "whose main purpose is to be passive recipients of tolerance" (21). In this process of assimilation, heterosexuality becomes normative, the yardstick against which everything else is measured and found to be similar or deviant. For this reason, alternative lifestyles are further marginalized.

Mian Lodalen's novels mirror the societal struggle outlined by Andersson, Barr, and Rydström. Margareta Lindholm discusses *Smulklubbens skamlösa systrar*, arguing that the novel mirrors the heteronormativity and the ambiguity toward homosexuality in contemporary society; on the one hand, same-sex couples can have their love legally recognized by the society through the partnership law, but on the other hand, their love does not get the same support from families and relatives as heterosexual love (Lindholm 2005, 29–30). This contradiction is present in *Trekant* as well. With their frequent depictions of the marginalization of lesbians in contemporary society, Lodalen's novels show that the long-standing construction of gays and lesbians as different in policy documents and legislation have consequences for lesbians. My becomes the victim of a hate crime, her friends are rejected by homophobic partners, and she learns that lesbian couples do not have the same right to assisted fertilization as heterosexual couples. These are stories that are not visible in policy documents and legislation, and by telling them, the novels contribute with new perspectives that challenge the image of Sweden as one of the most gay-friendly countries in the world. This image is also, of course, challenged by Andersson, Barr, and Rydström, as we have seen, but literature adds another dimension by its ability to tell more personal stories about lesbians who have to relate to the everyday implication of a sociopolitical construction of them as both equal to and also different from heterosexuals. As such, Lodalen's novels are political in Rancière's sense—they intervene in the shared idea of "gender-equitable Sweden" and add a specific sphere of experience that does not match. As we have seen, depictions of injustice and prejudice toward lesbians could be found in Svedberg's novels from the 1960s as well, but this perspective is more strongly articulated in Lodalen's novels. Despite the more marginalized status of lesbianism in the 1960s, Lodalen's novels from the 2000s are more preoccupied with describing the unjust treatment of lesbians in contemporary society than Svedberg's novels. This is probably due to the less tolerant attitude to homosexuality in the 1960s, which left much less room for gay and lesbian activism.

    While Boije af Gennäs's novel does not discuss society's marginalization of lesbians to the same extent as Lodalen's novels, it still depicts lesbianism in ways that add new dimensions to the common world and could thus be said to function as politics in this field, too. In *Stjärnor utan svindel*, lesbian love challenges and blurs different conventional social boundaries and opens up discursive space for a new kind of diversity. One boundary that love transgresses in Boije af Gennäs's novel is class. Sophie is an upper-class, aristocratic woman, and her friends are upper-class people who all follow their class conventions: they dress in expensive clothes, throw big parties with extravagant food and drinks, and vote to the right. Kaja works as a journalist, but she comes from a working-class background, and she is connected to left-wing activism. She participates in demonstrations, is a member of feminist groups, and wears vintage clothes and a Palestine scarf. The class difference in *Stjärnor utan svindel* is a prominent issue and a constant source of conflict between Sophie and Kaja. It is difficult to overcome, but both women work hard on bridging the class gap between them, and by the end of the novel they have succeeded. They attend an open debate about feminism, Kaja as part of the panel and Sophie in the audience. In the debate it becomes clear that they have learned from each other. Kaja is more open to cooperation between left-wing and right-wing feminists, and Sophie is more critical of right-wing politics. The progress is reflected not only in their opinions but also in their appearance and other people's responses; Kaja is wearing an Armani jacket that Sophie gave her, and after the debate Bengtsson, one of Kaja's friends who has been fairly hostile to Sophie, admits that she had been wrong and that Sophie is a great girl (*Stjärnor utan svindel*, 503–9).

When Sophie leaves her husband, she gives up her dream of the heterosexual nuclear family, but she gets a new family, the lesbian community. This family does not include children, at least not yet, but has a strong sense of female solidarity. Sophie dreams of starting a family with Kaja in the future, and in a conversation with Kaja's friend Liza she realizes that being a lesbian can, in fact, offer more opportunities than being straight: "We can offer so many more alternatives! Everything from marriage to cohabitation to living in different places to having a family with one dad and two moms to one partner having children and the other one having her own apartment to becoming lovers and then becoming just friends. And you can also be different things during different periods of time without people looking askance at you"[21] (*Stjärnor utan svindel*, 467). In this passage, love between women challenges the image of the traditional nuclear family as the goal of adulthood. While marriage is still a possibility, Sophie now sees different ways to have a family, thus opening the door to establishing new family boundaries. Like Krusenstjerna's *Fröknarna von Pahlen*, Boije af Gennäs's novel presents an idea that was important within radical feminism: Kate Millett's critique of the nuclear family (Millett [1970] 2000), as discussed in Chapter 1. Millett sees the family as the most influential institution in the perpetuation of the patriarchal society, since it mediates between the individual and the society and can effect control where political authorities cannot. In Liza's quoted statement, lesbianism opens up the definition of the nuclear family, and the alternative ways of organizing family life associated with lesbianism are connected to flexibility and freedom.

Furthermore, because it already exists outside the heterosexual norms, Boije af Gennäs's novel posits that lesbian love can transgress the gender dichotomy: "Love in all its variations, everything was allowed; nothing was impossible since the relationship per definition was an anomaly according to the norms of society. And because of that, everything became possible, and at the same time it was even more forbidden and exciting. You could be a woman, you could be like a man, you could live and play out all parts of your personality. You were a whole human being in the real sense of the word"[22] (*Stjärnor utan svindel*, 314). Lesbianism is defined as in a class of its own—like Agda in Krusenstjerna's novels—and this is possible since lesbians are already outsiders. It is precisely because love between women is seen as an "anomaly" that lesbians do not have to follow the norms of society. The lesbians in *Stjärnor utan svindel* can recognize what has traditionally been thought of as both masculine and feminine qualities: "They could fix a meal and fix the car. They could wear a dress and a suit, they could lick pussy and do each other with dildos. They were women and recognized their sensitive sides, but at the same time they did not deny their strength and aggression"[23] (*Stjärnor utan svindel*, 497). In this quote, traditionally feminine qualities are contrasted with traditionally masculine to make the argument that same-sex sexuality permits all these qualities to be expressed by one person. Lesbians are said to be whole human beings; they do not have to suppress certain sides of their personalities just because these parts are considered masculine according to society's norms.

While *Stjärnor utan svindel* depicts lesbianism as a realm of freedom that allows for a new kind of diversity, Lodalen's books poke fun at this view and offer a less idealized account of the lesbian community. Instead, Lodalen's novels focus on the marginalization of lesbianism in contemporary society, and My's account of the lesbian community should be viewed from this perspective. For Sophie, who is a privileged white upper-class woman, the lesbian community is a place of female solidarity and an escape from male-dominated society, but for My, it is a necessity. In the heteronormative society My describes, where lesbians are treated like second-class citizens and are victims of hate crimes, threats, homophobic parents, and prejudice, they have to stick together. Even if My pokes fun at the lesbian community, it is still clear that it is of paramount importance to her. The bond between My and her friends is depicted as very strong; they share each other's joys and sorrows. The friendships are a social safety net, and whenever one of the friends is going through difficulties, the others support her like a family would. As a matter of fact, My several times refers to her friends as her family or to other lesbians as family members or relatives. My has never had a traditional family—her biological parents were alcoholics and she grew up with various foster parents. Hedda and Mackan have taken care of her better than any mother, and she feels secure with them in a way she never did in any of her foster families (*Trekant*, 52–53). My grew up under difficult circumstances, but her experience as an outsider is not unique within the community; many lesbians in her circle of friends have been rejected by their biological parents who cannot accept their sexual identity, and they find a new family in the lesbian community. This allows for freedom as well; after Clara and Linn's wedding, My thinks about how lesbians have the possibility to create their own holidays and traditions and do not have to conform to family traditions and invite all their old relatives. But My also feels sadness, because what allows for this freedom is alienation—lesbians are outsiders, both in their biological families and in society (*Smulklubbens skamlösa systrar*, 164).

However, like *Stjärnor utan svindel*, Lodalen's novels also depict lesbianism as allowing for more diversity than heterosexuality. My's straight friend Mackan complains about her straight friends who believe that heterosexual coupling is the only way to happiness—and who will not invite single friends to a dinner party because it is only for couples (*Trekant*, 59–60). Mackan argues that it is easier to be a lesbian than a single straight woman; the lesbians are already outside of the frames of so-called normality, which allows for more flexibility in terms of lifestyles (*Trekant*, 150). Furthermore, My and her friends are critical of the nuclear family, primarily because it is repressive for women (*Trekant*, 150–51). However, they are hopeful about the future, since lesbians who have children have already started to challenge family norms, and Hedda believes that there will be more unconventional families in ten to twenty years: "Children with two moms, three dads, one mom and hopefully a bunch of cool people around the kid, not necessarily with biological bonds"[24] (*Trekant*, 152). Hedda's view of future families bears resemblance to Liza's statement in *Stjärnor utan svindel*. Both emphasize the flexibility and openness in these family constellations, and unlike the heterosexual nuclear family, biological bonds are of less importance. It is also similar to the women's commune at Krusenstjerna's Eka, although Hedda allows men into the picture.

The last chapter of *Trekant* indicates that Hedda's dream might be realized. In this novel My and her girlfriend Bob have a love relationship, a threesome, with the same married woman My had an affair with in *Smulklubbens skamlösa systrar*. The name of this woman is never revealed to the reader—My calls her "The C Cup," referring to the size of her breasts.

However, Bob leaves My for The C Cup, and My goes through a major crisis but is able to get through it with the support of her friends. Eventually she becomes friends with The C Cup's ex-husband Carl-Johan, and in the last chapter My and Mackan rent Carl-Johan's house in an affluent suburban neighborhood while he works abroad. Hedda and Karlsson stay with them every weekend, and in the end we learn that Hedda is probably pregnant. The four women have invaded a heteronormative space, an upper-class suburban neighborhood. They become a subversive force by appropriating some of the heteronormative attributes: they garden, expect a baby, and even have a dog. They behave like the average nuclear family but also challenge the idea through queer elements in the otherwise perfect facade; three of them are lesbians, two of which are in a relationship and are expecting a child together. Even the dog is different; she is not the typical dog but a big white poodle named Alice B after Gertrude Stein's female partner, Alice B. Toklas.

This ending and the attitudes expressed by Lodalen's characters, in fact, have much in common with Boije af Gennäs's character Sophie's view of the lesbian community: lesbianism allows for more flexibility when it comes to family constellations because lesbians are already outside of the norm, so they do not act like they are confined by it. It is also similar to Krusenstjerna's depiction of the women's commune at Eka, where women live together because of love and friendship. However, unlike the women in Lodalen's book, some of the women at Eka are biologically related, and some of them are also married to men but prioritize the bonds between women before those to their husbands. Children are born or are most likely about to be born in both novels.

Gender plays a less prominent role in Lodalen's novels than in Boije af Gennäs's novel, and the lesbians are rarely referred to in terms of masculinity or femininity. However, a few passages indicate that lesbianism can open up for more diversity regarding gender expression. When My takes a test for fun to see if she is butch or femme, the test shows that she is neither: "So what am I? Mixed breed, as I once said when I was six years old and was asked in preschool whether I was a boy or a girl"[25]

(*Smulklubbens skamlösa systrar*, 183). On a different occasion, when My and her friends are asked by a journalist what they would do if they were men for a day, My realizes that her life as a man would probably not differ too much from her life as a woman. These examples indicate that lesbianism is not strongly tied to specific gender roles in Lodalen's books; the lesbians are depicted as human beings rather than masculine or feminine, and they are not limited by gender divisions in the way they express their personalities. This allows for more flexibility in terms of gender than in *Stjärnor utan svindel*, where the lesbians are still referred to in terms of masculinity or femininity—or both. In Lodalen's books we seem to be closer to a society where gender does not matter when defining the self.

Thus the sexual-political dimensions of lesbianism in Boije af Gennäs's and Lodalen's books are both similar to and different from those found in Svedberg's books. Like Svedberg's novels, Lodalen's books depict the injustices lesbians encounter in contemporary society, and as we have seen, Lodalen's descriptions of the marginalization of lesbianism are more frequent and more detailed than Svedberg's. This could be due to the fact that lesbianism is less of a controversial subject in the 2000s than was the case in the 1960s, when lesbianism was still considered a disease in the Western world. Accordingly, Svedberg's novels are more preoccupied with the striving to "normalize" lesbianism by depicting lesbians as no different than heterosexuals. Boije af Gennäs's and Lodalen's books are written in the time of queer activism, and the in-your-face attitude can be found in the depictions of lesbianism in the novels. Lesbianism is "normalized" to a lesser extent in the turn of the millennium novels; instead there is an emphasis on the positive, norm-breaking qualities of lesbianism. In Boije af Gennäs's and Lodalen's novels, lesbianism gives rise to a new diversity in gender expression, family concepts, and intimacy that is not possible within the heterosexual system. A crucial point in these novels is that lesbianism challenges the old (heterosexual) system, and because of that it can give rise to a multitude of possibilities. Lesbianism is a norm breaker in a heteronormative society, making diversity and freedom also possible in other areas, such as gender expression, family constellations, and intimacy.

BODY POLITICS: CLAIMING SPACE IN THE WORLD

As in Krusenstjerna and Svedberg, the representations of lesbianism have political dimensions in Boije af Gennäs's and Lodalen's novels. New stories are told about gender inequality and the marginalization of lesbians in contemporary heteronormative society that challenge the image of Sweden as a model for gender equity and gay friendliness. This political dimension is apparent in the novels from the 1930s and 1960s as well, but in Boije af Gennäs's and Lodalen's novels, politics is also connected to representations of the body. The novels present two sorts of female bodies: the straight upper- or middle-class body and the lesbian working-class or left-wing-activist body. These two bodies not only differ from each other; they also oppose each other, and their meaning is thus produced partly through contrasts. The two different bodies are represented in different ways in the novels, and gender, sexuality, and class determine the bodies' possibilities for expressing themselves and claiming their space in the world. The body thus becomes a realm where different identities intersect—the lived experience and also the embodiment of abstract concepts such as gender, sexuality, and class.

In Lodalen's novel *Trekant*, My attends a dinner party at the home of lesbian couple Hedda and Karlsson when the doorbell rings:

A wild cackle breaks out when Linn, Clara, Leather Kim, Mackan, Horny Anette and two girls I do not recognize enter at the same time. I read them as straight in four seconds. They have to be Hedda's friends from work whom she has talked about. One of them has a tight top on that leaves her stomach bare and a short skirt that looks like a Swedish designer's waxed tablecloth. The other one is wearing a white short skirt with lace in folkloric style. It looks like she got stuck in her grandmother's lace curtain at the last family reunion. Over the lace curtain she's wearing something flowing and bright with a boat neck and ribbons impossible to trace the origin of, and her feet are tucked into small boots with 1980s heels. Her breasts are pressed up so that her nipples are in line with her armpits and her make-up makes you think of a Max Factor party commercial. No dyke would ever dress up like that. Suddenly I feel empathy for all the straight women in the world.[26] (*Trekant*, 108)

Her description of the two women is supposed to be funny but the message is clear: to be a straight woman means to dress up in strange ways. Femininity is performative; there are no core identities, since these are constructed through a stylized repetition of acts, to paraphrase Judith Butler. The costumes do not seem to be comfortable; one of the girls has to pull down her short skirt no less than three times in this chapter (*Trekant*, 111, 113, 117). The clothes described in this passage aim at controlling the body and keeping it in place, but they also make the body into an object, which My emphasizes by connecting the outfits to other objects: a tablecloth and a curtain. In another context, My attends a party where most of the female guests wear high heels and comments, "They can hardly run away from a rapist in those antifeminist stiletto heels"[27] (*Smulklubbens skamlösa systrar*, 81). To be a straight woman is the same as being accessible as a sexual object for men; their freedom is limited.

The controlled body ideal is connected to heterosexuality in Boije af Gennäs's novel as well. In *Stjärnor utan svindel*, it is important for a woman to be skinny. Already in the first chapter Sophie mentions that she is skinny: "too thin some people said, and I sometimes complained, but I was secretly very pleased with it"[28] (*Stjärnor utan svindel*, 15). But the thin ideal has its limits, limits that Sophie's anorexic friend, Nina, passes; she changes to the point where Sophie almost does not recognize her: "I was startled, looking right into a pair of familiar eyes. But that was the only thing. Her skin was stretched out tightly over her cheek bones, and she had watery wounds on her face. This was a woman who looked like she was at least fifty years old and had recently been released from a concentration camp. She would die soon, that was clear"[29] (*Stjärnor utan svindel*, 109–10). They talk about Nina's anorexia, and Nina tells Sophie that she works at a company where she is answering the phone since she cannot work anywhere where she can be seen. In Boije af Gennäs's novel, women control their bodies in order to stay thin and beautiful—they discuss diet pills and hold back on desserts, and Sophie, too, has suffered from eating disorders. To control the body is expected of an upper-middle-class woman, but to lose control over body control, like Nina, is not acceptable and is punished with alienation; Nina has to find a job where she is not in view, and she is not even in touch with her own family. This balance between thin and too thin is apparent when Nina talks about her brothers: "They are handsome, successful and gifted, and their wives have just the right amount of wit, weight and breasts"[30] (*Stjärnor utan svindel*, 111). Just the right amount (*lagom*)—repeated three times in the Swedish original, emphasizing its importance—is a key concept for women; they are not allowed to be noticed too much, at least not the straight women around Sophie. At a dinner party Sophie notices how a female friend has become thinner and thinner while her husband has put on weight (*Stjärnor utan svindel*, 248). In this passage a connection is made between the woman's policing of her body and heterosexuality: the man's body is literally allowed to take up more space at the cost of his wife's.

The straight female body in Boije af Gennäs's and Lodalen's novels is not supposed to be noticed too much. It has to be kept in place and policed in various ways, through makeup, clothes, and gestures. Sandra Lee Bartky adds a gender perspective to Michel Foucault's notion of docile bodies—that the rise of parliamentary institutions and greater political liberty brought with it a new discipline for the body. She argues that women's bodies are even more docile than men's and that all those practices directed toward the female body in order to make it feminine are, in fact, a process where the female body is constructed as subordinated. The disciplinary practices aim at producing a female body of a certain size (not too big), of certain gestures and body language (contained), and as an ornamented surface. Bartky connects these disciplinary practices to heterosexuality when arguing that a woman has to make herself an object and prey for a man and that she lives her body as if constantly seen by a patriarchal Other (Bartky 1990, 63–82). The straight women at the party in Lodalen's novel can be said to illustrate this idea: Even in a lesbian environment with no men present, they are dressed up as objects and with the level of discomfort for themselves. Straight female bodies described in Lodalen's novels—but also, as we have seen, in Boije af Gennäs's—are thus subordinated: they are supposed to be contained, ornamented, and sized, all with the goal of creating an object for the male gaze.

The body becomes a lived experience or an embodiment of the identities "woman" and "straight," located in a space where men still dominate. The male hegemonic space affects the body and its expressions; the straight female body is primarily supposed to be an object for male attention, at the cost of the body's ability to claim its own space, limiting it. Drawing on Simone de Beauvoir's account of female existence in patriarchal society as defined by a tension between immanence and transcendence, Iris Marion Young argues that the woman lives her body both as subject and as object. The patriarchal society defines the woman as an object: "An essential part of the situation of being a woman is that of living the ever present possibility that one will be gazed upon as a mere body, as shape and flesh that presents itself as the potential object of another subject's intentions and manipulations, rather than as a living manifestation of action and intention" (Young 1980, 154). This, in turn, explains the self-consciousness of the woman's relation to her body and also the distance she takes from it, according to Young.

In Boije af Gennäs's and Lodalen's novels, the bodies of the straight women function as objects for other subjects rather than "living manifestations of action and intentions." Even when men are not always present as subjects, living as a subordinate in a patriarchal society means that the female body must be kept in place and policed. The body interacts with the space that surrounds it; it embodies the meaning of space and becomes a physical manifestation of male hegemony, which limits the straight female body and turns it into an object. At the same time, the body affects space by being the foundation on which spatial interpretations of the world rest, perpetuating this hierarchical system.

The confinement of the female straight body becomes more pronounced when it is contrasted with the lesbian body in the novels. Kaja is described as thin but not in an unhealthy way, and Sophie thinks she looks strong and wiry (*Stjärnor utan svindel*, 93). Lesbian women are often said to be strong and take up space in *Stjärnor utan svindel*, as opposed to the straight women who always step aside for their men. The lesbian body, strong and taking up space, provides a physical contrast. This body is allowed to be natural—lesbians in the novels rarely wear makeup, while the straight women are described as well made up. When Sophie spends a weekend at Kaja's place, she dresses in more comfortable clothes, like Kaja and her lesbian friends, compared to the Laura Ashley creations with bows and cap sleeves that her straight friends wear at social events. The lesbian body does not have to be made up and dressed up in uncomfortable clothes but is allowed to take place as it is. The acceptance of the natural body is underscored when Kaja hosts a dinner party in her apartment and opens the door topless. Her friends then take a bath naked together in the bathtub (*Stjärnor utan svindel*, 255–56). Among the lesbians in the novel it is accepted to show the body "as it is," without clothes and makeup.

Lodalen's novels also depict the same acceptance of the natural lesbian body. As the quote describing Hedda's friends indicates, a dyke would never dress up the way the straight women do. My and her friends are usually dressed in comfortable clothes, and a recurring theme among the lesbians in the novel is the relinquishing of bodily control. The previously mentioned dinner party at Hedda and Karlsson's place runs late, and some of the lesbians fall asleep after drinking too much. They snore loudly, and one of them has snuff under her upper lip that leaves a brown trace of saliva on her cheek (*Trekant*, 127). The lesbian body does not have to be pretty but can prioritize bodily needs and wants over the demand to be an accessible object for the male gaze. Over all, bodily needs are given a considerable amount of space in Lodalen. My is not afraid to tell the reader about her need to fart or "take a crap"[31] (*Smulklubbens skamlösa systrar*, 54).

Another bodily need often discussed is sex. In *Smulklubbens skamlösa systrar*, My does not want a relationship but a mistress, and she is constantly complaining about how sexually starved

she is. Moreover, lesbian sexuality is not only seen as responding to other's needs, unlike heterosexuality. The novels describe
how both My and Hedda masturbate (*Smulklubbens skamlösa
systrar*, 66; *Trekant*, 54–58). In contrast, the married straight
woman, The C Cup, whom My has an affair with, is described as
passive in bed. My states that straight women are used to being
chased and seduced—that is even expected of them "unless they
wanted to be viewed as little horny bitches"[32] (*Trekant*, 158).
The C Cup tells My that she never had an orgasm with a man,
but with My she finally comes, and eventually she becomes
more sexually assertive with women.

Unsatisfied straight women are found in Boije af Gennäs,
too, and Sophie knows many women who hardly ever have
an orgasm with men (*Stjärnor utan svindel*, 501). On one
occasion Kaja does not want to have sex, and Sophie is devastated. They talk about it and realize that Sophie views the
relationship as a man–woman relationship, where the woman
cannot be refused sex or else she is seen as a whore, but the
lesbian relationship is not like that according to Kaja: "I am
not a man, you are not my wife and I am not more in charge
than you are in this relationship. We are both women; you are
my equal and have to take responsibility for when you want
to have sex. And when you do not want to. Just like I do"[33]
(*Stjärnor utan svindel*, 321). In this context, straight female
sexuality is framed as responding to men's needs, while lesbian sexuality is personal and independent. When Sophie visits
a lesbian club, she is struck by the fact that people's dances
look so liberated—it was like "embodied sexuality"[34] (*Stjärnor
utan svindel*, 262). Sophie thinks that straight women have
a lot to learn from the lesbians: "Straight women could use
the large amount of knowledge that lesbians have, knowledge
about sexuality and acceptance of one's body, about strength,
about the will and ability to survive in a patriarchy"[35] (*Stjärnor
utan svindel*, 262).

As an additional piece of the physical dimension of wom-
en's identities, lesbian women are mostly located in different
spaces than straight women. Men are missing from many of
these spaces, both in thought and in physical presence, and

hence the places are not pervaded by male hegemony. As stated before, men do not actually have to be present in order to affect the female body; it is the possibility of being viewed as an object that makes the tension between immanence and transcendence the core of feminine existence. In the lesbian space the male gaze is missing because the lesbians are not primarily accessible as sexual objects for men. Iris Marion Young defines the female body and feminine motility as more contained and inhibited compared to the male (Young 1980). However, this is not the case with the lesbian body in Boije af Gennäs's and Lodalen's novels, implying that Young's conclusion applies specifically to heterosexual norms. The male hegemonic space seems to only affect the straight female body, which has to be kept in place and becomes limited. Sandra Lee Bartky points out that the modern lack of formal public sanctions against the woman who chooses not to discipline her body does not mean that there are no sanctions at all. She suggests that lesbian women might be punished more indirectly, lacking access to a decent livelihood, for example (Bartky 1990, 76). Boije af Gennäs's and Lodalen's novels support Bartky's findings—as we have seen, various instances of discrimination against lesbians are highlighted and discussed—but lesbians still seem to enjoy a certain freedom from disciplinary body practices compared to heterosexual women. The marginalization of lesbians places them on the outskirts of male hegemony. Contrasts are key in connecting meaning to the body, so the lack of male hegemony in the lesbian space affects the lesbian body, which is allowed to take place without being held back. It embodies the meaning of a space where men are missing and thus becomes a physical manifestation of the lack of male hegemony, which allows the lesbian body to exist for itself and take up more space than the straight body.

The differences between the lesbian and straight bodies are also connected to class, especially in Boije af Gennäs, where class is a recurring topic. In Lodalen the class issue is less apparent, but it is clear that My and her friends are left-wing activists who do not care much about social etiquette. On the other hand, not only the formal tuxedo parties but even small dinner parties at home are governed down to the details in *Stjärnor utan svindel*. The first chapter depicts a dinner party at Sophie and her husband Lukas's house. Sophie cannot relax out of anxiety that something will go wrong, and she turns cold when Lukas almost forgets the welcoming toast (*Stjärnor utan svindel*, 26). At the same time, she has some ironic distance from the whole scene when she describes herself as a mechanical doll: "The duties of the hostess, she was almost like a wind-up doll. Tick, tick, tick; sharp heels against the hard-wood floors; red, shiny lips, matching red nails; jewelry; shiny eyes, shiny hair, which almost bounce-bounce-bounced when she moved"[36] (*Stjärnor utan svindel*, 18). The upper-class environment contributes another aspect to the male-dominated space where the straight female body is located and leaves a mark on it; the fear of a social faux pas, like forgetting the welcoming toast, affects Sophie's body: she turns cold. At one point Sophie even states that her class's neuroses and controlled behavior are part of their bodies (*Stjärnor utan svindel*, 464–65).

Through the lesbian community, Sophie encounters a different space than she is used to, and it becomes a sanctuary where she can leave behind her role as a straight, upper-class woman. It is no coincidence that Kaja lives in Södermalm, the part of Stockholm that historically has been the home of the working class. She lives in a neighborhood where Sophie has never been: "Apartment complexes, dirty facades; the whole neighborhood smelled like working class and misery"[37] (*Stjärnor utan svindel*, 119–20). Today this depiction might evoke laughter, since Södermalm has turned into a gentrified and affluent hipster neighborhood, but locating the lesbian commune on Södermalm has to be read as striving to place Kaja and her friends in a specific space: a working-class context far from the social context Sophie is used to. The first time she visits Kaja, she realizes that she has come to "a different world. There were no silver gravy pitchers here, no framed family portraits, no placemats with bird motifs. A closet was open and revealed piles of washed-out t-shirts and knitted sweaters. A striped rug was on the floor. Half-torn posters were nailed to the walls. There were plants everywhere. In the living room was a mismatch of dusty furniture which seemed to come from some kind of second-hand store"[38] (*Stjärnor utan svindel*, 121). This home appears to be alive and attuned to the people living there, as opposed to the homogeneity of the upper-class homes Sophie refers to in her "bird motifs" comment. The plants suggest the organic and natural in this space and its inhabitants. The lesbian life connected to the working class and left-wing activism comes across as more natural and contrasts with the straight upper-class life, which is depicted as artificial and limited (people are represented in framed portraits and nature on placemats).

As Rita Paqvalén has argued, *Stjärnor utan svindel* builds on a polarization between facade, represented by Sophie's previous life in the strictly controlled, straight upper class, and authenticity, in the shape of the lesbian community. Through her love for another woman, Sophie finds her original self, her true femininity, which had been hidden behind the false patriarchal constructions of femininity (Paqvalén 2002a). This polarization is part of the larger dichotomy of lesbianism and heterosexuality than can be found in both Boije af Gennäs's and Lodalen's novels; heterosexuality is represented as restricted and constructed and lesbianism as liberating and authentic. As fictional characters, these identities or positions are all cultural representations and thus all constructions to the same extent, but as stories of sexual identities, they contribute meaning to the shared world, adding to the understanding of how positions such as heterosexuality and lesbianism are perceived. Thus these representations have political implications.

As we have seen in this section, in Boije af Gennäs's and Lodalen's novels these political implications are strongly tied to the body, which encompasses identities such as gender, class, and sexuality and is located in different spaces that affect its expressions. The female, upper-class, heterosexual body is represented as a body governed by culture and society (and, thus, male hegemony); it is controlled to please the viewer but is not given much space to act on its own or to take up space. The female, working class/left-wing activist and lesbian body, on the other hand, is represented as natural and authentic and is allowed to take up space. This contrast suggests that the female body needs a space that is not governed by male hegemony in order to grow freely. The connection between the body and politics in the novels can be understood in light of contemporary feminist debate. With the emphasis on the private sphere and the personal as political within the second wave of feminism, the body took center stage in feminist debate. Contemporary media culture has been blamed for representing a feminine ideal that is impossible to attain for real women, causing eating disorders and a rise in cosmetic surgery (e.g., Bordo 1993). The representations of female bodies in Boije af Gennäs's and Lodalen's books can be seen as a statement in this debate, rejecting the feminine ideal; heterosexuality is blamed for the restricted construction of femininity, and lesbianism comes across as a refuge, a space where women's bodies are not regulated.

THE MEDICAL DISCOURSE: REINFORCING AND CHALLENGING THE THREE *M*s

Up to now, this chapter has mainly focused on the positive and empowering aspects of lesbianism in Boije af Gennäs's and Lodalen's novels. Lodalen's detailed depictions of the marginalization of lesbianism in contemporary society, for example, have been read as a way to challenge and change heteronormative society. However, these novels also contain negative representations of lesbianism—those that reinforce the connection between lesbianism and medicalization by referring to the medical discourse established at the turn of the twentieth century. The medical discourse is present in these novels to a lesser degree than in Svedberg's and Krusenstjerna's work, at least on an explicit level; in fact, medical explanations for homosexuality are rarely referred to explicitly. On the contrary, lesbianism is depicted as something that allows the characters to be more authentic and natural, as discussed, for instance, in the previous section on the body. Instead, the medical discourse can be found on a more implicit level, such as in imagery and often in passages that validate lesbianism on a more explicit level. It might seem like a stretch to trace back the medical discourse in novels from the turn of the millennium when homosexuality is no longer defined as a disease. However, evidence of its influence on modern portrayals of homosexuality shows a stronger legacy in the contemporary discourse on lesbianism than the progressive sociopolitical climate in Sweden may suggest.

As we have seen, the lesbians in *Stjärnor utan svindel* form a category of their own, beyond masculinity and femininity. In spite of this transgression of gender boundaries, the conventional distinction between masculinity and femininity is still used to define the lesbians in the novel; they inhabit a kind of borderland between masculinity and femininity. This in-between status is further reinforced by the frequent depictions of Kaja as androgynous or a tomboy. The novel's depictions of lesbians as androgynous or in between femininity and masculinity serves the purpose of depicting lesbianism as a realm of endless possibilities of gender expressions, but given the history of homosexuality and the medical discourse's descriptions of lesbians as a third sex, it is hard to ignore the connection to medicalization.

The *masculinity* explanation of female homosexuality is not the only turn-of-the-century explanation present in Boije af Gennäs's novel. The first time Sophie and Kaja make love, the other two *M*s are present, the *mirrors* explanation in particular. The act of love is referred to as "a familiarity"[39] (*Stjärnor utan svindel*, 238), and is described as natural and easy. Sophie thinks that giving oral sex to Kaja is an entirely different experience than giving it to a man, since Kaja's body is familiar: "likeness prevailed, not difference. Everything I did was done simultaneously to me, to my body"[40] (*Stjärnor utan svindel*, 241). In the depiction of this love encounter, familiarity and likeness are emphasized, and Sophie enjoys Kaja's body so much because it is the same as hers. Sameness is also emphasized in the imagery, as in the following passage. Sophie is licking Kaja, who says that she wants Sophie at the same time: "First I didn't understand what she meant. Then: to lick me at the same time. I was unsure of what to do, how to move in bed. Kaja showed me. She turned so that my vagina was close to her face. Twins in the same womb, nuts in one single shell. Pea pods, segments of orange, calves in their fold. Stars in the same constellation"[41]

(*Stjärnor utan svindel*, 240). This quote further highlights sameness, primarily through imagery: many different twin images are heaped together. The strong emphasis on likeness in the depiction of Sophie and Kaja's act of love, together with the fact that they are compared to twins—and therefore can be seen to mirror each other—suggests the medical discourse's *mirrors* explanation. Moreover, the *mothering* explanation can also be read into this quote, which mentions twins in the same womb. However, this is the only passage in the novel that alludes to mothers, and the allusion to *mirrors* is stronger. Overall, Sophie has a good relationship with her mother, and the reader never learns about Kaja's background.

Like androgyny, sameness is continually highlighted throughout the novel. Several images are used to depict lesbianism as love between two individuals who are alike, like-minded, and equals: symbiosis (*Stjärnor utan svindel*, 58), sisters (*Stjärnor utan svindel*, 315), soul mates (*Stjärnor utan svindel*, 439), and comments such as "she was exactly like me"[42] (*Stjärnor utan svindel*, 440). The emphasis on identification in Sophie and Kaja's relationship also suggests the psychoanalytic theory on lesbian merger, discussed in Chapter 2. This theory medicalizes lesbianism, further highlighting the connection between lesbianism and the medical discourse in the novel. However, it is important to note the fact that sameness is, without exception, a positive feeling for Sophie. For the first time in her life she is having an equal love relationship where she feels like she can be herself and grow. Freedom and equality are both linked to sameness; because Sophie and Kaja are "the same" (women with the same basic priorities in life) they can be free and equal. Nevertheless, sameness also alludes to the *mirrors* explanation and the psychoanalytic theory of lesbian merger in the same way as highlighting androgyny both represents lesbianism as a way of transgressing gender roles and suggests the *masculinity* explanation.

In Lodalen's novels, the medical discourse is present partly as a foil for the main characters, similar to the way the main characters in Svedberg's novels are distanced from deviant lesbianism or the way Bell von Wenden becomes a foil for Angela and Agda in Krusenstjerna's novels. Lodalen's novels sometimes refer to the historical medicalization of lesbianism when describing prejudice and lesbian stereotypes. For instance, when My watches the movie *Basic Instinct*, she starts thinking about lesbians in film history and realizes that they are often mentally ill, killers, or suicidal—and sometimes they are "cured" and become heterosexual (*Smulklubbens skamlösa systrar*, 27). When Hedda is asked to participate in a television debate on homosexuality, the reporter tells her that they want a good-looking lesbian and that these are hard to find because many lesbians look mannish (*Trekant*, 9). These two examples draw on various representations of lesbianism from the medical discourse: the mentally ill, the "lesbian evil" character, the tormented martyr, the lesbian whose deviant sexuality can be cured because it is acquired, and the third sex. However, the narratives dismiss these representations as stereotypes, and the main characters are described in contrast to them; My angrily defines the cinematic representations of lesbians as clichés, and the reader knows that Hedda is a feminine-looking beauty with long hair. Still, these examples show that the medical discourse influences how contemporary culture understands lesbianism.

Furthermore, the way of defining the characters' subjectivities outside of the frames of a binary gender model in Lodalen's novels can be seen as a way of challenging the medical discourse and its *masculinity* explanation to female homosexuality. As already mentioned, My and her friends are rarely defined in terms of femininity or masculinity. At the Pride festival, My makes herself up to look like a man for a night. When asked by some strangers whether she is a man or a woman, My responds, "I am a human being"[43] (*Smulklubbens skamlösa systrar*, 189). Her answer is representative of the attitude toward gendered identity in Lodalen's novels; it is not important. Still, the books are clear that lesbianism is what makes this diversity in expressing subjectivity possible. As we have seen, most of the straight women that My encounters are caught within the framework of conventional femininity created with a binary gender model and heterosexuality as the foundation (i.e., the heterosexual matrix). Thus, on the one hand, Lodalen's novels challenge the *masculinity* explanation by not defining lesbians in terms of masculinity or femininity, but on the other hand, they could be said to reinforce the medical discourse since resistance to gender categorization is possible only within a lesbian framework, in line with the medical discourse's understanding of the lesbian as a third sex. In other words, by limiting the freedom from the strict gender dichotomy to lesbianism, Lodalen's novels implicitly connect lesbianism to sexology's *masculinity* explanation and continue to define homosexuality as an Other, different from heterosexuality.

The *mirrors* explanation and the psychoanalytical theory of merging are also parts of the medical discourse that work as foils in Lodalen's novels. The idea of the so-called lesbian symbiosis, which brings these theories to mind, is always present in the novels, and My relates to it in different ways. In *Smulklubbens skamlösa systrar*, My constantly jokes about the idea of the lesbian symbiosis and distances herself from it. As we have seen, she does not want a relationship because she fears losing her freedom, and instead she looks for casual sex or a mistress. However, she never denies the existence of the lesbian symbiosis—she sees herself as the exception that proves the rule. In the end of the novel My meets a woman, Bob, whom she falls in love with, and the first chapter of *Trekant* describes how happy My is in her relationship with Bob. Even in a relationship, My's efforts to distance herself from the lesbian symbiosis continues—she jokes about it and acknowledges how she is about to enter "the world-famous lesbian symbiosis"[44] (*Trekant*, 25) or how she and Bob slowly fade into "the specifically lesbian symbiotic cohabitation"[45] (*Trekant*, 156). When My and Bob start a relationship with My's previous lover, The C Cup, My is proud of having distanced herself from the lesbian symbiosis and of being so queer that she can be in love with two women at the same time.

In the end, My's struggle to challenge the idea of the lesbian symbiosis fails; in *Smulklubbens skamlösa systrar* she falls in love with her mistress, The C Cup, and is devastated when the relationship ends, and in *Trekant* the threesome ends in disaster when Bob and C Cup fall in love and leave My.

However, as previously discussed, the ending of *Trekant* is truly queer; My lives together with her friends in a sort of commune-like house in the suburbs, and Hedda is probably expecting a baby. The constellation is queer, and the group is also queering its surroundings, the suburb, by appropriating some of its features, such as the house, the dog, and the baby, and turning it into a queer environment. Despite My's resistance, the strong presence of the lesbian symbiosis suggests the medical discourse's *mirrors* explanation and the psychoanalytic theory of lesbian merger, thus functioning as a kind of reinforcement of the medical discourse. At the same time, the medical discourse is challenged through My's resistance and through the queer ending of *Trekant*.

While the *masculinity* and *mirrors* explanations and the psychoanalytic theory of lesbian merger are simultaneously reinforced and challenged in Lodalen's novels, the *mothering* explanation is primarily reinforced, and it has a stronger presence than in Boije af Gennäs's novel. As already mentioned, My's biological parents were alcoholics, and she grew up in foster families. Her mother was literally absent, and My thus belongs to the large group of lesbian characters with absent mothers in Swedish twentieth- and early-twenty-first-century literature. But My seems to be looking for a mother substitute to a greater extent than some of the other characters I have discussed. Her first girlfriend is almost ten years older, and her name is Gun-Britt, which is a name more common in an older generation. My also describes Gun-Britt as older, and the two women soon start acting like mother and child; Gun-Britt nags My and tells her to behave like an adult (*Smulklubbens skamlösa systrar*, 20–21). My's second girlfriend nags her because she has a vocabulary like a teenager and because she is irresponsible (*Smulklubbens skamlösa systrar*, 22).

With her friends My often takes the role of a child; they treat her like an irresponsible teenager who can't keep track of anything. They care for her and are brought to tears when they talk about My's difficult childhood—and My doesn't mind; she enjoys the attention and love she gets (*Trekant*, 53). Hedda and Mackan sometimes act like her mothers, and when My first learns that Hedda wants to have children, she is afraid of losing her friend's care and attention (*Trekant*, 53). In her relationship with Bob, My is in constant need of love and attention: "All I want is to be close. Embraced. Taken care of. Seen. Loved"[46] (*Trekant*, 23). The words My uses are words associated with a parent's unconditional love for a child, given extra importance by making each word its own sentence, written with an initial capital letter. My continues to be upset and anxious when Hedda talks about her and Karlsson's plans to have a baby, and she is also afraid that Bob will want to have a baby soon—she thinks that she will not be able to compete for Bob's attention (*Trekant*, 126). My's relationship history, her complicated childhood, her childishness, and her longing for unconditional love all allude to the *mothering* explanation for female homosexuality. As opposed to the other parts of the medical discourse, the *mothering* explanation is never challenged or questioned in the novels.

As we have seen, Boije af Gennäs's and Lodalen's novels relate to the medical discourse on lesbianism in several different ways. In *Stjärnor utan svindel*, traditional images from the medical discourse are not connected to medicalization but associated with freedom. In Lodalen's novels, the medical discourse serves as a foil for the main characters or as images or parts of the plot that are never explicitly connected to medicalization. Still, the fact that images from the medical discourse established at the turn of the twentieth century are still present in these novels contributes to reinforcing the legacy of this discourse and suggests that it is still part of the discourse on lesbianism today. It is safe to assume that these connections between lesbianism and medicalization are not deliberate. As cultural representations, literature does not "belong" to the authors but is part of larger discourses. In line with Stuart Hall's argument discussed in the introduction, novels can be said to reflect contemporary discourses, but they are also meaning-making practices within those discourses. The Swedish state's relationship to homosexuality has been ambivalent: On the one hand, some advocates have framed homosexuality as similar to heterosexuality, therefore deserving the same treatment and legislation, but on the other hand, homosexuality had historically been treated differently. This ambiguity is reflected in Boije af Gennäs's and Lodalen's novels, partly because they describe a society where lesbians are both included and marginalized, but also because the medical discourse is present despite the novels' representations of lesbianism as nondeviant and even a better option for women than heterosexuality. Even though homosexuality was removed from the National Board of Health and Welfare's manual of psychological disorders in 1979, Boije af Gennäs's and Lodalen's novels suggest that medicalization is still part of the discourse on lesbianism, even today.

CHANGING THE WORLD: WRITING AS A POLITICAL STRATEGY

Boije af Gennäs's and Lodalen's novels are often referred to as autobiographical; *Stjärnor utan svindel* has been thought to depict Louise Boije af Gennäs's breakup from her marriage and her relationship with Mian Lodalen, while *Smulklubbens skamlösa systrar* has been read as a response to Boije af Gennäs's novel, an attempt to tell the other side of the story of this relationship. However, both writers officially deny these books are based on reality. *Stjärnor utan svindel* is dedicated to "Mian" but has an initial note stating that the story is fictional and that all similarities between characters, places, and situations and reality are coincidental. *Smulklubbens skamlösa systrar* also has an initial note explaining that some places in the book exist in reality, but not the people, so any similarities between the characters and real people are just coincidental. In addition to more personal speculations, the question of whether the novels are autobiographical or not directs the reader's interest toward writing and its more general relationship to reality. Writing about reality, about society, is also an important topic in all three novels, and the main characters in each book are writers; Sophie is a freelance writer, Kaja writes for a gay magazine, and My is a freelance journalist. Also, *Smulklubbens skamlösa systrar* is written in the form of My's journal. In the novels, writing works as a means to impact society, especially when it comes to feminist and to gay and lesbian politics.

In the scene following Sophie's encounter with her anorexic friend, she and Kaja enter into a discussion about the power of writing. They talk about the feminine ideal promoted by contemporary society, an ideal that pressures women to go on diets and make themselves sick. After a discussion about what they can do to change society, Sofie and Kaja reach the conclusion that writing can be their way of impacting society—they even talk about writing as a weapon (*Stjärnor utan svindel*, 114–15). The following day Sophie moves from theory to practice; she has been contracted to write a few columns for a health magazine and decides to write about eating disorders (*Stjärnor utan svindel*, 118). In another passage where Sophie reflects on her writing, she describes herself as a god who creates and makes decisions (*Stjärnor utan svindel*, 168). In these passages writing is connected to power; a writer is someone who can have impact on and change the world. This belief in the power of writing to change the world brings Rancière's theories to mind: literature is political in the way it adds new stories to the shared world. By pointing out how Sophie's stories can impact society the novel reminds us of the political nature of literature. Writing is also a substantial part of Sophie's life. For instance, when she is in the middle of the crisis caused by her love for Kaja and does not know what to do with her life, she knows that she has to stick to her writing because that will give her some stability (*Stjärnor utan svindel*, 245). Furthermore, even Sophie's dream of having a family is depicted in the light of her writing "like my books and TV shows, but this time made of flesh and blood and bones"[47] (*Stjärnor utan svindel*, 244). Sophie compares her written works to real children, which emphasizes the importance of her writing as an extension of herself.

Writing is also connected to lesbianism a couple of times in Boije af Gennäs's novel and to a lesbian literary history in particular. When Sophie tells a friend about Kaja and is worried that her love for another woman will ruin her career, he responds that she will be part of a great tradition: Selma

Lagerlöf, Karin Boye, and Edith Södergran—Swedish-speaking writers who had or at least were thought to have had erotic relationships with other women (*Stjärnor utan svindel*, 267–68). Furthermore, Kaja sometimes reads poetry to Sophie, after having asked if Sophie wants to hear what "the poet" has to say. The poets vary—Karin Boye or Edith Södergran, for example—but the two women seem to view the poet as an authority who can deliver a truth about their lives (*Stjärnor utan svindel*, 341, 520–21). Moreover, the title of the novel is taken from one of Edith Södergran's poems cited in the novel: the poem, "Violetta skymningar" ("Violet Dusks"), depicts women's community. The presence of the lesbian literary tradition in the novel emphasizes the crucial role of writing and its connection to lesbianism and women's emancipation. Moreover, on a metafictional level, the novel self-consciously places itself in that lesbian literary tradition.

The faith in writing in *Stjärnor utan svindel* is earnest and idealistic. Sophie believes that words from her pen can change the world, and that is one of the reasons she is so devoted to her writing. At first, the attitude toward writing seems to be different in Lodalen's novels. My is lazy and has to struggle to keep her deadlines, since she prioritizes late night parties and sleep before work. In one instance, she suffers from writer's block two hours before the deadline for a magazine column but manages to finish the text right on time, although she is not happy with her work (*Smulklubbens skamlösa systrar*, 17–18). My's attitude seems to be far from Sophie's idealistic faith in writing's ability to change the world. Still, writing and its abilities to impact society play a crucial part in Lodalen. My's work on the article about lesbians' struggles to have children covers six pages of the novel, so the reader gets to follow the process closely. In this case writing becomes a way of changing society, as My gives a detailed account of the injustices lesbians encounter when trying to have children. My's writing even prompts her to take action in the fictional reality of the novel; she tries to enlighten two straight mothers with small children that she meets in a public pool house by telling them about her findings (*Smulklubbens skamlösa systrar*, 34). As already mentioned, My writes another article about a lesbian who was thrown out from a restaurant because she kissed her girlfriend. Again writing becomes a way of raising awareness about injustices in society (*Smulklubbens skamlösa systrar*, 57–61). In both these cases, the otherwise lazy My becomes engaged and inspired and works hard until she has finished her articles.

Writing thus has a similar function in Boije af Gennäs's and Lodalen's novels as in Svedberg's novels from the 1960s. Like Svedberg, the autobiographical aspect and the belief in writing as a way to communicate "the truth" about the situation for lesbians and other women in contemporary society break down the boundaries between truth and fiction, life and art, putting a strong emphasis on writing as politics. By depicting the gender inequality and discrimination against lesbians in contemporary society, Boije af Gennäs's and Lodalen's novels provide another story of this society that contrasts with the image of Sweden as progressive and liberal. Since literature is part of the discourse of its time, it contributes with stories that set the boundaries for how different phenomena are viewed in the shared world. The theme of writing as holding the power for change in these three turn-of-the-millennium books clearly supports Ranciére's point that literature is politics just by being literature. This relationship is even stronger than in Svedberg's novels, since the belief in the world-changing dimension of literature is so strongly articulated in the novels. The metafictional ideas in Boije af Gennäs's and Lodalen's novels further contribute to highlighting the faith in writing as politics; these novels are themselves writing and might, as such, have an impact on their readers and be able to change the common world.

OTHER STORIES: LOUISE BOIJE AF GENNÄS, MIAN LODALEN, AND TURN-OF-THE-MILLENNIUM LITERATURE

In some ways Louise Boije af Gennäs's and Mian Lodalen's novels mirror contemporary Swedish society. The relative success of feminism in Sweden has led to a fairly gender-equitable society that provides the characters with more options in life compared to the women in Krusenstjerna's and Svedberg's novels. Furthermore, contemporary society's move toward acceptance of homosexuality gives the literary characters the opportunity to show their love for other women more openly than their forerunners. However, both Boije af Gennäs and Lodalen depict a society far from achieving gender equality and far from equitable for gays and lesbians. While lesbians in contemporary Sweden have generally the same legal status as men and heterosexuals, far closer than in the 1930s and 1960s, they still encounter prejudice and run the risk of being victims of hate crimes. In their novels, Boije af Gennäs and Lodalen focus on the less visible and quantifiable aspects of gender and sexual inequality and show that inequality exists on a structural level; Sweden—despite various political measures strengthening women's and gay and lesbian rights—is still a society dominated by men and guided by heteronormativity.

In contrast to the 1930s and 1960s, lesbianism is not an unusual topic in Swedish literature at the turn of the millennium. Because of the large number of lesbian-themed novels, I will not analyze each novel separately but instead discuss a few topics that can be found in these novels. Like in Boije af Gennäs's and Lodalen's novels, heterosexuality and men are dismissed in many of these texts. Men are depicted as suppressors to an even larger extent, since several novels describe how the protagonists are sexually abused by their fathers or another male relative. This is the case in Eva Lejonsommar's *Stilla tiger* (1991; *Silence is Quiet*) and *Återresa* (2002; *Return*), in Anna-Karin Granberg's *Där ingenting kan ses* (1992; *Where Nothing Can Be Seen*) and *Längre bort än hit* (1994; *Further Away Than Here*), and in Anna Mattsson's trilogy about Alexandra: *Alexandras rum* (1994; *Alexandra's Room*), *De ensammas hus* (2004; *The House of the Lonely*), and *Vägar utan nåd* (2006; *Roads without Mercy*). The protagonists are raped as adults in Lotta Lundberg's *Låta sig hända* (1998; *Let Oneself Happen*) and Hanna Wallsten's *I närheten av solen* (2005; *Near the Sun*). The sexual abuse that these women are victims of can be seen as a more direct expression of the structural subordination discussed in Boije af Gennäs's and Lodalen's novels.

Texts generally represent lesbianism as a refuge or a way to remember and heal from these traumatic experiences. Sofia in *Stilla tiger* was sexually abused by her uncle as a two-year-old, and these memories come back when she starts a relationship with another woman. In Granberg's novels, the protagonist is able to remember and process her difficult upbringing when she is in a relationship with a woman. In Mattsson's first two novels, the lesbian theme is not as prominent as in Granberg's, but the protagonist's love for women works as a temporary refuge. Lesbianism becomes more important in the third novel, where Alexandra loves women at a distance. Despite the fact that her love is unrequited, she still gains strength from it, and it gives her an identity. In *Låta sig hända*, high-schooler Ylva seeks support in her female teacher Marit, and the two women start a love relationship that becomes a source of strength for Ylva, helping her to heal from rape. Jessica in *I närheten av solen* becomes pregnant after having been sexually abused by two unknown young men, and she finds temporary comfort in the arms of the female protagonist. As we have seen, lesbianism is portrayed as a refuge in Boije af Gennäs's novel as well: It is liberation from male domination. The liberating aspects of lesbianism are particularly emphasized in the context of sexuality. While heterosexual sex is depicted as an invasion, Sophie feels equal when making love to Kaja in *Stjärnor utan svindel*, and this same dichotomy between heterosexual and homosexual love appears in many other turn-of-the-millennium novels with lesbian themes.

Furthermore, like in Boije af Gennäs and Lodalen, lesbianism is often connected to feminism and an awareness of male dominance in society in other turn-of-the-millennium novels. Anna in Eva Lejonsommar's *Att älska henne* (1995; *To Love Her*) is a dedicated feminist and schoolteacher who makes her students read Sappho. For the abused characters mentioned previously, lesbianism is liberating, an opportunity to lead a life without men, much like Sophie's idea of lesbianism in *Stjärnor utan svindel*. Anna Mattsson's Alexandra acknowledges that girls become weak and powerless in the presence of boys (Mattsson 2004, 267)—just as Sophie observes the dinner-party rituals of feminine submission in *Stjärnor utan svindel*. Love between women is also depicted as stronger and more emotionally intense than heterosexual love. In *Färdas på en blick* (2001; *Travelling on a Glance*), Lotta Lundberg's Laura falls head over heels in love with Marianne, and the power of the two women's love sharply contrasts to the colder and more distanced feelings Lotta had for her boyfriend, whom she just left. A similar contrast between heterosexual and lesbian love can be found in Boije af Gennäs's novel, where Sophie's love for Kaja is depicted as stronger and more powerful than the distanced relationship she has with her husband. The protagonist in Marlene Claesson's novel *Bisexuell* (2005; *Bisexual*) is bisexual and has relationships with both men and women throughout the novel. Her relationships with men are depicted as more distant, while her relationships with women are closer and more emotionally charged. They affect her more, and the love of her life is a woman, whom she refers to in second person, as "you," which shuts the reader out and emphasizes the closeness of the lovers—a narrative technique that we see in Svedberg's and Alexanderson's novels from the 1960s.

Since lesbianism generally comes across as a better and more equitable option than heterosexuality, it has political implications, just like in Boije af Gennäs's and Lodalen's novels. In *Stjärnor utan svindel*, lesbianism becomes a political statement in line with radical feminist thinking—a way for women to lead a life without men and have equal relationships. Furthermore, lesbianism becomes political in the sense that Sophie's relationship with Kaja is connected to an aim to change the world, something that is not possible in her heterosexual marriage. Also, a closer look at Lodalen's novels reveals a connection between lesbianism and feminism. My is aware of and reflects on the subordination of women in society and acknowledges that straight women have to adjust to men's needs. However, the main political focus in Lodalen's novels is on gay and lesbian rights. The novels depict several cases of homophobia, and My worries about as well as is the victim of hate crimes. Moreover, My describes how society often ends up treating lesbians as second-class citizens because legislation is based on heteronormative principles. Like Lodalen's texts, some of the other turn-of-the-millennium novels focus on gay and lesbian politics. For instance, homophobia is addressed in Eva Lejonsommar's *Att älska henne* and *En av oss* (1998; *One of Us*). Lesbianism also transgresses conventional boundaries in novels from this period. In Lejonsommar's *Att älska henne*, Anna and Marie come from different social classes, much like Sophie and Kaja in *Stjärnor utan svindel*. Lejonsommar's novel depicts a crisis in Anna and Marie's relationship, but they overcome the difficulties and in the end they have found a way back to each other, despite their differences. In Lotta Lundberg's *Låta sig hända*, which depicts the relationship between high-schooler Ylva and her much older teacher Marit, lesbianism transgresses age boundaries. The lesbian protagonist in Hanna Wallsten's *I närheten av solen* has a dysfunctional family and creates her own family together with the locals at the book café she runs. Jessica, who was raped, decides not to have an abortion, encouraged by the protagonist Moa, who even promises to help her take care of the baby. Here love and bonding between women transgress traditional family boundaries. As we have seen, similar boundaries are transgressed in Boije af Gennäs's and Lodalen's novels, too. In *Stjärnor utan svindel*, lesbianism transgresses boundaries such as class, family, and gender and opens up for a new kind of diversity allowing women to explore all sides of their personalities. While Lodalen's *My* pokes fun at the idea of the lesbian community as a realm of freedom, this community becomes an alternative family for My and her lesbian friends when homophobic birth families turn their backs on them, and the ending of *Trekant* is truly queer in terms of family constellations. Hence lesbianism does challenge conventional boundaries in Lodalen's novels, too. Lesbianism also gives rise to gender diversity in Lodalen's novels, but in a different way than in *Stjärnor utan svindel*. While the lesbian characters in Boije af Gennäs's novel can express both their feminine and masculine sides, the lesbians in Lodalen's novels are beyond gender polarization. They are rarely defined in terms of gender, which allows for even more gender flexibility than in *Stjärnor utan svindel*. Thus, in many of the novels from this period, lesbianism opens up for diversity and is portrayed as something intrinsically good.

The body plays an important role in all these turn-of-the-millennium novels. The dichotomy between the straight body and the lesbian body is not as apparent as in Boije af Gennäs's and Lodalen's novels, at least not initially. The body depicted in novels by Anna-Karin Granberg, Anna Mattsson, Lotta Lundberg, and Hanna Wallsten is the abused body. The body loses its value for the abused women, and they become self-destructive. Granberg's protagonist starts sleeping with boys when she is very young, and Mattsson's Alexandra wants to run away from home and plans to support herself through prostitution. Their bodies are depicted as already used, and the girls feel ashamed and dirty. In Granberg's, Lundberg's, and Wallsten's novels, the body can be redeemed, and the road to healing is usually enabled through love for another woman. This creates a dichotomy between the body abused by men within the heteronormative world and the body redeemed through lesbianism, similar to the portrayals of the heterosexual body and the lesbian body in Boije af Gennäs's and Lodalen's novels. In their novels, two opposite embodied identities are constructed, and the lesbian identity is represented as more liberating than the heterosexual identity. The body encompasses identities such as gender, sexuality, and class and is located in different spaces, which affect its expressions. The combination of female, heterosexual, and upper class creates a body governed by culture and society (and thus male hegemony); it is controlled and should please the viewer, but it is not given much space to act on its own or to take up space. The combination of female, homosexual, and working class/left-wing activist, on the other hand, creates a body that is depicted as natural and is allowed to take up space. While the effects of different experiences on the female body differ between texts, all these novels echo a similar oppression that the heteronormative, patriarchal society has on the female body.

Writing plays an important role in Lejonsommar's, Granberg's, Mattsson's, and Claesson's novels, as it does in Boije af Gennäs's and Lodalen's work, where both protagonists are writers and use their pens to influence society. Writing is thus tied to politics, like in Svedberg's novels, and becomes a political means to turn the world into a better place for lesbians and other women. Sofia in Lejonsommar's *Stilla tiger* has a typewriter, and the book ends with her starting to write in order to process her difficult childhood memories. Granberg's protagonist writes poetry, and her two novels discussed here are said to be autobiographical, like Boije af Gennäs's and Lodalen's. Mattsson's Alexandra writes a book and performs plays with her friends while growing up. After the trial against her stepfather, she writes a play about her experiences. Writing about experiences recalls Lodalen's My, who uses her pen as a journalist to write about injustices lesbians experience in society. Claesson's novel is a fictional journal, like Lodalen's *Smulklubbens skamlösa systrar*. For the protagonists, writing becomes a way of processing their experiences but also something that gives them strength and identity, a positive force that might even influence people and make this world a better place to live for young women. As in Boije af Gennäs and Lodalen, the pen becomes a weapon in the hands of the protagonists—through writing they get the opportunity to tell their stories and thereby regain power over themselves.

It is striking that so many contemporary novels with lesbian themes deal with sexual abuse. In Lejonsommar's *Stilla tiger*, Sofia was sexually abused by her uncle when she was two. In *Återresa*, Lena was sexually abused by her father during her upbringing, and she also had a complicated relationship with her mother. Granberg's protagonist grows up being sexually abused not only by her father but also sometimes by her mother. Mattsson's Alexandra is sexually abused by her stepfather, who controls the entire family, and her mother is too weak and repressed to stand up for her daughter. Lundberg's Ylva is raped by her classmates, and her parents are too preoccupied with their social facade to understand the gravity of what happened to their daughter, who instead seeks love and support in her teacher.

Dysfunctional families permeate these novels. In Mattsson's novels, the adults around Alexandra assume that her lesbianism is caused by her being abused, but this cause-and-effect perspective on lesbianism is not presented as a message in the novels as a whole. The reader rather sides with Alexandra and dismisses the adults as prejudiced and ignorant. Even if the cause-and-effect perspective is not emphasized in these or other novels, lesbianism and mental-health issues are still connected. All the protagonists have complicated relationships with their mothers, and some of them fall in love with older women, which suggests the *mothering* explanation from the medical discourse established a century before. Wallsten's Moa's mother, for example, has mental-health problems, and this affected the entire family and her upbringing. The other two *M*s, *masculinity* and *mirrors*, are not present in these novels, but the *mothering* explanation is more strongly emphasized in the books discussed in this section in comparison to many other novels discussed in this study. Furthermore, the fact that so many lesbian characters come from dysfunctional families and suffer from mental-health issues establishes a connection between lesbianism and medicalization, which reinforces the medical discourse.

The connection between lesbianism and the medical discourse is to some extent expressed differently in Boije af Gennäs's and Lodalen's novels and the other novels discussed in this section. Both groups refer the three *M*s, but they do so in different ways. In Boije af Gennäs and Lodalen, there are no explicit connections between lesbianism and the medical discourse, but the medical discourse is still present in imagery and plots or as negative representation from which the characters distance themselves. Further complicating this discourse is the fact that the same aspects of lesbianism the protagonists experience as positive and empowering (sameness, diversity in gender expression) are the ones that are connected to the medical discourse (*mirrors*, *masculinity*). In the other turn-of-the-millennium novels, the medical discourse has a much stronger presence. The *mothering* explanation is implicitly used as an explanation for lesbianism, since most of the characters have troubled relationships with their mothers. Moreover, the striking presence of lesbian protagonists who have been victims of sexual abuse and have dysfunctional families recalls

turn-of-the-twentieth-century explanations of female homosexuality as acquired. As discussed in Chapter 1, Freud and
his psychoanalytical followers saw homosexuality mainly as a
result of an abnormal psychosexual development. In line with
this idea that homosexuality is acquired, the traumatic experiences could be read as what cause the protagonists to turn
to lesbianism, even if no explicit connections between sexual
abuse and lesbianism are made in the novels. In implying that
lesbianism is acquired, these novels parallel Svedberg's lesbian characters from the 1960s and Krusenstjerna's Bell von
Wenden from the 1930s. Even if the turn-of-the-millennium
novels never explicitly medicalize their protagonists the way
Krusenstjerna's and Svedberg's do, they all rest firmly on ideas
of lesbianism that are found within the turn-of-the-twentieth-
century medical discourse.

Both Liv Saga Bergdahl and Rita Paqvalén have acknowledged
the darker sides of turn-of-the-millennium, lesbian-themed novels (Bergdahl 2010, 241–42; Paqvalén 2002a). While Bergdahl
notices the connections to abuse and dysfunction more in passing and focuses on the theme of openness, Paqvalén explores
the darker themes in contemporary literature more deeply. She
highlights how the novels present a dichotomy between the
nuclear family and men on the one hand and lesbianism on
the other. While the nuclear family is associated with violence
and sexual abuse and men are represented as threats, the lesbian community is depicted as a refuge for the abused women
and lesbianism as a way for the female protagonist to become
whole and find her own self (Paqvalén 2002a). According to
Paqvalén's reading, the darker sides of these novels are associated with heterosexuality, while lesbianism comes across as a
positive and empowering alternative.

This chapter presents an added complexity to Paqvalén's
reading. While acknowledging this opposition between heterosexuality and lesbianism, these readings emphasize that
the representations of lesbianism are not just a polarization
between traumatic heterosexuality and empowering lesbianism. In the literary discourse, positive descriptions of lesbianism
as empowerment and freedom are intertwined with depictions

that suggest the medical discourse on lesbianism established at the turn of the twentieth century. Turn-of-the-millennium Swedish novels thus represent lesbianism in the same ambiguous way as the novels from the 1930s and the 1960s do, despite the fact that the conditions for gays and lesbians have improved significantly in Sweden since then. Today Sweden has some of the most progressive laws on homosexuality in the world, but as we have seen in this chapter, the state still treats homosexuality with a certain amount of ambivalence. The conflict evident in the literary discourse, where positive representations of lesbianism are interlaced with images that can be traced back to the medical discourse almost a century before, corresponds to and contributes to the same conflict in the sociopolitical discourse. As such, it challenges the image of Sweden as a gay-friendly country but also challenges the notion of the Western discourse on homosexuality, which is based on an idea of progression. The conditions for the lesbian characters in the contemporary novels are, of course, different than those in the novels from those of the 1930s and 1960s; Sophie, Kaja, My, and the others are surrounded by an openness that makes it easier for them to live as lesbians in society. This shows that some progress has been made. Still, close readings of turn-of-the-millennium novels suggest that the core of the Swedish literary discourse on lesbianism has not fundamentally changed from the discourse of the 1930s.

CONCLUSION

THE LITERARY DISCOURSE
ON LESBIANISM

The novels discussed in this book were published during a period of 75 years, a period associated with great societal change, especially when it comes to LGBTQ issues in Sweden. Based on the changes in laws and the more general sociopolitical discourse, we might expect the literary representations of lesbianism to undergo a similar change during this period. However, despite the 75 years—Agnes von Krusenstjerna's *Fröknarna von Pahlen* came out in the 1930s, Annakarin Svedberg published her lesbian-themed novels in the 1960s, and Louise Boije af Gennäs and Mian Lodalen wrote their novels at the turn of the millennium—lesbianism is represented in surprisingly similar ways in these novels. All these works present both positive images of lesbianism and negative generalizations linked to the medical discourse to different degrees.

As stated in the introduction, there is a fairly established consensus about how homosexuality has been viewed in the Western world during the twentieth century. With the rise of sexology and psychoanalysis in the end of the nineteenth century, homosexuality was medicalized. The medical discourse was strong in the beginning of the twentieth century and led to the decriminalization of homosexuality in the Western countries—this happened in 1944 in Sweden. The gay and lesbian liberation movement starting in the 1960s and 1970s increased public awareness of gay and lesbian rights and led to a more open and tolerant attitude toward homosexuality. Although gays and lesbians still suffer from marginalization and stigmatization in the Western world today, the general tendency is to view the Western attitude to homosexuality during the twentieth century as one of progression—as a development from repression, persecution, and medicalization to liberation, visibility, and civil rights. Sweden, with its progressive laws for the gay and lesbian community, can be seen both as representative of this course of change and, at the same time, as a pioneer. Though same-sex legislation did not pass through the parliament smoothly, and though there is an ambiguity and ambivalence toward homosexuality in state policy documents, Sweden is still seen as one of the most gay-friendly countries in the world.

One of the aims of this book has been to explore the ways the literary discourse relates to these sociopolitical discourses on the Western progression of thought and on gay-friendly Sweden. As discussed in the introduction, Anglo-American literature seems to confirm and reinforce the discourse of progression; according to Anglo-American research, pre-Stonewall literature is generally populated by lesbian sickies and martyrs, while post-Stonewall literature celebrates lesbianism as a better option than heterosexuality and as a source of strength and empowerment for women. However, Swedish literature does not clearly confirm this idea of progression—despite the fact that Sweden is seen as one of the most liberal and progressive countries when it comes to homosexuality.

Instead, we have seen how lesbianism is represented in the same ambiguous way between 1930 and 2005; all these books reinforce but also challenge the medical discourse on lesbianism. In Agnes von Krusenstjerna's work, lesbianism is connected to a medical discourse established at the turn of the twentieth century, thus contributing to reinforcing 1930s sociopolitical understandings of lesbianism as medicalized. This pathologized understanding is present both in the stereotypical depictions of the lesbian as vampire or monster, as in Bell von Wenden, and in the positive depictions of, for instance, Angela and Agda's equal and empowering relationship. In Annakarin Svedberg's novels from the 1960s, the medical discourse established at the turn of the century is continually referred to, even more so than in Krusenstjerna's novels. For instance, the characters reflect on themselves in Freudian terms, and cause-and-effect connections are established between childhood traumas and adulthood lesbianism. In Louise Boije af Gennäs's and Mian Lodalen's turn-of-the-millennium novels, references to the medical discourse established at the end of the nineteenth century are less explicit and more subtle, but the medical discourse is present in, for example, the characterization of lesbians that the protagonists reject. The medical discourse has an even stronger presence in many other novels from the turn of the millennium, since so many of their lesbian characters come from dysfunctional families and suffer from poor psychological health.

On the other hand, the very same medical discourse is challenged in all the novels discussed in this study. In Krusenstjerna, the medical discourse's *masculinity* explanation to female homosexuality is challenged through the depiction of Angela and Agda as "real women"—their love for each other does not place them in the sexologists' "third sex" category. The challenging of society's (medicalized) understandings of lesbianism is articulated more strongly in Svedberg's novels compared to Krusenstjerna's. Svedberg's novels draw attention to the marginalization of lesbianism in contemporary society, and there is an attempt to "normalize" lesbianism by portraying it as not fundamentally different from heterosexuality. Moreover, these novels depict lesbian relationships as a better alternative for women. Heterosexuality and men are dismissed, and lesbianism is presented as empowering, allowing women to lead a life outside of male-dominated society. In Svedberg, men are dismissed as either inept or misogynists, leaving lesbianism as the only option for women to have equal and satisfying erotic relationships. In Boije af Gennäs and Lodalen, the dichotomy between heterosexuality and lesbianism is particularly emphasized in the representations of the body; the heterosexual body is controlled and policed in various ways, while the lesbian body is allowed more freedom. Furthermore, lesbianism opens up for a new kind of diversity in terms of gender expression and family constellation. Both Lodalen's and Krusenstjerna's novels end with the description of women living together in commune-like settings that allow for both same-sex relationships and children. By contributing with new dimensions of lesbianism that add to and challenge sociopolitical understandings, the novels become political in Rancière's sense. The books I have studied all contribute with affirming stories of lesbianism—as a better alternative than heterosexuality and as connected to a feminist project—and these stories, especially the ones from the 1930s and 1960s, directly oppose how lesbianism was understood in society. These novels also tell stories about the subordination of women and the marginalization of lesbianism, stories that contribute knowledge to a society that might not be as progressive when it comes to gender equality and LGBTQ rights as both Sweden and the rest of the world believe. In these two senses, the novels are political in an affirmative way; they add positive images of lesbianism and point to injustices in society in ways that call for change, and they even suggest a tool for change: the pen. But as we have seen, the novels also contribute with stories of medicalization of lesbianism, and hence they are also political in a way that conflicts with the affirmative politics these novels also represent. By holding onto a medical discourse, these novels might in fact be contributing to the marginalization of lesbians despite their more explicit intention to do the opposite.

Thus Swedish literature challenges both the discourse of a Western progressive attitude to homosexuality during the twentieth century as well as the discourse on a gay-friendly Sweden. In Swedish literature, lesbianism is not only represented as medicalized in the beginning of the century; it is also connected to a feminist project and depicted as a better option than heterosexuality. Conversely, the turn-of-the-millennium literary discourse on lesbianism not only is open and tolerant but also contains ideas based on the medical discourse, almost a century old. These representations in literature thus have far-reaching implications for every citizen, not just lesbians. An inclusive society is a fundamental principle in a democratic state like Sweden, and marginalizing specific groups undermines the society as a whole. As stated in the introduction, cultural representations are key to our understanding of the social reality, since the material world, as argued by Stuart Hall and others, has no meaning in itself; rather, meaning is shaped through language when we describe, or represent, the world. Furthermore, as argued by Sherrie A. Inness and Niall Richardson, cultural representations are of specific importance when it comes to the construction of homosexuality, since cultural representations provide many people with their only images of the LGBTQ community.

The ambiguous literary discourse on lesbianism that consistently appears throughout the twentieth century must then be considered a part of the broader Swedish discourse on lesbianism. The literary representations suggest that there are alternative ways of understanding lesbianism throughout this period. The representations of lesbianism as a way to escape male dominance in Krusenstjerna's novels from the 1930s and in Svedberg's from the 1960s suggest that what was later termed "radical feminist thinking" has been part of the discourse on lesbianism even before the rise of the radical feminist movement around 1970. As we have seen, Krusenstjerna's novels can even be more radical than the contemporary novels: While the misses von Pahlen actually start a women's commune, where women and children will live happily outside of the patriarchy, Sophie in *Stjärnor utan svindel* only dreams of living happily in a house with only women and no men. What was possible in Krusenstjerna's novels has become a utopian ideal at the turn of the millennium.

The broader sociopolitical discourse on lesbianism in the beginning of the twentieth century is hardly associated with positive aspects of lesbians and lesbian life, but this study of the literary discourse suggests that lesbianism not only was medicalized but could also have empowering dimensions and be connected to a feminist project. The readings also suggest that the discourse on lesbianism at the turn of the millennium is not only one of openness and tolerance, as the more general Western discourse on homosexuality indicates. Instead, the literary texts reveal that the medicalization of lesbianism has lasting power even today. The ambiguous discourse does, in part, correspond to the political ambiguity toward the LGBTQ community; the recurring discussions of homosexuality as "different" in policy documents reinforce a discourse where heterosexuality is the norm and homosexuality is deviant.

Negative aspects of today's discourse on homosexuality have been acknowledged by previous scholars, who have challenged not only the discourse but also the "affirmative turn" in queer criticism, with the mainstreaming and normalization of gay and lesbian culture as one of its aims (Edelman 2004; Love 2007). However, key to this book is that both affirmative and negative aspects exist in the literary discourse on lesbianism *at the same time* and that this contradictory discourse shows remarkable continuity during the twentieth century. For instance, while Lee Edelman argues that queers—as outsiders and representatives of the figure of negativity and the death drive—oppose a widely embraced discourse of reproductive futurism, manifested in the figure of the child, the Swedish literary discourse on lesbianism can encompass both queer negativity and reproductive futurism, sometimes even in the same characters. For example, the women at Eka in Krusenstjerna's *Fröknarna von Pahlen* decide to lead their lives without men, but in the end of the book series three of the women are pregnant and give birth to children. Mary and Agneta in Svedberg's *Se upp för trollen!* also give birth to a child. In both cases, imagery is used to stress the fruitful and loving aspects of the lesbian environment, which put a new twist on the Swedish family politics of the time, aimed at the heterosexual nuclear family. In the end of Lodalen's *Trekant*, Hedda is probably expecting a child with her female partner, and they live together in a house with a few other women and a dog, queering the surrounding heteronormative suburban environment. Despite the reproductive futurism, all these novels contain more or less explicit references to the medical discourse on lesbianism.

Foucault's definition of discourse—as a group of statements that provide a language for that which can be said and thought about a certain topic in a given context—emphasizes the importance of language in discursive practices (Foucault [1969] 2002; Foucault [1976] 1990). The novelists discussed in this book are forced to use the language of discourse when referring to phenomena in the world, and if the discourse on lesbianism contains medical dimensions, they might have no choice but to reinforce medicalization when writing about lesbianism. Monique Wittig illustrates this point when arguing that heterosexual language/discourse governs the way people think and perceive the world: "These discourses of heterosexuality oppress us in the sense that they prevent us from speaking unless we speak in their terms" (Wittig [1980] 1992, 25). However, Wittig suggests a way out of the oppressive discourses of heterosexuality. Since the concept of *woman* can only have meaning within the frames of heterosexuality as opposite and subordinate to men, lesbians are not women. According to Wittig, lesbianism is a kind of free space since it exists beyond the categories of *man* and *woman* in heterosexual discourse. What constitutes *woman* in a discourse governed by heterosexuality is a particular relation to *man*, a subordinate relation, but lesbians escape this relationship by refusing to be heterosexual (Wittig [1981] 1992, 9–20).

Wittig thus acknowledges how lesbianism can become a subversive force that challenges heterosexual discourse and its oppressive nature, and this has much in common with the way the Swedish literary discourse on lesbianism works. Despite the medicalizing dimension of the discourse, which sets boundaries for what can be said, lesbianism can offer freedom and empowerment for women. Furthermore, the literary representations of lesbianism as not any different from or even as a better alternative than heterosexuality are stories of lesbianism that become part of the common world. As part of this shared world, these stories open up discursive space for lesbianism and change society's understanding.

Writing plays an important role, both in lesbian-themed novels from the 1960s and from the turn of the millennium, and the faith in writing in these novels illustrates Rancière's idea of an essential connection between literature and politics. In fact, writing plays a significant role in Krusenstjerna's book series, too. In the last novel, *Av samma blod*, Petra von Pahlen finds her aunt Laura's old diary hidden in the seat of a chair. Laura used to live at the mansion as a widow, but the diary reveals that she had a love affair with a Romany man from Spain, an affair that resulted in a child. The child, Rosita, later gave birth to three daughters, and two of them turn out to be Agda and Frideborg. Moreover, Agda's father was, in fact, Petra's father, so Petra and Agda are half sisters—and Petra, Angela, Frideborg, and Agda are all related. Writing in the form of Aunt Laura's diary reveals "the truth" of the kinship and prompts Petra to invite Agda and Frideborg to Eka and include them in the women's commune.

In Krusenstjerna's novel, but also in Svedberg's, Boije af Gennäs's, and Lodalen's, writing becomes a means of telling "the truth" about lesbianism and women and to make an impact on society. The idea of "the truth" is, of course, a discursive construction, the result of meaning-making practices, but cultural representations are an important part of the construction of reality, especially when it comes to how we understand and make sense of homosexuality. The themes of autobiography and writing in these books highlight the need for new and "more true" stories of lesbianism that contribute to changing the shared world and revealing the connection between literature and politics. However, our language for these stories is intricately connected to a discourse tainted by medicalization. As a result, the stories of lesbianism told in twentieth-century literature both confirm and challenge sociopolitical discourses, and they contain negatively charged references to the medicalization of homosexuality as well as positive depictions of lesbianism. Hence the Swedish literary discourse on lesbianism is an ambiguous affair.

NOTES

INTRODUCTION

1. For a more detailed overview of the Western history of homo-sexuality, see, for instance, Hekma 2006, Rizzo 2006, and Tamagne 2006.
2. For a more detailed overview of the Swedish history of homo-sexuality, see, for instance, Norrhem, Rydström, and Winkvist 2008.
3. Gabriele Griffin describes a similar image of the lesbian literary history, although she mentions how post-Stonewall literature sometimes focused on women's rights to the extent that lesbian experiences are overlooked (Griffin 1993). Research has tended to focus on pre-Stonewall literature, but some work has been done on post-Stonewall literature as well.

   Faderman's "no lesbians before 1900" theory, as Terry Castle refers to it, has been criticized for making desire between women invisible prior to the rise of the science of sexuality, and many scholars have shown that, both in literature and in real-ity, eroticism between women existed in people's minds even before the rise of sexology (Castle 1993; Donoghue 1993; Marcus 2007; Moore 1997; Vanita 1996).

   Still, the late nineteenth century and the first part of the twentieth century come across as a dark period in lesbian literary history. Some scholars discuss how pre-Stonewall writers depict lesbianism as the impossible (Rohy 2000), the unrepresentable (Wachman 2001), or the secondary in Western culture during this period (Jagose 2002). Other scholars find that lesbianism in pre-Stonewall literature is a threat (Duggan 2000; Inness 1997), a problem (Abraham 1996; Smith 1997), or connected to loss and psychological disorder (Allen 1996; Coffman 2006). Despite a few exceptions (Johnston 2007; Kent 2003), research on pre-Stonewall literature generally confirms this period as a dark era for lesbianism in literature.

Similarly, research on post-Stonewall literature generally confirms the Faderman/Zimmerman view. Lesbian narratives are seen as utopian and deconstructive, since the lesbian subject rebels against male narrative structures and creates her own space (Farwell 1996). Post-Stonewall literature is seen as less homophobic (Smith 1997) and connected to feminism (Palmer 1993). However, Palmer (1993) notices a shift in the mid-1980s toward more diversity in lesbian writings, and in some research that deals with the post-Stonewall period, there are efforts to challenge the Faderman/Zimmerman view (Allen 1996; Hoogland 1997; Roof 1996). Some of these studies focus on other genres than literature as well or take literature from the pre-Stonewall period into account.

4. Eva Borgström is also working on a book on desire between women in Swedish literature from 1900 to 1930.

5. In fact, Scandinavian literary history provides a large variety of differentiated material for queer readings already in pre-modern times. Dodo Parikas's bibliographical overview of LGBTQ themes in literature is more than 400 pages. Parikas does not have scholarly intentions with his book, and his selection is arbitrary to some extent, but Swedish and Scandinavian literature still takes up more than half of the book, which says something about the frequency of queer themes in Scandinavian literature (Parikas 2009).

CHAPTER 1

1. The first monograph on her work, Stig Ahlgren's *Krusenstjerna-studier* (*Krusenstjerna Studies*), was published in 1940. Ten years later, Olof Lagercrantz's *Agnes von Krusenstjerna* ([1951] 1980) was the first dissertation on Krusenstjerna to be defended. Lagercrantz's work has been reprinted several times, and he was viewed as an authority on Krusenstjerna for many years. In 1989, Birgitta Svanberg published her dissertation *Sanningen om kvinnorna* (*The Truth about the Women*), contributing a feminist perspective on Krusenstjerna's work. A third dissertation on Krusenstjerna was published in 2007: Rita Paqvalén's *Kampen om Eros* (*The Struggle for Eros*). Paqvalén continued Svanberg's work by reading Krusenstjerna from a feminist perspective but adds a queer theory perspective as well. Merete Mazzarella published her book *Agnes von Krusenstjerna* in 1992, and in 2008 an anthology with essays on Krusenstjerna's

work, *Tänd eld!* (*Light the Fire*), was released (Björklund and Williams 2008). In 2013 Anna Williams published a biography of Krusenstjerna: *Från verklighetens stränder* (*From the Beaches of Reality*). Aside from the book-length studies, there are several book chapters and articles on Krusenstjerna. Barbro Backberger has published articles in two different anthologies (1968; 1981), and Eva Adolfsson has published two book chapters on Krusenstjerna (1983; 1991). Kristin Järvstad writes about Krusenstjerna's Tony trilogy published in the 1920s in her dissertation on women's coming-of-age novels in Sweden (1996). Anders Öhman has a chapter on Krusenstjerna's *Fattigadel* (*Poor Nobility*) in his book on Swedish confessional literature (2001), and Krusenstjerna is one of the writers Gunilla Domellöf focuses on in her book on women writers in Sweden during the 1930s (2001). Liv Saga Bergdahl has a long chapter on the 1930s in her dissertation on identity and (in)visibility in Swedish lesbian novels, which includes a discussion on Krusenstjerna (Bergdahl 2010). Both Anna Williams and Rita Paqvalén published book chapters and articles on her work before their monographs came out (Williams 2002; 2004; Paqvalén 2002b; 2003; 2004a; 2004b). I have published four articles and book chapters on Krusenstjerna (Björklund 2006; 2008a; 2008b; 2009).

2. "ett stort och kärleksfullt rike för barn och kvinnor." All English translations from *Fröknarna von Pahlen* are my own in collaboration with line editor Rebecca Ahlfeldt. The book series contains the following seven novels (the year of the original editions in parentheses): I. *Den blå rullgardinen* (1930; *The Blue Curtain*); II. *Kvinnogatan* (1930; *Women's Street*); III. *Höstens skuggor* (1931; *Shadows of the Fall*); IV. *Porten vid Johannes* (1933; *The Gate at Johannes's*); V. *Älskande par* (1933; *Loving Couples*); VI. *Bröllop på Ekered* (1935; *Wedding at Ekered*); VII. *Av samma blod* (1935; *From the Same Blood*). The second volume was translated into English in the 1980s by Janet E. Thompson, and the translation is available at Lund University Library. The manuscript is typed and bound but does not seem to be in print; it lacks an ISBN number. Ingalill Sandberg and Christina Swedberg at the Uppsala University Library have not been able to locate any other copies of the translation, despite much effort. I have also been in contact with Ingemar Perup at Krusenstjerna's publishing house Albert Bonniers Förlag, and

he could not find any information about the translation or the translator in their archives.

3. "Hon såg på kvinnorna, som en man ser på dem: med begärelse och heta önskningar. För henne var det helt naturligt att åtrå en ung kvinna, vilkens kropp blommade och doftade."

4. See also Greger Eman (1993), who makes a similar argument. However, he dates the shift of paradigms to 1920 and refers to the period before 1920 as the period of "the feminist friendship-love" and the period after 1920 as "the homosexual period." The homosexual period, as Eman defines it, is similar to Lundahl's definition of the individual-oriented view after 1930; like Lundahl, Eman emphasizes the influence of medical science. Also, Eman's definition of feminist friendship-love bears resemblance to Lundahl's definition of the practice-oriented view, but in addition to Lundahl's ideas, Eman views love between women during this period as a feminist statement with connections to the women's movement; women distanced themselves from men and chose to live with each other (13–28).

5. "Också väninnor kunna älska varandra. Det vet jag. Den kärleken är lättare att förstå. Jag tycker det. Män äro så olika oss. Aldrig förstå de oss. De leva i sig själva. Jag har aldrig träffat en man som inte var egoist. En man suger sin näring ur sitt eget starka jag. En kvinna måste alltid ha en annan att älska, att uppoffra sig för, att gråta och skratta tillsammans med. Hon är starkast då. Borde inte kärleken vara lyckligast, då den man har kär är lik en själv—också kroppsligen? De behag man själv äger beundrar man hos en annan i starkare grad. Man får ju icke kela med sig själv eller smeka sig själv. Det kallas narcissism. Men att famna en bild snarlik en själv, fastän vackrare och mera utvecklad, det är att söka forma sig efter fullkomligheten. Då mognar man, då blir man helt kvinna. Jag tror att vi måste nå utom oss själva, men vi förlora oss och gå alldeles vilse, om vi söka en tvillingsjäl så helt olika oss som en man är. Förstår du mig?"

6. "en ung kvinnas kropp"

7. "ett litet underligt huvud med hår som ålande ormar"

8. "hon hade älskat sig själv, njutit sig själv, ätit upp sitt hjärta, så att blodet nu dröp om hennes läppar"

9. "Ur den första förskräckliga rädslan för att få stryk växte så småningom upp ett underligt begär därefter. Ett rasande, kittlande begär, som gjorde hennes strupe torr och brännande och som jagade henne ända in i nattens drömmar. När föreståndarinnan fingrade på knapparna till hennes byxor, klängde hon sig fast

vid henne, snyftande, med vidöppna ögon och ryckande som i spasmer. Skammen, blygselkänslan, allt smalt bort för denna längtan efter den svidande smärta de där händerna tillfogade henne. Hon krängde och vred sig över föreståndarinnans knän blott för att i allt högre grad få känna njutningen av rappen, hettan i kroppen, de bultande pulsslagen. Hon begick handlingar, vilka stämplades som okynne och elakhet, endast för att ånyo skälvande få ledas fram till föreståndarinnan och mottaga straffet."

10. "det perversa barnet"

11. "Hon liknade en av dessa ljust röda blommor, som trivas i kärren och slingra sina slemmiga rötter allt djupare ned i dyn. De blomma i solskenet med huvudena ovanför den blanka vattenytan, medan de hämta all sin näring och allt sitt liv från den underjordiska och mörka ruttenhet, som de stå fast i. Likt dessa blommor levde Bell ett dubbelliv, tvingad därtill av dunkla drifter och av den miljö hon vuxit upp ur."

12. "Denna förnimmelse av kroppens och själens frihet hade hon aldrig förr haft."

13. "i synnerhet fruktade han dem, när de sökte nästla sig in hos kvinnobarn, som han själv ville beskydda eller få älska"

14. "Genom fönstret föll en svagt ljusgul solstrimma in. Angela tyckte att den såg ut som en påsklilja, då den fladdrade mot tapeten: ett tidigt budskap om att våren snart stod för dörren. Då, i april, skulle hon få sitt barn. Det skulle väckas av solen och växa med blåsipporna och vitsipporna."

15. "Rummet var ett drivhus där deras plötsliga kärleksblomma slagit ut. Den bedövade dem med sin vällukt. De sökte sig intill varandra, darrande av åtrå. [...] Detta var som i livets barndom då ingen ännu ätit av kunskapens träd på gott och ont. Det låg ljus och renhet och ett saligt lugn däri."

16. "Ja, Eka gamla gård var denna tid som ett drivhus."

17. "—Det är väl inte som när man blir kär i en man, sade [Agda] tankfullt. En man är så olika oss. Vi måste söka länge. Vi måste jämföra med oss själva. Vi äro helt enkelt på okänd mark. En kvinna förstår strax en annan kvinna därför att de äro så lika varandra, ha samma förutsättningar. Så där brukade åtminstone Bell förklara det."

18. "riktiga kvinnor, fast vi inte ha några män och inte behöva några heller nu"

19. "Lundstedt inte bara yrkade på straffrihet, han jämställde också homosexuella förbindelser med heterosexuella" (my translation).

20. Lundstedt argued that homosexual actions were as natural as heterosexual since both actions were natural expressions of a person's sexual drives, and according to Lundstedt this was true of both congenital and acquired homosexuality. He based his argument on a scientific paper attached to his motion, written by an anonymous physician arguing that homosexuality was not a disease but a "variety" (Lundstedt 1933, 15–20, 105–7).

21. On one occasion, Petra reflects on Angela and Agda's relationship and worries that they might have gone further in their love than "what was considered permissible" ("vad som betraktades som tillåtligt"; Av samma blod, 315). The passive tense suggests that Petra is expressing a common attitude in society rather than her own, which makes the passage somewhat ambiguous; other parts of the text seems to suggest that this normative attitude could be questioned.

22. "Jag har endast i högst sällsynta fall av heterosexuell kärlek funnit en så fullständig inlevelse, en så öm hängivenhet som man undantagslöst kan konstatera i homosexuella förhållanden mellan kvinnor" (my translation).

23. "endast två kvinnor och ett barn som de väntade och som de båda skulle vårda sig om och beskydda, när det kom. En familj skulle de vara. En liten helig familj på två kvinnor och ett barn, säkert en blivande kvinna också det."

24. "Charlie gick tidigt till sängs och låg och bläddrade i ett litet album med amatörfotografier. De föreställde alla Sara. Hon lade det under huvudkudden, släckte sin lampa och föll i en djup, sund sömn. Lakansspetsen höjde och sänkte sig med hennes jämna, långa andetag. Hon hämtade nya krafter i ungdomens helhjärtade, obrutna vila, som fullbordar det som växer.

   Hennes kropp var nu mogen att börja leva det liv, för vilket vår Herre behagat skapa henne" (my translation in collaboration with line editor Rebecca Ahlfeldt).

Chapter 2

1. Liv Saga Bergdahl reads one of Svedberg's novels in her dissertation, and Svedberg's work is discussed by Birgitta Holm in an article on the 1960s in Nordisk kvinnolitteraturhistoria (Bergdahl 2010; Holm and Schottenius 1997).

2. "Det fick inte vara så, att jag var kär i Carola. Det tog emot överallt. Carola var så olik mig på alla möjliga områden. Carina var lik mig, så henne fick jag älska. Inga var en modersgestalt, så henne fick jag älska. Men Carola? En pojkflicka. En flicka, med alltför stor önskan att vara man, att uppträda som man, att bli betraktad som man. Jag ville inte." All English translations from Svedberg's work are my own in collaboration with line editor Rebecca Ahlfeldt. The language of Svedberg's novels is often poetic and experimental, and I have tried to keep some of these characteristics in the translations.

3. "Det är något fel på min mor. En brist någonstans. En ödesdiger skavank, som gjorde henne nästan lika oduglig i livet, nästan lika motståndslös som en—som en nervklen, ja, men är det inte det hon är—är det inte . . . ?"

4. "Vem är Inga? Modern är anonym. Som jorden. Modern har inget ansikte. Bara ymniga, skänkande bröst, som aldrig sinar."

5. "Moder, moder min. Vem är du? Jag söker någon. Jag söker en mor. Här vilar kring mig moder kosmos, som den havande modern vilar kring det ofödda fostret. Här vilar jag som i sammetsnatt under gnistrande stjärnor och bidar min födelsetid. Här vilar. Jag.

Det fanns en annan kvinna. Det fanns en annan mor. Var hon, som dessa djupa oceaner? Var hon, som denna varma vind och jord och himmel? Någonstans skedde en felräkning. Hennes öde slogs sönder mot en obarmhärtighet. Det är hon, som gör så ont i mig, som splittrat glas i mina ådror. Det är hon. Moder. Moder min. Jag låg i hennes famn en gång, kanske. Moder, Moder min. Dina kristaller var krossade långt innan min tid. Kan du förstå det?

Jag kände Ingas hårda bröstvårta mot min tungspets, och fann mellan väldiga lår ett drypande kvinnosköte."

6. "Aldrig tidigare hade hon känt en sådan sorg över att behöva skiljas från någon. Jo, som barn, då modern varit tvungen att resa bort för sin svåra sjukdoms skull och senare, ännu värre, då modern oåterkalleligen dött."

7. "Aldrig tidigare i sitt liv hade hon ens varit i närheten av en sådan känsla.—Den enda människa, inför vilken hon nånsin hyst jämförbara känslor, var hennes döda mor."

8. "obotlig hysterika"

9. "Fuktiga blygdhår trasslar in sig i varandra och brösten pressas samman. Hand söker bröst. Mun söker bröstvårta."

10. "I din kropp känner jag igen en kvinnas kropp. Din kind är mjuk mot min och inte sträv."
11. "Då blir hon bara kär i dig, och så blir du aldrig av med henne."
12. "Nej, jag vågar inte, för då blir jag kanske aldrig av med dig sen. Jag vet, hur tjejer är. De suger sig fast."
13. "den *falska* tron på den homosexuella kärlekens starkare känslomässiga engagerande"
14. "Och hur nära madrasser än ligger varandra, så är också en liten sprutta en sprutta, som förhindrar älskande att krypa in i varandra och somna så tätt hopslingrade, som de önskar."
15. "Hon gjorde verkligen inget djupare intryck på mig, verkade snarast lite tråkig, charmlös och trist.—Typisk flata, tänkte jag och tittade på hennes långbyxor, mörkblå tröja, kort klippta hår och ograciösa rörelser."
16. "Carina var mycket vacker i sin stol, hade höga klackar och rak, åtsittande klänning, och hon tittade på mig med sina gröna ögon."
17. "—Det där är inte någon vanlig väninna, sa han bistert till sin kvinnliga kollega. Jag har väl varit med förr.—Men det är konstigt, jag förstår det inte. De är ju så kvinnliga båda två."
18. For a more detailed overview, see Lennerhed 1994, 70–88, and Söderström 2000.
19. "inte känsligare än en gammal traktor"
20. "Jag sa ingenting. Jag hörde och visste, att jag inte ville hålla med honom. Jag visste, att jag ville säga helt andra saker, men sa ingenting."
21. "—Vicka karlar vi har omkring oss! säger hon och skakar på huvudet."
22. "I en bok har vi funnit en bild av en man, ritad av en prostituterad.
    —En penis med ett huvud på! sa Brita.
    —Och en så slankig en, sa jag. Den är ju impotent!
    —Ja, den duger inte mycket till. Så nu vet vi det."
23. "Sekelgammal uppfattning om kvinnan som en sig mannen underordnande varelse trängde sig på dem. Inför vilken man det vara må, stod de där plötsligt utan vilja och val och utan bestämmanderätt över sina egna handlingar. Det var inte bara deras kärlek som reagerade. Det fanns en än djupare och mer allmänmänsklig klangbotten av muttrande ovilja. Där fanns en stark irritation över, att dessa män betraktade sitt eget sällskap som något så självklart attraktivt, att varje kvinna, om inte lycklig, så dock smickrad, väntades svara mot deras handtryckningar och omslingringar."

24. "Det var något ceremoniellt över det sätt, varpå de grekiska männen hoppades nå kontakt med en kvinna—mannen spelade sin roll, den han från barndomen identifierat sig med, och han väntade med samma självklarhet, som en skådespelare väntar, att hans medaktörer skall hålla sig till pjäsen, att kvinnorna skulle spela sin."

25. "Samtliga tre kvinnliga turnémedlemmar beredde han stort besvär, inte enbart genom att oförtrutet söka deras sällskap, utan framför allt genom sina fysiska närmanden. Trots deras ideliga avvisanden, gick han varje afton hoppfullt till ny attack. Men ingen var hågad."

26. "ty hur det än var, så var hon beroende av hans kärlek. Om den skulle försvinna—ja, vart skulle hon då ta vägen i tillvaron?"

27. "tråkig stämning i hemmet"

28. "Mary lutade sig över Edvin och kysste honom.
    —Nu, min älskade, sa hon, vill jag ha ett barn. Jag vill inte vänta längre. Vad väntar vi på? Vi har allt vi behöver—lägenhet, badrum, modernt kök med elspis, två rum—det räcker i alla fall de första åren—gott om skåp och garderober, trevliga möbler, kylskåp, ett bra skafferi, god köksutrustning, tjugo par lakan, sextio örngott, fyra dussin handdukar och fyra dussin kökshanddukar, två dussin frotté och fyra utmärkta badlakan."

29. "Det där uppslaget med att 'sy själv era sängkammargardiner' hade hon fått från Husmodern. 'I ljuvligt blått, skirt rosa eller vitt'."

30. "Men förtroende kan inte framtvingas—det hade hon läst i Damernas Värld och ofta hört i radio."

31. "Skulle inte jag vara karl nog att själv kunna försörja hustru och barn?"

32. "Och han satte upp henne på sadelknappen, svepte sin mantel kring henne och red i sporrsträck i väg. Ett moln av damm virvlades upp kring dem och fradgan stod kring hästens mun.—Inne i manteln sprattlade Mona, skrek och levde rövare, slog med knytnävarna, bet omkring sig i vild ilska. 'Jag vill inte jag vill inte!' Men *han* ville. Och det var i denna stund den avgörande faktorn."

33. "efter små gröna strån i den svarta jord, som de besått"

34. "var övervuxen av blommor och grönt: murgröna, ringblommor, rosor, tulpaner, narcisser—allt möjligt växande klängde utmed väggar och grodde i rabatter"

35. "En gång hade hon varit den lockande sirenen med oemotståndlig dragningskraft. Varenda karl hade blivit knasig av att se

henne. Så jobbig den tiden varit! Ett himla besvär att hålla dem på lagom avstånd utan att de tappade intresset!"

36. "Rabatterna prunkar, träden står i blom."
37. "Där är det igen. Får kvinnor älska kvinnor. Och i så fall hur?
    Det är svårt att komma över det. Man tror ibland, att man har gjort det, men så dyker tvivlet upp igen som en syl genom hjärtat. Somom homosexuella känslor inte vore riktiga känslor. Somom homosexualitet inte vore riktig sexualitet. Men den är riktig, jag vet det. Lika nyanserad, lika betydelsefull, lika intensiv och innerlig som annan sexualitet."
38. "två förvridna individer"
39. "det mångfacetterade begrepp som går under ett enda namn: kärlek"
40. "Måhända är just därför sådana förbindelser i vissa kretsar en aning illa sedda. Man brukar i sammanhanget tala om 'njutning utan ändamål', vad de nu kunna mena med det, eller vilka erfarenheter som ligger bakom ett sådant yttrande!"
41. "—Men dit borde man ju gå! Det verkar festligt! Vad gör de där? Sitter och diskuterar hur de skall påverka den allmänna opinionen med broschyrer och möten och kampanjer . . . och återigen börjar jag skratta på ett otillbörligt muntert sätt åt dessa olyckliga människor.
    —Å, det är allvarligt, säger Carola, som själv är allvarlig nu och lite generad över min munterhet och sina egna komplex.—De vill naturligtvis vara som alla andra.
    —Men det blir de ju inte! Inte på det sättet! Så att de vill införa legitimerade homosexuella förbindelser, som äktenskap då?"
42. "De såg patetiska ut i den mulna dagern. Kantiga, ensamma—två under träden i allén. Med bleka händer klibbande samman i den råa luften. Längre bort kom en man och en kvinna. Mjukt och självfallet höll de om varandra, log, pratade. Var lyckliga."
43. "där män och kvinnor ännu har kvar sin identitet"
44. "flutit isär"
45. "Jag vill skriva, skriva, skriva. Låta skiten välla ur mig. Allt, skiten, lyckan, slagget och de glimrande välsignade ögonblicken—det glimrande, välsignade livet, växandet, hoppet, tron, kärleken och döden."
46. "nu"
47. "Stella sitter nu i mitt knä. Lite svårt att skriva, men det går."

48. "Jag säger så fåniga saker i det du skriver. Det är en vrångbild av mig. Varför säger du inte hur tjusig jag är? Varför står det inte: Nu går Brita så vackert ned mot pinjen, till exempel."

CHAPTER 3

1. I have discussed the coming-out process in contemporary Swedish youth novels elsewhere (Björklund 2013). See also Bergdahl 2010, 259–70.

2. Rita Paqvalén has written an article on *Stjärnor utan svindel*, and the novel is discussed in Liv Saga Bergdahl's article on lesbian literature and in her dissertation (Paqvalén 2002a; Bergdahl 2006; Bergdahl 2010). Sociologist Margareta Lindholm has written about *Smulklubbens skamlösa systrar* and Eva Alexanderson's *Kontradans* (1969) from a sociological perspective, comparing the situation for lesbians in the 1960s and in contemporary society (Lindholm 2005).

3. "Detta skedde för att vi kvinnor sakta men säkert, från Askungen som barn och fram till Pretty Woman i vuxen ålder, hade övertygats om att en man i ett heterosexuellt romantiskt föhållande var själva grunden för vår existens, och att vi aldrig skulle bli lyckliga utan den. I avsaknad av en man skulle vi förbli anställda slavar eller horor, det var sens moralen i dessa berättelser." All English translations from Boije af Gennäs's and Lodalen's novels are my own in collaboration with line editor Rebecca Ahlfeldt.

4. "Han var söt och lockig, och jag behövde inte ta på mig alla andras problem. Vi i vår kokong, vi i vår trygghet. Nyhetsuppläsaren pratade om kriget i Bosnien, men jag blundade och koncentrerade mig intensivt på att bara andas."

5. "Som ett vårdtecken omsluter oss denna ring, likt ett band av metall. Från guldring till järngrepp."

6. "Kvinnor är vackra, kloka, intelligenta och duktiga. Män är fula, dumma, meningslösa och inkompetenta. Det är samma sak hela tiden. Vart man än tittar. I familjer, i förhållanden, på jobbet, i politiken. Varenda gång någonting meningsfullt blir gjort— sjukvård, omsorg, ta hand om gamla och fattiga, bistå flyktingar och krigsoffer—så är det kvinnors verk. Och alltid när någon sorts skit händer—nedskärningar, starta krig, våldtäkter, hustrumisshandel, barnmisshandel, oprovocerat våld på gatorna—så är det män som ligger bakom. Hela tiden. Utan undantag."

7. "varför kan vi inte bo tillsammans du och jag och några andra tjejer i ett hus fullt av lyckliga kvinnor?"
8. "Men det känns också som om Kaja förlöser mig, på ett annat sätt, efter åratal av jobbiga relationer till män. Och jag tänker att om fler tjejer insåg att vi kan vara tillsammans med varandra, så skulle MYCKET stora delar av det kvinnliga, heterosexuella utbudet försvinna från marknaden."
9. "Det här var inte en man som ville förtrycka mig, bestämma över mig, förnedra mig, spruta in sin säd i mig. Det här var en kvinna som var kåt tillsammans med mig, som älskade mig och därför ville göra mig lycklig."
10. "Lukas var upphetsad, men jag kände att han var långt borta."
11. "Ingen, jag säger ingen, flata skulle spöka ut sig sådär. Får en plötslig emapti för all världens heterokvinnor. Är detta vad som krävs för att vara gångbar på dagens marknad? Varför skulle de annars slösa så mycket tid, energi och stålar på sitt yttre?"
12. "Det räcker att lesbiska har sex en gång för att börja fumla med förlovningsringarna.

    Men jag är undantaget som bekräftar regeln. Behöver faktiskt inte identifiera mig med hela flatsamhället. Kan fatta egna beslut om mitt eget liv. Ska trotsa normen och satsa på att träffa en Älskarinna."
13. "Här trycks fyrahundra brudar in på ett och samma ställe och nästan alla har legat med en eller flera, eller haft relationer med varandra och minst trettio stycken är fortfarande intresserade av den förra som nu redan limmar på en ny som dessutom råkar vara ens gamla ex och så vidare och så vidare i en enda sörja."
14. "tröttsam radikalfeminism"
15. "Fattaru hur vidrigt det är att ständigt behöva befatta sig med fienden? Tror du man kan träna upp sig till flata?"
16. "Jävla skata—äckliga flata"
17. "Som om det vore en gång man gör det och sedan är det över. Jag kommer ut varenda dag."
18. "Folk utgår ifrån att man inte kan vara homo. Inte ens när man säger det rakt ut."
19. This was the case when *Smulklubbens skamlösa systrar* was written, but the laws have changed since then. In 2005, lesbians gained the right to assisted reproduction in Swedish hospitals.
20. "Jag betalar lika mycket skatt som alla andra, men jag kan inte åtnjuta samma rättigheter."
21. "Vi har så många fler möjligheter att erbjuda! Allt från äktenskap till samboförhållande till att vara särbo till att ha en familj

med en pappa och två mammor till att en har barn och den andra har en egen våning till att man övergår till att vara älskarinnor till att man bara blir väninnor. Och dessutom kan man vara olika saker under olika perioder utan att folk tittar snett."

22. "Kärlek i alla former, allt var tillåtet; ingenting var omöjligt eftersom hela relationen per definition var en anomali enligt samhällets normer. Och därmed blev istället allting möjligt, samtidigt som det blev extra förbjudet och spännande. Man kunde vara kvinna, man kunde vara som en man, man kunde leva ut och leka fram alla sin personlighets sidor. Man var i ordets rätta bemärkelse en hel människa."

23. "De kunde både laga mat och laga bilen. De kunde både klä sig i klänning och kostym, de kunde både slicka fitta och sätta på varandra med dildo. De var kvinnor och bejakade sina känsliga sidor, samtidigt som de inte förnekade sin styrka och aggressivitet."

24. "Barn med två mammor, tre farsor, en mamma och förhoppningsvis en bunt av coola människor runt ungen, inte nödvändigtvis med biologiska släktband"

25. "Vad är jag då? Blandras, som jag en gång sa när jag var sex år och på lekskolan fick frågan om jag var en pojke eller flicka."

26. "Ett vilt kackel bryter loss när Linn, Clara, Läder-Kim, Mackan, Kåta Anette och två tjejer som jag inte känner igen gör entré samtidigt. Jag scannar av att de är hetero på fyra sekunder. Måste vara Heddas jobbarpolare som hon har pratat om. En av dem har en tajt topp som blottar magen och en kort kjol som liknar en vaxduk från 10-gruppen. Den andra bär vit, kort kjol med spets i allmogestil. Ser ut som om hon fastnat i sin mormors spetsgardin på förra släktträffen. Ovanpå gardinen har hon något sladdrigt och grällt med båtringning och snören som man inte hajar var de kommer ifrån och fötterna är nedstoppade i små stövletter med åttiotalsklack. Brösten är uppressade så att bröstvårtorna är i linje med armvecken och sminkningen för tankarna till en festreklam för Max Factor. Ingen, jag säger ingen, flata skulle spöka ut sig sådär. Får en plötslig empati för all världens heterokvinnor."

27. "De kan knappast springa ifrån en våldtäktsman i de där antifeministiska stilettklackarna"

28. "för smal sa en del och jag beklagade mig ibland, men i hemlighet var jag mycket nöjd med detta faktum"

29. "Jag studsade till och såg upp, rakt in i ett par bekanta ögon. Men det var också det enda. Skinnet spände och stramade över

hennes kindben, och hon hade vattniga sår i ansiktet. Det var en kvinna som såg ut att vara minst femtio år gammal och nyligen utsläppt från ett koncentrationsläger. Hon skulle snart dö, det framgick tydligt."

30. "De är vackra, framgångsrika och begåvade, och deras fruar är lagom kloka och lagom smala och har lagom stora bröst."
31. "lägga en kabel"
32. "Om de inte vill bli betraktade som små kåta hyndor."
33. "Jag är ingen man, du är inte min fru och jag är inte mer drivande än du i den här relationen. Vi är kvinnor båda två, du är min jämlike, och måste själv ta ansvar för när du vill ha sex. Och när du inte vill. Precis som jag."
34. "förkroppsligad sexualitet"
35. "Hos de lesbiska fanns en stor mängd kunskap som heterosexuella kvinnor kunde dra nytta av, kunskap som rörde sexualitet och bejakande av den egna kroppen, som rörde styrka, som rörde vilja och förmåga att överleva i ett patriarkat."
36. "Värdinneskapets plikter, man var som uppvridbar. Tick, tick, tick; vassa klackar mot parketten; röda, blanka läppar, lika röda naglar; ädla stenar, glänsande ögon, skinande hår som liksom studs-studs-studsade medan man rörde sig."
37. "Hyreskaserner, smutsiga fasader; hela kvarteret andades arbetarklass och misär"
38. "en annan värld. Här fanns inga såssnipor i silver, inga inramade släktporträtt, inga bordstabletter med fågelmotiv. Ett skåp stod öppet och avslöjade travar av urtvättade T-shirts och stickade tröjor. En randig trasmatta låg på golvet. Halvt sönderrivna affischer satt uppnålade på väggarna. Överallt stod växter. I vardagsrummet dammiga, omatchade möbler som föreföll att komma från någon typ av second-hand-affär."
39. "ett igenkännande"
40. "likhet rådde och inte olikhet. Allt jag gjorde skedde simultant med mig, med min kropp."
41. "Först förstod jag inte vad hon menade. Sedan: att slicka mig på samma gång. Jag kände mig oviss om vad jag skulle göra, hur jag skulle flytta mig i sängen. Kaja visade. Hon vände sig om, så att jag hamnade med mitt sköte precis i höjd med hennes ansikte. Tvillingar i samma moderliv, filippinnötter i ett, enda skal. Ärtskidor, apelsinklyftor; kalvar i en fålla. Stjärnor i samma tecken."
42. "hon var precis som jag"
43. "Jag är en människa"

44. "den världsberömda lesbiska tvåsamheten"
45. "det särskilt för lesbiska symbiotiska samboskapet"
46. "Allt jag vill är att vara nära. Omhuldad. Omhändertagen. Sedd. Älskad."
47. "Som mina böcker och TV-program, men denna gång av kött och blod och ben"

References

Abraham, Julie. 1996. *Are Girls Necessary? Lesbian Writing and Modern Histories*. New York: Routledge.

Adolfsson, Eva. 1983. "Drömmen om badstranden: Kvinnobilder i trettitalslitteraturen, särskilt hos Agnes von Krusenstjerna och Moa Martinson." In *Kvinnor och skapande: En antologi om litteratur och konst tillägnad Karin Westman Berg*, edited by Birgitta Paget, Birgitta Svanberg, Barbro Werkmäster, Margareta Wirmark, and Gabriella Åhmansson, 207–19. Stockholm: Författarförlaget.

———. 1991. *I gränsland: Essäer om kvinnliga författarskap*. Stockholm: Bonnier.

Ahlgren, Stig. 1940. *Krusenstjerna-studier*. Stockholm: Bonnier.

Ahmed, Sara. 2006. *Queer Phenomenology: Orientations, Objects, Others*. Durham: Duke University Press.

Alexanderson, Eva. 1964. *Fyrtio dagar i öknen*. Stockholm: Bonnier.

———. 1969. *Kontradans*. Stockholm: Bonnier.

Allen, Carolyn. 1996. *Following Djuna: Women Lovers and the Erotics of Loss*. Bloomington: Indiana University Press.

Andersson, Catrine. 2011. *Hundra år av tvåsamhet: Äktenskapet i svenska statliga utredningar 1909–2009*. Lund: Arkiv.

Andreasson, Martin. 2000. "Samhällsfara eller samhällsgrupp? Riksdagens syn på homo- och bisexuella." In *Homo i folkhemmet: Homo- och bisexuella i Sverige 1950–2000*, edited by Martin Andreasson, 36–58. Göteborg: Anamma.

Backberger, Barbro. (1966) 2003. *Det förkrympta kvinnoidealet*. Stockholm: Pocky.

———. 1968. "'Vi skulle inte inbilla oss att vi voro fria': Den urspårade kvinnorevolten i Krusenstjernas romaner." In *Könsroller i litteraturen från antiken till 1960-talet*, edited by Karin Westman Berg, 140–67. Stockholm: Prisma.

———. 1981. "Samhällsklass och kvinnoliv: En studie i Agnes von Krusenstjernas och Moa Martinsons författarskap." In *Kvinnornas litteraturhistoria*, vol. 1, edited by Marie Louise Ramnefalk and Anna Westberg, 368–97. Stockholm: Författarförlaget.

192 REFERENCES

Barr, Bonnie. 2009. "Regnbuefamilier i Danmark, Sverige og Norge." In *Regnbågsfamiljers ställning i Norden: Politik, rättigheter och villkor*, edited by Jennie Westlund, 17–173. Oslo: NIKK.

Bartky, Sandra Lee. 1990. *Femininity and Domination: Studies in the Phenomenology of Oppression*. New York: Routledge.

Beauvoir, Simone de. (1949) 2010. *The Second Sex*. Translated by Constance Borde and Sheila Malovany-Chevallier. New York: Alfred A. Knopf.

Bergdahl, Liv Saga. 2006. "Fredade zoner och offentliga rum: Om 'lesbisk litteratur' och 'öppenhet.'" *lambda nordica* 11 (1–2): 47–59.

———. 2010. *Kärleken utan namn: Identitet och (o)synlighet i svenska lesbiska romaner*. Umeå: Institutionen för kultur- och medievetenskaper, Umeå universitet.

Björk, Nina. 1996. *Under det rosa täcket: Om kvinnlighetens vara och feministiska strategier*. Stockholm: Wahlström and Widstrand.

Björklund, Jenny. 2006. "Frihet, jämlikhet, systerskap: Samkönat begär och gränsöverskridande kärlek i Agnes von Krusenstjernas *Fröknarna von Pahlen*." *Tidskrift för litteraturvetenskap* 35 (3–4): 65–83.

———. 2008a. "Angela + Stanny = sant: Samkönad kärlek som politik i Agnes von Krusenstjernas *Fröknarna von Pahlen*." In *Tänd eld! Essäer om Agnes von Krusenstjernas författarskap*, edited by Jenny Björklund and Anna Williams, 119–56. Stockholm: Norstedts Akademiska Förlag.

———. 2008b. "Kärlekens gränsland: Kvinnlig homosexualitet i Agnes von Krusenstjernas *Fröknarna von Pahlen*." In *Gränser i nordisk litteratur/Borders in Nordic Literature, IASS XXVI 2006*, vol. 2, edited by Clas Zilliacus, Heidi Grönstrand, and Ulrika Gustafsson, 544–51. Åbo: Åbo Akademis förlag.

———. 2009. "Den heliga familjen: Heteronormativitet och kvinnlighet i Agnes von Krusenstjernas *Fröknarna von Pahlen*." In *En bok om genus: Nyfikenhet, nytänkande, nytta*, edited by Christina Angelfors and Eva Schömer, 57–78. Växjö: Växjö University Press.

———. 2013. "Coming Out, Coming In: Geographies of Lesbian Existence in Contemporary Swedish Youth Novels." In *Sexuality, Rurality, and Geography*, edited by Andrew Gorman-Murray, Barbara Pini, and Lia Bryant, 159–71. Lanham: Lexington Books.

Björklund, Jenny, and Anna Williams, eds. 2008. *Tänd eld! Essäer om Agnes von Krusenstjernas författarskap*. Stockholm: Norstedts Akademiska Förlag.

Boije af Gennäs, Louise. 1996. *Stjärnor utan svindel.* Stockholm: Norstedt.

Bordo, Susan. 1993. *Unbearable Weight: Feminism, Western Culture, and the Body.* Berkeley: University of California Press.

Borgström, Eva. 2008. *Kärlekshistoria: Begär mellan kvinnor i 1800-talets litteratur.* Göteborg: Kabusa.

Boye, Karin. 1934. *Kris.* Stockholm: Bonnier.

Butler, Judith. (1990) 1999. *Gender Trouble: Feminism and the Subversion of Identity.* New York: Routledge.

Caprio, Frank S. (1954) 1958. *Kvinnlig homosexualitet.* Translated by Erik Janson. Stockholm: Centralpress.

Castle, Terry. 1993. *The Apparitional Lesbian: Female Homosexuality and Modern Culture.* New York: Columbia University Press.

Claesson, Marlene. 2005. *Bisexuell.* Uttran: Anormativa.

Coffman, Christine E. 2006. *Insane Passions: Lesbianism and Psychosis in Literature and Film.* Middletown: Wesleyan University Press.

Domellöf, Gunilla. 1986. *I oss är en mångfald levande: Karin Boye som kritiker och prosamodernist.* Umeå: Umeå universitet.

———. 2001. *Mätt med främmande mått: Idéanalys av kvinnliga författares samtidsmottagande och romaner 1930–1935.* Hedemora: Gidlunds.

Donoghue, Emma. 1993. *Passions between Women: British Lesbian Culture 1668–1801.* London: Scarlet Press.

Duggan, Lisa. 2000. *Sapphic Slashers: Sex, Violence, and American Modernity.* Durham: Duke University Press.

Dworkin, Andrea. (1987) 2007. *Intercourse.* New York: Basic Books.

Edelman, Lee. 2004. *No Future: Queer Theory and the Death Drive.* Durham: Duke University Press.

Edenheim, Sara. 2005. *Begärets lagar: Moderna statliga utredningar och heteronormativitetens genealogi.* Stockholm/Stehag: Symposion.

Ellis, Havelock. (1901) 1920. *Studies in the Psychology of Sex.* Vol. 2, *Sexual Inversion.* 3rd revised edition. Philadelphia: F. A. Davis.

Eman, Greger. 1993. *Nya himlar över en ny jord: Om Klara Johanson, Lydia Wahlström och den feministiska vänskapskärleken.* Lund: Ellerström.

Faderman, Lillian. (1981) 2001. *Surpassing the Love of Men: Romantic Friendship and Love between Women from the Renaissance to the Present.* New York: Perennial.

Farwell, Marilyn R. 1996. *Heterosexual Plots and Lesbian Narratives.* New York: New York University Press.

Fjelkestam, Kristina. 2002. *Ungkarlsflickor, kamrathustrur och man-haftiga lesbianer: Modernitetens litterära gestalter i mellankrigs-tidens Sverige*. Stockholm/Stehag: Symposion.

———. 2005. "Tale of Transgression: *Charlie* and the Representation of Female Homosexuality in Interwar Sweden." *NORA—Nordic Journal of Feminist and Gender Research* 13 (1): 9–19.

Foucault, Michel. (1969) 2002. *Archaeology of Knowledge*. Translated by A. M. Sheridan Smith. London: Routledge Classics.

———. (1976) 1990. *The History of Sexuality*. Vol. 1, *An Introduction*. Translated by Robert Hurley. Harmondsworth: Penguin.

Freud, Sigmund. (1905) 1953. "Three Essays on the Theory of Sexuality." In *The Standard Edition of the Complete Psychological Works of Sigmund Freud*, vol. 7, 123–245. Translated under the general editorship of James Strachey in collaboration with Anna Freud. London: Hogarth Press and the Institute of Psycho-Analysis.

———. (1914) 1957. "On Narcissism: An Introduction." In *The Standard Edition of the Complete Psychological Works of Sigmund Freud*, vol. 14, 67–102. Translated under the general editorship of James Strachey in collaboration with Anna Freud. London: Hogarth Press and the Institute of Psycho-Analysis.

———. (1920) 1955. "The Psychogenesis of a Case of Homosexuality in a Woman." In *The Standard Edition of the Complete Psychological Works of Sigmund Freud*, vol. 18, 145–72. Translated under the general editorship of James Strachey in collaboration with Anna Freud. London: Hogarth Press and the Institute of Psycho-Analysis.

Friedan, Betty. 1963. *The Feminine Mystique*. New York: W. W. Norton.

Gilbert, Sandra M., and Susan Gubar. (1979) 2000. *The Madwoman in the Attic: The Woman Writer and the Nineteenth-Century Literary Imagination*. New Haven: Yale University Press.

Granberg, Anna-Karin. 1992. *Där ingenting kan ses: En familjeberät-telse*. Stockholm: Wahlström and Widstrand.

———. 1994. *Längre bort än hit*. Stockholm: Wahlström and Widstrand.

Griffin, Gabriele. 1993. *Heavenly Love? Lesbian Images in Twentieth-Century Women's Writing*. Manchester: Manchester University Press.

Halberstam, Judith. 1998. *Female Masculinity*. Durham: Duke University Press.

Hall, Stuart. 1997. "The Work of Representation." In *Representation: Cultural Representations and Signifying Practices*, edited by Stuart Hall, 13–74. London: Sage.

Hallbeck, Nils. 1969. *En kvinnas älskarinna*. Stockholm: Hson.

Hallgren, Hanna. 2008. *När lesbiska blev kvinnor—När kvinnor blev lesbiska: Lesbiskfeministiska kvinnors diskursproduktion rörande kön, sexualitet, kropp och identitet under 1970- och 1980-talen i Sverige*. Göteborg: Kabusa.

Hekma, Gert. 2006. "The Gay World: 1980 to the Present." In *Gay Life and Culture: A World History*, edited by Robert Aldrich, 333–63. London: Thames and Hudson.

Hirdman, Yvonne. 1990. "Genussystemet." In *Demokrati och makt i Sverige: Maktutredningens huvudrapport*, SOU 1990:44, 73–116. Stockholm: Allmänna Förlaget.

———. (1992) 2004. "Kvinnorna i välfärdsstaten: Sverige 1930–1990." In *Kvinnohistoria: Om kvinnors villkor från antiken till våra dagar*, edited by Birgit Janrup-Dünkelberg, Christina Florin, and Yvonne Hirdman, 203–18. Stockholm: Utbildningsradion.

———. (2001) 2003. *Genus: Om det stabilas föränderliga former*. Malmö: Liber.

Holm, Birgitta, and Maria Schottenius. 1997. "Att ge sig världen i våld: Nya litterära fronter." In *Nordisk kvinnolitteraturhistoria*. Vol. 4, *På jorden 1960–1990*, edited by Elisabeth Møller Jensen, Unni Langås, Anne-Marie Mai, Anne Birgitte Richard, Maria Schottenius, and Lisbeth Larsson, 88–96. Höganäs: Bra Böcker.

Hoogland, Renée. 1997. *Lesbian Configurations*. Cambridge: Polity.

Inness, Sherrie A. 1997. *The Lesbian Menace: Ideology, Identity, and the Representation of Lesbian Life*. Amherst: University of Massachusetts Press.

Isaksson, Emma. 2007. *Kvinnokamp: Synen på underordning och motstånd i den nya kvinnorörelsen*. Stockholm: Atlas.

Jagose, Annamarie. 2002. *Inconsequence: Lesbian Representation and the Logic of Sexual Sequence*. Ithaca: Cornell University Press.

Järvstad, Kristin. 1996. *Att utvecklas till kvinna: Studier i den kvinnliga utvecklingsromanen i 1900-talets Sverige*. Stockholm/Stehag: Symposion.

———. 2008. *Den kluvna kvinnligheten: "Öfvergångskvinnan" som litterär gestalt i svenska samtidsromaner 1890–1920*. Stockholm/Stehag: Symposion.

Johnston, Georgia. 2007. *The Formation of 20th-Century Queer Auto-biography: Reading Vita Sackville-West, Virginia Woolf, Hilda Doolittle, and Gertrude Stein*. New York: Palgrave Macmillan.

Kent, Kathryn R. 2003. *Making Girls into Women: American Women's Writing and the Rise of Lesbian Identity*. Durham: Duke University Press.

Key, Ellen. 1903. *Lifslinjer*, vol. 1. Stockholm: Bonnier.

Krafft-Ebing, Richard von. (1886) 1998. *Psychopathia Sexualis: With Especial Reference to the Antipathic Sexual Instinct: A Medico-Forensic Study*. Translated from the 12th German edition by Franklin S. Klaf (1965). New York: Arcade.

Krusenstjerna, Agnes von. 1944–46. *Samlade skrifter*. Commented and edited by Johannes Edfelt. Stockholm: Bonnier.

Kuhlefelt, Eva. 2009. "Manhaftig lesbian eller gentlemannabutch? Om konstruktionen av kvinnomaskulinitet i Margareta Subers roman *Charlie* (1932)." In *Bloch, butch, Bertel: Kontextuella litteraturstudier*, edited by Michel Ekman and Kristina Malmio, 69–83. Åbo: Litteraturvetenskap, Åbo Akademi.

Lagercrantz, Olof. (1951) 1980. *Agnes von Krusenstjerna*. Stockholm: Bonnier.

Laskar, Pia. 1997. "Sexualfrågan som verktyg i könsdebatten: Två texter från mellankrigstiden." In *Seklernas sex: Bidrag till sexualitetens historia*, edited by Åsa Bergenheim and Lena Lennerhed, 187–203. Stockholm: Carlsson.

Lazarsfeld, Sofie. (1931) 1938. *Hur kvinnan upplever mannen: Andras bekännelser och egna betraktelser*. Translated by Karin Alin. Stockholm: Natur och Kultur.

Lejonsommar, Eva. 1991. *Stilla tiger*. Stockholm: Författares bokmaskin.

———. 1995. *Att älska henne*. Göteborg: Anamma.

———. 1998. *En av oss*. Göteborg: Anamma.

———. 2002. *Återresa*. Göteborg: Alfabeta/Anamma.

Lennerhed, Lena. 1994. *Frihet att njuta: Sexualdebatten i Sverige på 1960-talet*. Stockholm: Norstedt.

———. 2000. "Rätten att vara annorlunda: Homosexualitet i sextiotalets debatt." In *Homo i folkhemmet: Homo- och bisexuella i Sverige 1950–2000*, edited by Martin Andreasson, 132–41. Göteborg: Anamma.

———. 2002. *Sex i folkhemmet: RFSUs tidiga historia*. Hedemora: Gidlunds.

Lindén, Claudia, and Ulrika Milles, eds. 1995. *Feministisk bruksanvisning*. Stockholm: Norstedt.

Lindeqvist, Karin. 2006. "'Den där lilla . . .': *Charlie* och inversionsdiskursen i *Ensamhetens brunn*." *lambda nordica* 11 (3): 7–25.

Lindholm, Disa. 1961. *Ficklampsljus*. Helsingfors: Söderström.

Lindholm, Margareta. 1990. *Talet om det kvinnliga: Studier i feministiskt tänkande i Sverige under 1930-talet*. Göteborg: Göteborgs universitet.

———. 2005. *Kärlek: Situationer*. Ystad: Kabusa.

Lodalen, Mian. 2003. *Smulklubbens skamlösa systrar*. Stockholm: Forum.

———. 2005. *Trekant*. Stockholm: Forum.

Love, Heather. 2007. *Feeling Backward: Loss and the Politics of Queer History*. Cambridge: Harvard University Press.

Lundahl, Pia. 2001. *Intimitetens villkor: Kön, sexualitet och berättelser om jaget*. Lund: Lunds universitet.

———. 2005. "Den blockerade sexualiteten: Kvinnors inkorrekta begär 1930–1960." In *Queersverige*, edited by Don Kulick, 260–87. Stockholm: Natur och Kultur.

Lundberg, Lotta. 1998. *Låta sig hända*. Stockholm: Bonnier.

———. 2001. *Färdas på en blick*. Stockholm: Bonnier.

Lundstedt, Vilhelm. 1933. *"Otukt mot naturen": Bör den vara straffbar?* Stockholm: Bonnier.

Magnusson, Jan. 2000. "Från tragiskt öde till fritt vald livsstil: Bögar och lesbiska i det sena nittonhundratalets litteratur." In *Homo i folkhemmet: Homo- och bisexuella i Sverige 1950–2000*, edited by Martin Andreasson, 59–75. Göteborg: Anamma.

Marcus, Sharon. 2007. *Between Women: Friendship, Desire, and Marriage in Victorian England*. Princeton: Princeton University Press.

Mattsson, Anna. 1994. *Alexandras rum*. Stockholm: Wahlström and Widstrand.

———. 2004. *De ensammas hus*. Stockholm: Wahlström and Widstrand.

———. 2006. *Vägar utan nåd*. Stockholm: Wahlström and Widstrand.

Mazzarella, Merete. 1992. *Agnes von Krusenstjerna*. Stockholm: Natur och Kultur.

Mencher, Julie. 1997. "Intimacy in Lesbian Relationships: A Critical Reexamination of Fusion." In *Women's Growth in Diversity: More Writings from the Stone Center*, edited by Judith V. Jordan, 311–30. New York: Guilford.

Millett, Kate. (1970) 2000. *Sexual Politics*. Urbana: University of Illinois Press.

Moore, Lisa L. 1997. *Dangerous Intimacies: Toward a Sapphic History of the British Novel*. Durham: Duke University Press.

Norrhem, Svante, Jens Rydström, and Hanna Winkvist. 2008. *Undantagsmänniskor: En svensk HBT-historia*. Stockholm: Norstedts Akademiska Förlag.

O'Connor, Noreen, and Joanna Ryan. 1993. *Wild Desires and Mistaken Identities: Lesbianism and Psychoanalysis*. London: Virago.

Ohlander, Ann-Sofie, and Ulla-Britt Strömberg. 2008. *Tusen svenska kvinnoår: Svensk kvinnohistoria från vikingatid till nutid*. Stockholm: Norstedts Akademiska Förlag.

Öhman, Anders. 2001. *Apologier: En linje i den svenska romanen från August Strindberg till Agnes von Krusenstjerna*. Stockholm/Stehag: Symposion.

Pallesen, Henning. 1964. *De avvikande*. Stockholm: Bonnier.

Palmer, Paulina. 1993. *Contemporary Lesbian Writing: Dreams, Desire, Difference*. Buckingham: Open University Press.

Paqvalén, Rita. 2002a. "Att bli ett autentiskt subjekt." In *Men det var hennes kläder: Nedslag i den samtida svenskspråkiga kvinnolitteraturen*, edited by Rita Paqvalén and Tiia Strandén, 121–32. Helsingfors: Söderström.

———. 2002b. "Den kvinnliga författarens kropp." *Parnass* 2002 (2): 18–22.

———. 2003. "Perversion, dekadens eller kärlek? Pahlenforskningen ur ett queerperspektiv." *lambda nordica* 9 (1–2): 121–29.

———. 2004a. "Love as a Feminist Project: A Reading of the *Pahlen* Series by Agnes von Krusenstjerna." In *The New Woman and the Aesthetic Opening: Unlocking Gender in Twentieth-Century Texts*, edited by Ebba Witt-Brattström, 181–91. Huddinge: Södertörns högskola.

———. 2004b. "Om doror, perversioner och moderskap." *Naistutkimus* 17 (1): 36–48.

———. 2007. *Kampen om Eros: Om kön och kärlek i Pahlensviten*. Helsingfors: Nordica, Helsingfors universitet.

Parikas, Dodo. 2009. *HBT speglat i litteraturen*. Lund: BTJ Förlag.

Rancière, Jacques. (2006) 2011. *The Politics of Literature*. Translated by Julie Rose. Cambridge: Polity.

Rich, Adrienne. 1980. "Compulsory Heterosexuality and Lesbian Existence." *Signs* 5 (4): 631–60.

Richardson, Niall. 2010. *Transgressive Bodies: Representations in Film and Popular Culture*. Farnham: Ashgate.

Rizzo, Domenico. 2006. "Public Spheres and Gay Politics since the Second World War." In *Gay Life and Culture: A World History*, edited by Robert Aldrich, 197–221. London: Thames and Hudson.

Rohy, Valerie. 2000. *Impossible Women: Lesbian Figures and American Literature*. Ithaca: Cornell University Press.

Roof, Judith. 1996. *Come as You Are: Sexuality and Narrative*. New York: Columbia University Press.

Rosenberg, Tiina. 2002. *Queerfeministisk agenda*. Stockholm: Atlas.

Rydström, Jens. 2003. *Sinners and Citizens: Bestiality and Homosexuality in Sweden, 1880–1950*. Chicago: University of Chicago Press.

———. 2005. "Tvåsamhetens brunn: Registrerat partnerskap i Norden." In *Queersverige*, edited by Don Kulick, 308–35. Stockholm: Natur och Kultur.

———. 2011. *Odd Couples: A History of Gay Marriage in Scandinavia*. Amsterdam: Aksant Academic Publishers, Amsterdam University Press.

Sanner, Inga. 2003. *Den segrande Eros: Kärleksföreställningar från Emanuel Swedenborg till Poul Bjerre*. Nora: Nya Doxa.

Smith, Patricia Juliana. 1997. *Lesbian Panic: Homoeroticism in Modern British Women's Fiction*. New York: Columbia University Press.

Söderström, Göran. 2000. "Kejne- och Haijbyaffärerna." In *Homo i folkhemmet: Homo- och bisexuella i Sverige 1950–2000*, edited by Martin Andreasson, 92–117. Göteborg: Anamma.

Statistics Sweden. 2012. *Women and Men in Sweden: Facts and Figures 2012*. Örebro: Statistics Sweden, Population Statistics Unit.

Suber, Margareta. 1932. *Charlie*. Stockholm: Bonnier.

Svanberg, Birgitta. 1983. "Förtryck och uppror: En analys av grundtematiken i Karin Boyes roman *Kris*." In *Kvinnor och skapande: En antologi om litteratur och konst tillägnad Karin Westman Berg*, edited by Birgitta Paget, Birgitta Svanberg, Barbro Werkmäster, Margareta Wirmark, and Gabriella Åhmansson, 220–34. Stockholm: Författarförlaget.

———. 1989. *Sanningen om kvinnorna: En läsning av Agnes von Krusenstjernas romanserie Fröknarna von Pahlen*. Stockholm: Gidlunds.

———. 1996. "Den mörka gåtan: Kärlek mellan kvinnor som litterärt motiv." In *Nordisk kvinnolitteraturhistoria*. Vol. 3, *Vida Världen 1900–1960*, edited by Elisabeth Møller Jensen, Margaretha Fahlgren, Beth Juncker, Anne-Marie Mai, Anne Birgitte Rønning, Birgitta Svanberg, and Ebba Witt-Brattström, 430–36. Höganäs: Bra Böcker.

Svedberg, Annakarin. 1962. *Vingklippta*. Stockholm: Bonnier.

———. 1963a. *Det goda livet*. Stockholm: Bonnier.

———. 1963b. *Se upp för trollen! eller: Äntligen en bok om livet sådant det är*. Stockholm: Bonnier.

————. 1966. *Din egen*. Stockholm: Bonnier.

Swedish National Institute of Public Health. 2005. *Homosexuellas, bisexuellas och transpersoners hälsosituation: Återrapportering av regeringsuppdrag att undersöka och analysera hälsosituationen bland hbt-personer*. Report No. A 2005:19.

Tamagne, Florence. 2006. "The Homosexual Age, 1870–1940." In *Gay Life and Culture: A World History*, edited by Robert Aldrich, 167–95. London: Thames and Hudson.

Tiby, Eva. 1999. *Hatbrott? Homosexuella kvinnors och mäns berättelser om utsatthet för brott*. Stockholm: Kriminologiska institutionen, Stockholms universitet.

Tiby, Eva, and Anna-Maria Sörberg. 2006. *En studie av homofoba hatbrott i Sverige*. Stockholm: Forum för levande historia.

Ullerstam, Lars. 1964. *De erotiska minoriteterna*. Göteborg: Zindermans.

Vanita, Ruth. 1996. *Sappho and the Virgin Mary: Same-Sex Love and the English Literary Imagination*. New York: Columbia University Press.

Wachman, Gay. 2001. *Lesbian Empire: Radical Crosswriting in the Twenties*. New Brunswick: Rutgers University Press.

Wallsten, Hanna. 2005. *I närheten av solen*. Stockholm: Forum.

Warner, Michael. 1991. "Introduction: Fear of a Queer Planet." *Social Text* 29: 3–17.

Wikander, Ulla. 1992. "Delat arbete, delad makt: Om kvinnors underordning i och genom arbetet: En historisk essä." In *Kontrakt i kris: Om kvinnors plats i välfärdsstaten*, edited by Gertrud Åström and Yvonne Hirdman, 21–84. Stockholm: Carlsson.

Williams, Anna. 2002. *Tillträde till den nya tiden: Fem berättelser om när Sverige blev modernt: Ivar Lo-Johansson, Agnes von Krusenstjerna, Vilhelm Moberg, Moa Martinson*. Stockholm/Stehag: Symposion.

————. 2004. "Unge herr Agda: Omklädningsmotivet i Agnes von Krusenstjernas *Fröknarna von Pahlen*." In *Omklädningsrum: Könsöverskridanden och rollbyten från Tintomara till Tant Blomma*, edited by Eva Heggestad and Anna Williams, 101–19. Lund: Studentlitteratur.

————. 2013. *Från verklighetens stränder: Agnes von Krusenstjernas liv och diktning*. Stockholm: Bonnier.

Wittig, Monique. (1980) 1992. "The Straight Mind." In *The Straight Mind and Other Essays*, 21–32. Boston: Beacon.

————. (1981) 1992. "One Is Not Born a Woman." In *The Straight Mind and Other Essays*, 9–20. Boston: Beacon.

Young, Iris Marion. 1980. "Throwing Like a Girl: A Phenomenology of Feminine Body Comportment Motility and Spatiality." *Human Studies* 3 (2): 137–56.

Zimmerman, Bonnie. 1990. *The Safe Sea of Women: Lesbian Fiction, 1969–1989.* Boston: Beacon.

INDEX